INHERITANCE

Inheritance

Ontario's Century Farms Past & Present

John and Monica Ladell

Illustrations by Bert Hoferichter, MPA

Dundurn Press
Toronto & Reading
1986

Printed and bound in Canada by T. H. Best Printing Company Limited. This publication was originally published by Macmillan of Canada Limited in 1979.

The writing of this manuscript and the publication of this book were made possible by support from several sources. We wish to acknowledge the generous assistance and ongoing support of the Canada Council and the Ontario Arts Council.

J. Kirk Howard, Publisher

Dundurn Press Limited
1558 Queen Street East
Toronto, Canada
M4L 1E8

Dundurn Press Distribution
Athol Brose, Wargrave
Reading, England
RG10 8DY

Canadian Cataloguing in Publication Data

Ladell, John, 1924-
   Inheritance : Ontario's century farms past & present

Includes index.
ISBN 1-55002-008-0

1. Family farms - Ontario - History. 2. Ontario - Rural conditions. I. Ladell, Monica, 1925- II. Title

S451.5.06L33 1986   630'.9713   C86-094611-8

Contents

To Lindsay and Simon

Preface

*C*entury farm signs are a familiar sight to those who live in the country. But no doubt there are many from the towns and cities who on noticing these signs for the first time have wondered what they are and what they mean. Quite simply they indicate a farm that has been owned and worked by the same family for a hundred years or more.

The signs were first issued by the Junior Farmers' Association of Ontario as a centennial project in 1967, and to place the project in perspective something should first be said about the Junior Farmers themselves.

In 1944 a group of government officials and forty-eight young men and women from rural Ontario met in an attic of the Parliament Buildings in Queen's Park, Toronto. As a result of this meeting, the Junior Farmers' Association of Ontario was formed. Its objectives were to create a deeper and more permanent interest in the agricultural and social life of the community and to encourage self-help and community betterment. The membership of the Association grew rapidly, until in 1978 there were more than 7,500 members between the ages of sixteen and thirty in 121 clubs across Ontario. The Junior Farmers' Association to some degree continues and complements the work of the 4-H Clubs, whose membership is confined to young people between the ages of twelve and twenty-one, and both organizations share a magazine, now aptly called *The Enthusiast*.

In 1967 Canada was to celebrate her first century as a confederation. In the spring of 1965, Don Lazenby, a columnist for the *Junior Farmer and 4-H Quarterly*, wrote: "What will we — the Junior Farmers' Association of Ontario — give to our country during her centennial celebration? I believe a centennial project should be a fitting tribute to the past, something that it is possible to do in the present, and one that will be of value and use in the future."

The centennial project he proposed was the allocation of roadside signs to farms in Ontario that had been in the same family since

1867 — the year of Canadian confederation. "The signs erected during such a project would serve a threefold purpose in the future," Don Lazenby continued. "They would create a pride in ownership, indicate Century Farms to visitors . . . and remind future generations of their heritage."

During the spring and summer of 1966 Junior Farmers spent many hours locating owners of century farms throughout the province. The sign itself was designed by Sue Forth, an Ancaster girl, who later married Bill Dyment, a farmer who qualified for the sign in 1975 and a noted breeder of Holstein cattle. By September 1966, initial work was completed and 5,000 signs were distributed to interested farmers at a nominal cost of one dollar each. After the signs were put up there was a futher demand, bringing the total number issued to some 6,200.

Thus century farm signs became common landmarks along country roads. However, the signs had been designed to last only one year, the year of the Centennial. Some have survived to this day, but many have long since succumbed to the wind and weather and have rusted away. In 1974, the Junior Farmers' Association reactivated the project. Old signs can now be replaced by new ones and as farm families reach their hundredth year they can apply for a sign to hang at their gate.

This book is a tribute to the century farmers of Ontario and to the imaginative 1967 project of the Junior Farmers' Association of Ontario. Century farm families symbolize a heritage of which we can all be proud. What these families contributed to their communities in the past and what they are contributing still; the history of their ancestors and of their homes; the progressive development and sophistication of their farming operations; their memories of things past and their appraisal of things present, all combine to create a rich and varied tapestry of which this book can provide only a brief and imperfect glimpse.

Of the many century farms still extant, the few that appear in this book constitute a minute sample from what the scientist would consider a large and far from homogeneous population. And lest even the word "sample" may be taken to indicate that this book has scientific pretensions, it must be stated flatly that it has not. Some farms were deliberately sought out; others were stumbled upon by chance. Finding a farm even when its location was known brought moments of frustration. Rural Ontario has concession roads and side-roads that are clearly marked on a map but have an uncanny facility for eluding the stranger. In most cases, the interviews, which were recorded on tape, took place in the evenings, for farmers are busy people and work to an inexorable schedule. The authors wish here to express their appreciation of the welcome and hospitality they received in many farm homes.

The interviews on which this book is based took place in the summers of 1977 and 1978 and in the intervening winter. In all, some twelve thousand miles was covered in a series of journeys across most of southern Ontario. In sum those journeys might well be described as an odyssey, for each brought its adventures in terms of new knowledge gained, new vistas opened up, and new friends made.

Acknowledgements

This book could not have been written without grants
from the Canada Council and the Ontario Arts Council,
or without the co-operation of the Junior Farmers' Association of
Ontario.

The authors also wish to record their appreciation of help received
from the staff of the Ontario Archives, the Toronto Reference
Library, the Marine Museum of Upper Canada, and the Ontario
Agricultural Museum at Milton.

The Ruth Konrad Canadiana Collection of the Mississauga Central Library was invaluable. Staff of the Mississauga Library System
patiently answered hundreds of queries and borrowed much material on our behalf.

Thanks are due to officials of the Ontario Ministry of Agriculture
and Food, Toronto, who gave freely of their time and advice, among
them Don Beeney, Ken Knox, Rod Stork, Janet Horner, and Basil
Madigan. The Ministry's Agricultural Representatives in the various
county seats were sources of local information available
nowhere else.

It would be impossible to list the names of all the people across
Ontario to whom the authors are indebted, but among them are
Mrs. Elsa Neil, formerly of Thornhill; Councillor Patricia Wright,
Cumberland Township; Mr. Harry Pettypiece, Essex; Mrs. Viola
Reid, Pakenham Township; Miss Barbara Coffman and Mrs. Joseph
Wismer, Sr., Louth Township; Mr. and Mrs. Gordon King,
Woodstock; Mrs. Pat Kerr, Acton; Mrs. Alfred Cairns, Ameliasburgh Township; Mlle Rose-Marie Benoit, Paincourt; Mrs. Gordon
Hill, Huron County; Mrs. Thorold Lane, Ingleside; Mr. George
Jackson, Milton; Mrs. Abner Martin, West Montrose; Professor
Michael Hornyansky, St. Catharines; Dr. Hess, Sr., Kitchener; Mr.
Melvin Weber, Elmira; Professor and Mrs. Walter Martin, Waterloo;
the Bolus family, Blenheim; Mr. Alec Mullen, Cornwall; Mrs.
Elizabeth Blair, U.E.L., Toronto; Mr. Patrick Folkes, Tobermory;

Mr. Christopher Porter and Mr. Glenn Cunningham, Upper Canada Village; Mr. Henry Clement, Dover Township; Professor Douglas Richardson, Toronto; Professor Douglas Hoffman, Guelph; Mrs. Barbara Humphreys, Ottawa; Dr. and Mrs. Ruth Humphreys, Toronto; Professor Desmond Morton, Erindale; Mr. and Mrs. Herman Sallmen, Ottawa; Mr. Bob Lord, Oakville; Mrs. Patience Morrisey, Mrs. Joan Musselman, and Mr. Angus Robertson, Mississauga.

Thanks are due to Bert Hoferichter for his skill and cooperation in taking the photographs.

Finally, a particular debt of gratitude is owed to those century farmers who gave freely of their time and knowledge, but whose stories, regrettably, could not be included in this book.

Introduction

*T*he word "farm" is a deceptively simple one. Everyone knows what a farm is, of course, but to define it precisely takes a few moments' thought. First, there is the understanding that a farm constitutes land on which something is produced that was not there before. A piece of land may yield quantities of gravel, but a gravel pit is not a farm. Second, the word farm implies some human effort and action. Unaided by man, trees may appear on a tract of land and eventually yield timber, but such land cannot be called a farm.

It seems that a farm implies a process, an interaction, between man and the land; a process that involves using the land to grow something that will be of benefit to him, usually but not always food, that food either to be consumed directly or to be eaten by animals which in turn will be consumed.

The one small word farm, then, expresses a complex idea in which man, the land, and what men do to that land are intimately connected. There can be few forms of human activity that see a closer interaction between man and his work, each moulding the other. It is sometimes said of an old seaman that he has salt-water in his veins, so great is the impression that over the years the man has become one with the sea that has given him his living. But the analogy between farmer and seaman cannot be taken very far. For while both the sea and the land may affect the man who works them, the seaman can do little to change the sea, while the farmer can, and does, do a great deal to change the land.

On a century farm this continuous transformation — of the land by the farmer and of the farmer by the land — has gone on for generations. Some century farm families in Ontario have been on their land, not for one hundred, but for nearly two hundred years. To find a century farm that can boast six generations is common; a few go back eight or more. Much of what is described in this book applies to all farmers in Ontario; but the century farmers, what of them? What are those qualities that won them the right to hang the century farm sign at their gate?

If there is one quality that is peculiarly theirs, it is tenacity. Nowadays tenacity is not always one of the prized virtues. If something doesn't work right away, it seems smart to give up and try something else. Yet nothing could have been more alien to those who stayed on their land year after year, generation after generation. The century farmer continued to farm through years when what little cash there was went to pay the mortgage; years when the farm produced well but markets were poor, or years when markets were good but, through drought, floods, disease, or maybe just plain bad judgement, harvests were disappointing. In some seasons his cattle throve and brought in good money at the sale-barn or prizes, perhaps, in the show-ring; in others, disease struck his animals and no one wanted any part of them. And there were occasions in some parts of Ontario when an enemy raided his farm, stole his produce, burnt his house and barns, and ruined his crops. Up years and down years, a hundred of them or more.

For the century farm family, past triumphs and disasters are the stuff of long family history, and so closely are the fortunes of the farm interwoven with this history that it is often impossible to draw a line between them. A century farmer today may find himself having to live with a decision made by his grandfather, be it a barn that could have been better sited or an option on land that was never taken up. And he knows that his heirs, when they take over the farm, will have to live with *his* decisions.

To the urbanite who may tend to think of land merely as a salable commodity, the determination of some farmers to hold on to the family holdings through thick and thin may well be incomprehensible. But to a farmer, the land is the basis of his existence, the stuff from which everything literally springs. And for a century farmer that stuff, that soil, has been tended and nurtured by his father before him and his grandfather before that. The land remains a link between him and his forebears, one that is not to be broken lightly.

Furthermore, he knows that his land remains fertile only with wise and constant care. Untended, the best of farmland goes quickly to ruin and it may take years to restore it to its former productive state. The farmer is conscious of the amount of care and hard work that previous generations have put in — invested, if you like — to keep the land healthy and productive. And in some cases that effort has been put into poor land that through the years has been gradually upgraded. In sum, the quality of his land, though less tangible, is as constant a reminder of his inheritance as his home, his animals, his silos, and his barns.

However, what is more immediate and real is the prospect that a son — or, in some cases, a daughter — will be taking over the farm and that even as he has cherished the land, his son or daughter will do likewise. For farming is nothing if not a family affair. Indeed, therein lies the source of the strength that the early farmers were able to impart to the communities that they took so large a share in building. Today, with the cost of hired help beyond the reach of many, it is only through the efforts of the family that the farm keeps going at all.

It would be difficult to do justice to the contribution of women to Ontario farming. There are women today who are running their own farms — some farms have been handed down from mother to daughter — while there are thousands of others playing a pivotal role as they always have done in managing the farms, often to the extent of undertaking hard physical work alongside their menfolk, in addition to their roles as wives and mothers.

Many farm children now as always have their chores to do before and after school. And as they grow older they take on an increasing share of the work. Older still they may become full-time partners in the farming operation, or they may leave home to follow an occupation or a profession that may have little or nothing to do with farming. However, many family operations depend on sons or daughters returning at week-ends or at harvest-time to help out.

A farming family's involvement with, and commitment to, their land reveals an attitude towards inheritance that differs fundamentally from that commonly prevailing in our urbanized society, where the concept that one generation holds the family's possessions in trust for the next is rare indeed. The average urbanite, however settled he may feel, knows that he will almost certainly be moving on some day and that there will come a time when his house and his garden will pass into the hands of strangers. It is of course true that a man hopes that what is in the bank will not be squandered when he is gone; as for his other possessions, the best he can hope for is to divide them in such a manner that their distribution will not lead to unseemly family squabbles.

A farmer, on the other hand, far from thinking of dividing his inheritance, is concerned in most cases with handing down a dynamic whole that cannot be divided in the physical sense without destroying it. There are some century farmers who, though anxious that the farm should continue in the family name, have no sons or daughters — or for that matter any other relatives — to whom the farm may be left. For some, there is more than a touch of personal tragedy in this, though when speaking of it the farmer may treat the matter philosophically, if not lightly. But there are many more cases where there are heirs but none willing to follow in their fathers' footsteps. And here we come up against some hard economic facts.

In a recent year with a farmer deriving, on the average, less than a third of his net income from his farming operation, over half the farmers in Ontario were augmenting their income by earning money off the farm. Frequently the farmer, or those of his family who were contributing to the family income, worked off the farm by choice. Indeed, sometimes the farm operation was secondary to a preferred profession or career. Nevertheless, it was often true that without an income from other sources, the farm could not be kept going at all.

The century farmer is not immune to the basic laws of economic survival. Thus, however strong the dynastic urge may be, after taking a long, hard look at the farm's prospects he may well encourage his children to take up professions offering a greater degree of security in return for less strenuous labour. The location of the farm, its productivity, the increasingly heavy investment in machinery, not to mention the cost of borrowing money to pay for that machinery, may be some of the factors that bring the farmer to the point of advising his children to seek their fortunes elsewhere.

But with the family gone and off the farm for good, what then? The farmer may sell, or he may rent his land. The latter option leaves the land in the family and provides an income while it is kept in working condition. In their time many century farms have seen some or all of their acreage rented, to be taken over again as soon as circumstances permitted, and in such cases renting is one chapter in the farm's long history. In others, renting is the final episode.

Of the six thousand and more century farms that received the farm sign so proudly in 1967, many have passed out of the family in the twelve years that have followed. Many of the earliest farms were closely associated with, if not actually part of, the first settlements in the province, and as those settlements expanded to become towns the first farms disappeared. Towns grew into cities, bringing outlying farms within the urban shadow in a process that continues to this day, at an accelerating pace.

But many century farms remain. And the story of those farms and of the families that own them is in large part the story of Ontario. Their forebears settled the land and put many of our villages, towns, and cities literally on the map, and from being leaders in their own communities, many went on to frame our laws, to found industries and lead governments, while others went to fight in our wars, some to die in them.

The stories that century farmers have to tell do not dwell exclusively on the farm's past prosperity or lack of it, or on the way their houses came to be built, or what it was like to farm in early days. Their stories touch on and illuminate almost every facet of Ontario's past, and so we find chains of circumstance that lead us to the mainsprings of events on the wider stages of history. To listen to those stories was to be impressed again and again by the fact that the story of Upper Canada did not begin with the American Revolution that brought the Loyalists north to found a new province, but with events in Europe that led their forebears to begin new lives in North America. Some were the victims of religious persecution, while others were displaced persons who had lost everything in the wars that lacerated seventeenth-century Europe. Mounting rivalry between Britain and France in the century that followed led to the extinction of New France and so paved the way for the Upper Canada that was still to come, while towards the end of that same century the age-old Anglo-French conflict culminated in the Napoleonic Wars that profoundly affected the history of settlement once Upper Canada was founded. Born out of war, it was another war and its aftermath that shaped the infant province. Thus the story of many century farm families begins, not with the day that saw an ancestor take up land as a settler, but in earlier times. Hence the historical framework in which these family histories have been set.

But however disparate their origins, and however different the imperatives that brought the first settlers, they all faced much the same problems once they were here. For the majority, starting again in a new country meant first clearing a small patch of land upon which to grow enough food to stay alive. Acre by acre, the land was slowly reclaimed from the forest, the removal of each tree-stump involving back-breaking labour. With the area of cleared land growing larger each year, there might be produce to sell or, more likely, to barter for food and implements. A mill to grind the precious wheat into flour might be as far as fifty miles away and the journey there and back was often made on foot, with heavy sacks carried on the shoulders.

For some it would be years before they held ready cash in their hands. Many earned it by making potash, lime, or maple syrup. Others built mills or tanneries or sold their special skills as carpenters, blacksmiths, or masons. In effect, these craftsmen started businesses which they carried on in addition to their farming. Then, as the villages and towns grew, so did the markets for the farmers' produce, and the farms that we know began to emerge.

Through all this the centre of the family's activity, the operations room as it were, was the family home — the farmhouse. Those who expect that an old farmhouse will be an architectural gem, a period piece dating back in all particulars to the time when it was built, may be disappointed. A farmhouse is, quite rightly, a working house and as such may well have been remodelled several times in the interests of efficiency. Thus a house whose exterior design is in keeping with a specific period may well contain an almost completely modern interior. More commonly, the old and the new comfortably co-exist, with a hallway much as it would have been in the nineteenth century and a kitchen that gleams with chrome and stainless steel.

In fact a century farm family will probably have lived under a number of roofs. Typically, the first log dwelling or shanty made way for something more substantial, or perhaps was absorbed into a larger building where the original logs — the reminder of earlier poverty — disappeared behind siding. In its turn, the second house may have been replaced by a more spacious structure, possibly of stone or brick. This will be the house that is visible today.

While the houses and the men and women who lived in them have come and gone, the land remains — the vital link between one generation and the next. From their land the century farm families have derived the strength that helped them build the Ontario that we know; and on those acres they developed and passed on to their sons and daughters the qualities and skills upon which the agricultural industry of Ontario now largely rests.

CHAPTER ONE

Loyalists Along the Front

*T*ake of conspiracy and the root of pride three handfuls, two of ambition and vain glory. Pound them in the mortar of faction and discord. Boil it . . . until you find the scum of falsehood . . . rise to the top. Then strain it through the cup of rebellion. . . ."[1]

So began a satirical recipe for a potion that would turn a man into an American rebel. The author of the recipe, Oliver Parker, a loyal citizen of New Hampshire, was hauled before a revolutionary committee and sent to prison for his impudence, as were many hundreds of others in the thirteen colonies who could not bring themselves to see eye to eye with the rebels and who made their feelings known.

Earlier in the revolution a spell in the pillory was thought to help bring a Loyalist — or Tory, as he was then known — to his senses. Later, as feelings began to rise, those who were adamant in their loyalty to the king ran the risk of being tarred and feathered, and not a few were, while the common lot of the Loyalists was insult and abuse, with threats of violence to their persons and property.

With the Declaration of Independence in 1776 and the outbreak of war, oaths of allegiance to the Patriot cause were required. Those failing to subscribe were interrogated and if their conduct was found inimical to the revolution they might be imprisoned or exiled, their property forfeited to the Patriot government. In Massachusetts, for example, many convicted Loyalists were banished to Europe or the West Indies, with a spell in squalid cells on a guard-ship in Boston harbour often a harrowing prelude to transportation overseas. Later, as the armed conflict deepened, Loyalists who had fled to the British had their property confiscated, and when adherence to the Crown was construed as treason, those who joined the king's forces ran the risk of death by hanging if captured. Summary executions after a battle were not infrequent.

In its conflict of ideas and ideals and in all its cruelty and inhumanity, what came to be called the War of Independence was in its
essentials the first American civil war. Of the two and a half million
American colonists, something like half a million, or one man in
five, were to be numbered among the Loyalists. They came from all
walks of life — government officials, merchants, lawyers, farmers,
clergymen, tradesmen, teachers — all to be caught in the terrible
dilemma that civil war engenders, a dilemma compounded of con-
flicting and irreconcilable loyalties, a dislike of violent solutions, and
an innate urge to survive. And to escape it no fewer than a hundred
thousand Americans fled to other lands.

In 1783, when the rebellious American colonies had finally won
their independence, the land that was to become Ontario was part of
the province of Quebec. It was virtually an empty land of forests,
lakes, rivers, and streams, reserved by government decree for the
Indians whose home it had been for time out of mind. There were
few white people. Apart from a few hundred soldiers and fur-
traders in their forts and trading posts scattered thinly along the
Great Lakes, there were only two European settlements worthy of
the name. One was at Niagara and had sprung up during the war
that had just ended. The other — and much older one — was
situated in the vicinity of Detroit, where the French had built Fort
Pontchartrain in 1701, a settlement that had eventually spilled over
on to the Canadian side of the Detroit River.

This then was the land to which the Loyalists came — about 2,100
families in all, comprising some 5,700 men, women, and children.
Not many chose this wilderness, given the tens of thousands of
Loyalists who had fled the American colonies, but few as they were,
they were to find themselves founding members of a new province.
Among their descendants are a number of the century farm families
described in this book.

In 1789, six years after the first Loyalist settlements had been
established, Sir Guy Carleton, then Lord Dorchester and governor-
in-chief of all Britain's remaining possessions in North America,
proposed that "the families who had adhered to the Unity of the
Empire, and joined the Royal Standard in America before the Treaty
of Separation in the year 1783" should be given a "Marke of Honour".[2] As a result of his proposal what became known as the U. E.
Lists were prepared, giving the names of all those — both men and
women — who had risked and lost so much in their demonstration
of loyalty to the British Crown during the Revolution. The letters
"U. E." reflected Dorchester's phrase "Unity of Empire", and it was
from the same phrase that the term United Empire Loyalist was
derived later.

But what was this empire to which the Loyalists adhered? Empire is a term we tend to associate with all the grandeur, pomp, and circumstance of Queen Victoria's reign when the British flag was flying in almost every corner of every continent, the empire that was the precursor of today's Commonwealth.

The empire that the Loyalists knew, however, was somewhat different. Sometimes called the "first British empire", it had been acquired in the course of international struggles that started early in the sixteenth century when Spain and Portugal established their first colonies in the New World. England and France joined in the race to acquire overseas sources of wealth, and later, the Dutch, whose sudden emergence as a major maritime power was one of the wonders of seventeenth-century Europe.

With the French claiming most of what is now eastern Canada, the English and the Dutch focussed their attention on the Atlantic seaboard to the south. There the first English colony to survive and flourish was Virginia, founded in 1615 to grow tobacco for the home market. Massachusetts followed in 1620 with the arrival of the Pilgrim Fathers, and two years later New Hampshire was established. Maryland came next in the 1630s, with Connecticut and Rhode Island hiving off Massachusetts. The latter half of the seventeenth century saw three colonies — later known as New York, New Jersey, and Delaware — pass from Dutch into English hands, as well as the establishment of Carolina and Pennsylvania. With the splitting of Carolina into two parts early in the 1700s and with Georgia carved out of South Carolina some time later, the last of the thirteen colonies had been formed. The American component of that first British empire was complete.

By this time the Dutch had fallen out of the imperial race, leaving France and Britain as the principal protagonists in a world-wide struggle for empire. In 1763, at the conclusion of the Seven Years War — sometimes called the French and Indian War in Canada — Britain and France had been at each other's throats for twenty-eight of the first sixty-three years of the eighteenth century.

The Seven Years War ended with a British victory, and the architect of that victory was William Pitt, whose son — also a William — was to steer his country successfully through the Napoleonic Wars.

The establishment of the earlier colonies had as their primary object the acquisition of wealth. There was also a feeling that England was becoming overcrowded, though at the time the American colonies were founded the population of that island was less than a tenth of what it is today. But such reasons for expansion overseas remained ill-defined. In William Pitt, the Elder, however, the motives became crystallized and were embodied in the man. Though a chronic invalid and subject to fits of madness — he was a manic depressive — Pitt possessed what we now call charisma to a remarkable degree. Such was the quality of his leadership that the British nation was brought to share in his vision of the future: a vision of a greater Britain whose wealth would come from overseas trade. To carry out his grand design two things above all were necessary: naval supremacy and the elimination of Britain's major trading rivals — the French.

Pitt supervised the conduct of the war down to the last detail. Thus, for example, he not only devised the overall strategy that led to the extinction of New France, but also directed the navy to make a detailed survey of the St. Lawrence which was to contribute not a little to the capture of Quebec in 1759 by the British under General Wolfe. One of the officers who carried out the survey was James Cook, working from H.M.S. *Pembroke*, a ship commanded by Captain John Simcoe, the father of John Graves Simcoe, who was to become the first lieutenant-governor of Upper Canada.

The Seven Years War ended with New France in British hands — and a lot more besides. Referred to by Sir Winston Churchill as "the first world war", the conflict was global in extent. An idea of just how wide-ranging it was can be gained from the terms of the Treaty of Paris that ended it in 1763, just twelve years before the American colonists broke into open rebellion. In the West Indies, Britain acquired a number of islands, while others were returned to France. One of them, Guadeloupe, was an island of such richness that the British almost kept it, the French to receive nothing less than Canada in exchange. Clive had put an end to the French hopes of expansion in India. Manila and Havana were given back to the Spaniards, who had become involved in the latter stages of the war. Another Spanish possession, Florida, Britain decided to keep.

This then was the empire that the Loyalists knew: West Indian islands, Florida, Bermuda, Nova Scotia, Quebec, Newfoundland, a few trading posts in Africa, parts of India under the dubious control of the East India Company, and the thriving colonies along the Atlantic seaboard from which the Loyalists themselves came. As yet the British flag did not fly in Australia or New Zealand, or on other islands in the Pacific. Nor in Malaya, Singapore, Burma, or Ceylon. Nor in any of those outposts of empire known to the Victorians such as Hong-Kong, Cape Colony, and Aden at the tip of the Arabian peninsula. And no claim could be laid to India in its entirety, destined one day to become the most illustrious jewel in Queen Victoria's crown.

Besides its meagre size compared with the mammoth imperial enterprise of the nineteenth century, the empire of the Loyalists differed from the later in a very important particular. It belonged traditionally to the Crown, and though management of colonial affairs was entrusted to committees and councils of various kinds, it had long been accepted that these bodies were answerable to the monarch and not to Parliament.

The constitutional struggle to curb the power of the king reached a climax with the so-called Glorious Revolution of 1688 when William III, better known as William of Orange or Good King Billy, was allowed to mount the throne that Parliament had offered him only after he had agreed to certain conditions that placed limits on his royal prerogatives. But the tradition that colonial matters were the business of the king and no one else tended to persist, and here we touch on the heart of the American colonists' quarrel with Britain. Their allegiance was to the king, not to Parliament; and especially not, when matters came to a head, to a Parliament in which they were not represented and which enacted laws to their discomfort.

By the same token the allegiance to the king that the Loyalists could not bring themselves to renounce had in those days of heightened loyalties something of an almost personal nature in it. For many their allegiance to the Crown was something that touched their very honour. As one Loyalist put it as he hurried to help the British at Lexington where the opening shots of the War of Independence were fired: "I have always eaten the King's bread and always intend to."[3]

There was no political oppression in the American colonies — at least no more than there was in Britain at the time, where in the mid-1700s an increasingly well-educated, and (since the coming of daily newspapers) well-informed, public was beginning to give thought to such questions as the nature of man's freedom. But political corruption and the abuse of power were causing great concern, and unrest was in the air. This discontent did not go unnoticed by thinking men in the colonies. While there had been extensive settlement by the Germans, Dutch, and French, the majority of colonists were of British stock and links with the mother country were still strong. And we tend to forget how much coming and going there was across the Atlantic. While to us a six-week ocean voyage implies isolation, to men whose fastest mode of travel on land was by horse, a few weeks at sea was quite acceptable.

The Americans, then, kept in close touch with what was going on in Britain, and, when their troubles started to mount, they found more than a few sympathizers and supporters there. Much that was subsequently decreed for the colonies by George III and his government was done in the teeth not only of the Opposition in Parliament but of protesting citizens throughout the British Isles. And sometimes the colonists did more than just keep in touch. When John Wilkes, a publisher and politician, became embroiled in 1763 in a celebrated case involving civil liberty, Virginia shipped over turtles and tobacco to solace him in prison.

The primary causes of the revolution were economic, not political. There were long-standing grievances connected with England's Navigation Acts, which placed irksome restrictions on colonial trade and commerce. In the northern colonies there was resentment at a tax placed by the British on "foreign" molasses. From molasses the colonists produced rum, much of which was used in Africa to pay for slaves. The sale of rum was a valuable source of revenue, and to obtain molasses in the amounts required, smuggling was common — as were attempts to evade the Navigation Acts, all of which led to continual friction with enforcing authorities.

Down south the plantation owners were sinking into debt as the tobacco they shipped to often-unscrupulous agents in England failed to cover the expense of the goods they ordered from that country. For many southern planters, a break with Britain raised the happy prospect of debts cancelled — some so massive as to be handed down as a dismal legacy from father to son.

Then in 1759 the British took Quebec. Montreal capitulated a year later, and in 1763, with the ending of the Seven Years War, the province of Quebec became part of the British empire. Ironically for the British, it was the removal of the French threat to the American colonies that triggered the events that led to their loss. Under the terms of the Proclamation of 1763, the British defined the western boundary of the province of Quebec as being along the Ottawa River (much as it is today), and they placed a moratorium on any further westward expansion of the American colonies. All lands to the west of the Ottawa and the Appalachians were henceforward to be reserved for the Indians and licensed fur-traders.

For the colonists who had fought alongside the British in three wars against the French and who had contributed to their final North American defeat, the Proclamation of 1763 came as a rude shock. Enterprising Americans with their eyes on the western lands had already formed land-settlement companies. All this was now to come to nothing, and for many colonists the Proclamation was but another instance of a rigid and authoritarian Britain standing in the way of local initiative and free enterprise.

And then came the new taxes. The British not only were having to pay for a very expensive war, but were now committed to guarding their new possessions. In England disgruntled country gentlemen complained that taxes were gobbling up an outrageous fifteen per cent of their income. It was surely only fair that the American colonies should contribute to their own defence?

Among the taxes now imposed on the colonists was one on newspapers and legal documents of various kinds. It was a small tax, such as had been paid in Britain for years, but the Stamp Tax, as it was called, was the first direct tax to be imposed on the colonists and as such it aroused their anger. A wave of violence swept through the colonies; officials concerned with the distribution of the stamps were abused or hanged in effigy; in some places their offices were wrecked; in others, their homes.

The attempted imposition of the Stamp Tax brought latent antagonisms into the open for the first time. "Liberty Boys" or "Sons of Liberty" appeared, out of nowhere it seemed, to egg on the rioters. Quite a few Loyalists were to remember that it was during the Stamp Act riots of 1765 that their allegiance to the Crown was first tested.

Following the disturbances — and the imposition of a boycott on British goods — the British backed down. The Stamp Act was repealed and the year 1766 saw the colonists in a state of high jubilation. Church bells rang, thanksgiving services were held, and the people of New York went so far as to erect a statue of George III made of gilded lead.

The colonists' joy was short-lived, however, for even as it was repealing the Stamp Act, Parliament, prodded by the king, reasserted its right to legislate for the colonies and the next year passed a bill that placed new import duties on a range of articles, including tea.

Once again the colonists resorted to violence and riot. A renewed boycott of British goods was organized, ominously accompanied this time by blacklists giving the names of "Tories" who persisted in trading with the British. In Boston the renewed zeal of the customs officers was particularly unwelcome, and when in 1768 they boarded and searched a ship belonging to a prominent Patriot, they were driven off it by his supporters. The Governor of Massachusetts asked for troops to help restore order. These duly arrived from Halifax to become the object of an active resentment which culminated in 1770 in the "Boston Massacre" — an incident that saw a platoon of British troops under a Captain Preston baited by the crowd until they opened fire, leaving several citizens dead in the snow and others wounded.

Captain Preston and his men were promptly placed under arrest, but blood had been shed and the Patriots made the most of it. The names of those who co-operated with the British were duly noted: Robert Auchmuty and Sampson Blowers, for example, lawyers for the defence in Captain Preston's trial; James Barrick, a ropemaker, who served on the jury; Newton Prince, a pastry cook, who gave evidence, presumably of the wrong kind; one Mary Brown, who made shirts for the British troops; William Hill, who made bread for them; and a Joseph Coffin, who went so far as to turn his distillery and sugar-house into a barracks for them.

On the very day that Captain Preston and his men got themselves into trouble in Boston, steps were being taken in London to remove import duties imposed three years earlier. Only those on tea were to be retained. As a result the colonial boycott of British goods was gradually abandoned, and in general, matters seemed to be on the mend.

And then in 1773, after three years of calm, a disastrous decision was made in London. In order to help the East India Company, which was on the verge of bankruptcy, an act was passed that would allow the company to dump its surplus tea in the American colonies, such tea to be free of any English duty. Even with the import duty that still had to be paid, the tea would be cheaper than anything that the American merchants — or the smugglers — could supply. However, what really caused the uproar was the principle involved, it being generally understood that the king insisted on the retention of the import duty as a symbol of his royal authority.

The Patriots swung into action again and in every port the arrival of tea was awaited by furious citizens. From New York the ships were sent back to sea without unloading; in Charleston the tea got ashore only to be locked up; while in Boston enraged citizens who forbade the unloading of the vessels clashed with Thomas Hutchinson, the governor and later a prominent Loyalist, who ordered that the tea be landed. Matters seemed deadlocked; then on December 16, 1773, a band of Patriots, rather ineffectively disguised as Indians, swarmed aboard the ships and sent 340 cases of tea floating down the tide.

This was too much for London. Ignoring all pleas for moderation, Parliament took a series of drastic measures designed to bring Massachusetts, and in particular, Boston, to heel. The colony's charter was amended, General Thomas Gage, British Commander-in-Chief in North America, was appointed military governor, and the port of Boston was to be closed until the tea, valued at £10,000, was paid for.

These Coercive Acts, as they were called, marked a parting of the ways. Up to this point, the Patriots were a minority, though a vociferous and a well-organized one. But from that point on their star was to be in the ascendant, and with increasing momentum political power was to move into their hands. There were many thoughtful men — and not a few of them later became active Loyalists — who for years had been seeking a reasonable solution to the colony's problems, a political formula whereby the colonies could retain their autonomy while yet remaining within the British Empire. Now their voices were to go unheard as the power of the legally constituted colonial assemblies dwindled and the possibility of changing the course of events by legal means became increasingly remote.

Shocked and angry at the provisions of the Coercive Acts, the colonists received another jolt when the news reached them of the passage of the Quebec Act, which was given royal assent in May 1774.

This far-sighted piece of legislation, which superseded the Proclamation of 1763, was the joint work of James Murray and Sir Guy Carleton, both of whom had served under General Wolfe at the time of the British conquest of Quebec. Murray was Quebec's first governor and Carleton had succeeded him in 1766. Both men felt strongly that liberality and understanding were essential if the loyalty of the Québécois to the British Crown was to be retained and fostered. Thus the Quebec Act confirmed the right of French-speaking Canadians to pursue the Roman Catholic religion; provided for a dual legal system, with British common and French civil law existing side by side; and retained the traditional seigneurial system of land holdings. This last provision, whereby the habitant or settler could continue to occupy land only on a rental basis and on payment of tithes to the church, was well received by the seigneurs who held the land and by the priests, but not by the settlers. The Quebec Act also redefined the province of Quebec, which now became a huge L-shaped area, stretching from Labrador to Lake Superior with an arm reaching southwards to include all or part of what are now the states of Michigan, Ohio, Illinois, Minnesota, and Wisconsin.

To many dissenting American colonists this easy acknowledgement of the Roman Catholic religion came as a betrayal, while the new boundaries of Quebec, which placed limits on the western expansion of New York, Pennsylvania, and Virginia, further irked those who still dreamed of highly profitable western settlements. Relations between the colonies and Britain were now being strained to breaking point, and as the tensions mounted, the active harassment and maltreatment of Loyalists began.

    . . . he was stript Stark naked, one of the severest cold nights this winter, his body covered all over with Tar, then with feathers, his arm dislocated in tearing off his cloaths [sic], he was dragged in a Cart with thousands attending, some beating him with clubs and knocking him out of the Cart then in again. They gave him several severe whippings, at different parts of the Town. . . .[4]

That was how one eye-witness described the treatment meted out in 1774 by a Boston mob to Jonathan Malcom, a Loyalist customs officer. Malcom later claimed that he was the first Loyalist to be tarred and feathered, a punishment that at one point was widely used as a threat to keep Loyalists in line, even if it were not always carried out.

In May of the same year, General Gage arrived in Boston. In June, the port of Boston was officially closed and before the summer was out, five thousand British troops had been landed. In September what was called the First Continental Congress met in Philadelphia. A Declaration of Rights was prepared. Respectful in tone and addressed, significantly enough, to the king and not to Parliament, it asserted the right of the colonists to legislate for themselves, while recognizing that external matters should remain the responsibility of the home government.

In London the stubbornness of the king and of a Parliament that was not only obsessed with the need to raise money but blinded by the assumption that the colonies existed only to serve British interests combined against the Americans. Their Declaration was rejected.

Following the Continental Congress, what were generally called "Committees of Public Safety" began to form in the various colonies. With wide powers to arrest, detain without trial, and punish all those who were considered "obnoxious", they intensified the hounding of Loyalists. Rebel militia gathered here and there and the stockpiling of arms began. The Loyalists, like the Patriots, were also thinking in terms of armed force. Late in 1774 what was probably the first Loyalist corps was formed in Massachusetts, but its existence was to be short-lived.

The inevitable clash of arms occurred in April of 1775 when a British force was confronted at Lexington by rebel militiamen. Somebody fired a shot, the British opened fire, and the American War of Independence had begun. Following a further engagement at Concord the British withdrew to Boston through an increasingly hostile countryside and suffering casualties all the way.

Within a month the Second Continental Congress was meeting in Philadelphia, where George Washington was elected to command the Continental Army, a grand name for what was as yet an undisciplined rabble, most whom were then on the outskirts of Boston where the British were bottled up. At the same time Congress drew up another petition to George III, which was carried to England by the Loyalist Richard Penn. The king refused to see him.

Meanwhile the Americans had invaded Canada.

In 1775 the defences of the province of Quebec were in a precarious state. Early in the year, however, a Lieutenant-Colonel Maclean was authorized to raise a new provincial regiment to be called the Royal Highland Emigrants, these to be accoutred and dressed like the Black Watch, with one difference. Their sporrans were to be of raccoon skin. This regiment, largely composed of Highlanders who had taken up land in eastern Canada following their discharge after the Seven Years War, was to serve with such distinction during the siege of Quebec as well as on other occasions that it was later elevated to the status of a line regiment — the 84th.

The Royal Highland Emigrants had been formed just in time. To defend the entire province of Quebec, Sir Guy Carleton had little more than a thousand regular troops at his disposal. And these, with the Emigrants and a small number of irregulars, were spread thinly from the city of Quebec to remote forts on the Great Lakes over six hundred miles away.

The Americans came very close to success. For five months the future of Canada rested with Carleton and his small garrison beleaguered in Quebec. In its beginnings, however, the American invasion of 1775 had all the elements of a comic opera. Early in that year, Ethan Allen, who had a vision of an independent Vermont (which was known at that time as the New Hampshire Grants), set off with a motley crew of followers to capture the British forts at Crown Point and Ticonderoga, which, situated as they were at the southern end of Lake Champlain, guarded the only practicable north-south valley between the St. Lawrence and the colonies to the south, a route to be much travelled by opposing armies and by northbound Loyalists in the years to come.

Ethan Allen succeeded in his enterprise, surprising the commanding officer at Fort Ticonderoga in his night-shirt and inviting him to surrender "in the name of the Great Jehovah and Continental Congress". Crown Point, with its garrison of a single platoon, was also captured, though by this time Ethan Allen had been joined in an uneasy alliance by Benedict Arnold, then a colonel, who was acting under official instructions to carry the revolutionary war on to Canadian soil.

This farcical overture was followed by events that had little of humour in them. Assuming that the hopefully dissident province of Quebec could be brought into the American fold as the fourteenth colony, a two-pronged invasion was planned. One force was to take the Lake Champlain route to Montreal; the other, further east, was to strike directly at the city of Quebec through the forested hills of Maine.

Following the surrender of another British fort at St. Johns (now St. Jean), about twenty miles north of Lake Champlain, the way to Montreal was open. Seeing little hope of holding it with the forces at his disposal, Carleton set off downstream for Quebec, taking with him stores and all the hundred or so regulars he had left in a flotilla of small sailing boats. Though he did not know it, he was being pursued by the American advance guard racing along the southern St. Lawrence shore. They caught up with him near Sorel, where he had been delayed by adverse winds and the grounding of one of his boats. Under the guns of the Americans, Carleton transferred to a smaller craft when night came and slipped quietly downstream to reach Quebec and safety a few days later. As a captain in the Quebec militia put it: "We saw salvation in his presence."

The Americans moving down the St. Lawrence then joined the second force which had been struggling northwards through the wilderness of Maine and which had finally emerged on the south shore of the St. Lawrence near Quebec in mid-November. It had taken them six nightmarish weeks to cover the three hundred miles, during which seven hundred of the original twelve hundred men had been lost to desertion, disease, or sheer exhaustion. In mid-December, the combined force appeared before the city of Quebec and laid siege to it.

To defend the city of five thousand inhabitants, Guy Carleton had about twelve hundred men, of whom three hundred or so were Royal Highland Emigrants and nearly eight hundred were militiamen or volunteers, more than half of them French. The remainder of his force was made up of marines, artillerymen, and seamen off ships that had been laid up for the winter.

With the bitter cold and disease adding to its miseries the American army was soon reduced to only a thousand effectives, and in a desperate attempt to take Quebec they launched an attack in the teeth of a raging blizzard in the very early hours of New Year's Day, 1776. One American general was killed at the head of his assaulting party, whereupon his men retreated. The second force fought its way into the lower town, to be defeated when Carleton ordered a sortie and took them in the rear.

The attempt to capture Quebec had failed and the Americans did not try again. The siege of the city, however, was not lifted for another five months. In May, British warships landed two hundred regulars and marines, and with their assistance Carleton went on the offensive the same day. By nightfall the Americans were in full retreat. With the arrival in June of General Burgoyne with a number of British and German regiments, the retreat of the Americans became general and the invasion was over. It was to be another thirty-six years before the Americans tried, and failed, to take Canada again.

Meanwhile the Declaration of Independence had been signed on July 2, 1776, to be promulgated two days later, and the British had evacuated Boston. Following the Battle of Bunker's Hill, when the rebels were dislodged from the heights overlooking the city but only at heavy cost, the British subsided into inaction while the Continental Army blockaded the port on its landward side. With the installation of cannon on the heights overlooking it, Boston became increasingly untenable and it was decided to withdraw.

Loyalists by the hundreds had been taking refuge in Boston since 1774 and to them the decision to abandon Boston came as a betrayal. They had only a few days to make up their minds whether to go with the British or stay, and those who did decide to abandon their homeland had to leave with only what they could carry. The British sailed to Halifax in March 1776, and with them went eleven hundred Loyalists in what was the first mass exodus from the American colonies. Dr. Sylvester Gardiner, a physician from Cambridge, Massachusetts, and one of the evacuees, was to say: "I found I could not remain in Boston and trust my person with a set of lawless rebels whose actions have disgraced human nature and have treated all the King's loyal subjects . . . with great cruelty."[5] Another Loyalist was of a more practical turn of mind: "All we poor refugees must be made good our losses and damage. Hanging people won't pay me for what I have suffered. . . . And after damages are sufficiently compensated, then hang all the Massachusetts rebels by the dozens, if you please."[6] From Halifax most of those first refugees made their way to Britain, which before the war ended was to receive from the various colonies perhaps as many as ten thousand Loyalists, some to return later to their homeland, many to live as unhappy exiles in England and to die there. It was said that there was a scarcely a village in England that did not have an American grave.

In July 1776, four months after the evacuation of Boston, the British under General Howe appeared off New York and began landing troops on Staten Island, and a month later on Long Island — fifteen thousand British and five thousand Hessians, the largest army ever seen in North America. Outnumbered and out-manoeuvred, General Washington's rebel forces were badly mauled in a battle that developed on Long Island, and after further defeats, Washington withdrew across the Delaware into Pennsylvania, leaving New Jersey and New York itself in British hands, the latter to remain so until the war ended seven years later.

With the return of the British to New York, serious recruiting for the Loyalist regiments began. The Royal Highland Emigrants had been raised earlier, as were two other units, the Royal Fencible Americans and the Nova Scotia Volunteers, these officered and manned as far as possible by ex-British regulars. The first Loyalist regiment proper seems to have been the New York Volunteers, which was raised in January 1776 and whose members had managed to slip away north to join the British forces. However, with two important exceptions, the integration of the Loyalist regiments into the Provincial Line, as it was called, did not begin until the British took New York.

Among the first regiments to be formed were the New York Loyalists, sometimes called De Lancey's Brigade, after the man who raised them. About the same time, the New Jersey Volunteers was formed, as was the Queen's Rangers, a regiment about which we shall hear more. Later came the King's Regiment, the King's Orange Volunteers, and the Loyal American Regiment. And there were to be many others, such as the Pennsylvania Loyalists, the Maryland Loyalists, and the British Legion, a highly mobile force with its core of hard-riding Pennsylvanians that later was to cut a swathe in South Carolina under its brilliant, if ruthless, British commander, Banastre Tarleton. From the southern colonies were to come such regiments as the North Carolina Highlanders and the East Florida Rangers named after the British-occupied territory from which they had operated since the start of the war.

Before the war ended, between twenty and thirty thousand Loyalists had served at one time or another in the more than fifty Loyalist regiments, while thousands more saw service in the militia units. Towards the end of the war, ten thousand men were serving simultaneously in the Provincial Line, which at one point outnumbered Washington's Continental Army.

From the point of view of our story the two most important regiments formed prior to the British occupation of New York were the King's Royal Regiment of New York, raised by Sir John Johnson, and Butler's Rangers. Important because the men discharged from these regiments helped spearhead the settlement of Upper Canada, while Sir John Johnson himself was to become Canada's leading and most influential Loyalist.

Sir John came from Albany, New York, where his father, Sir William, owned large estates. Sir William had been Superintendent of Indian Affairs in New York and over the years had built a remarkable rapport with the Mohawk Indians, as his son was also to do. In 1773 Sir William, though not a Scot himself — he was Irish by birth — encouraged the settlement on his estate of a number of Highlanders, some of whom were to slip away to join the Royal Highland Emigrants. On Sir William's death in 1774, his son assumed his father's patriarchal role with respect to the Highlanders, and when, as a prominent Loyalist, he was threatened with arrest by the Patriots, he fled north to Montreal, taking 175 of his retainers with him. On his arrival, Sir John was asked to raise a regiment, and so the King's Royal Regiment of New York came into being, popularly known as the Royal Yorkers; or, because of the colour of their jackets, Johnson's Royal Greens.

John Butler was originally from Connecticut but later settled near Albany, New York, where he was a neighbour of the Johnsons. Like Sir William Johnson he had taken a leading role in rallying loyal Indians to the support of the British in the Seven Years War and had led them in battle. Marked down as a Loyalist early in the American Revolution, John Butler made his way to Niagara with his son, Walter, to become a deputy Superintendent of Indian Affairs and to raise the regiment to which he gave his name.

Operating from Niagara, Butler's Rangers, sometimes acting in concert with loyal Indians under their leader Joseph Brant, or with the Royal Yorkers and detachments of regulars, made it their business to harry outlying settlements in upper New York and Pennsylvania; and when the British went on the offensive in the north in 1777, the Rangers were among the Loyalist units that took an active part in it.

It was the appearance of General Burgoyne that had put an end to American hopes of taking the province of Quebec in 1776. It was then that Burgoyne evolved a plan that called for a northern army — under himself — striking south through Lake Champlain and the Hudson Valley to meet a southern army coming north from New York. Burgoyne was so taken with his plan that he returned to London to promote it and there it was enthusiastically approved.

General Howe in New York, however, had his own ideas and was intending, as London well knew, to move, not north, but south to

Philadelphia. In the absence of any clear directives from home, Howe saw no reason to change his plans. And so Burgoyne marched south to meet a supporting army that never appeared and to a disaster that had a profound effect on the course of the war.

At first all went well, with Fort Ticonderoga on Lake Champlain retaken early in July. Then things started to go wrong. Much as the Americans had done the year before, Burgoyne had fallen into the error of expecting massive local support. In fact, the further he went, the more numerous were the forces opposing him. Two hundred miles from his base, with only a few days' rations left, and with no word of any relieving force coming up from the south, Burgoyne finally surrendered at Saratoga, taking with him into captivity a quarter of the British forces in North America.

At about the same time, the Royal Yorkers, Butler's Rangers, and loyal Mohawks under Joseph Brant were heavily involved in an unsuccessful attempt to force a passage through the Mohawk Valley. Loyalists also took part in the Battle of Bennington, which came not long before Burgoyne's surrender when he had sent a mixed force to destroy a rebel cache of arms. The force was ambushed and before it was all over, nine hundred men had been lost. There were many Loyalists among the dead and wounded, and those who were taken prisoner were treated as common felons, as was the usual practice. Among them on this occasion was a Captain John Dafoe or Defoe, whose descendants now farm near Morrisburg.

The accommodation of a mounting number of Loyalist prisoners, both civil and military, became a problem in the northern rebel colonies, a problem that was at least partially resolved by converting the disused Simsbury copper mines into a prison. Located near what is now called East Granby, Connecticut, the prison became notorious for its subterranean cells which could only be reached by a ladder. It was here that Captain Dafoe was incarcerated until he managed to escape, as many did before the war ended. In one mass break-out in 1781 most of the prisoners got away after a battle in which several of the guards were killed.

Among the many Loyalists who experienced the murky horror of the Simsbury mines, the most distinguished was William Franklin, governor of New Jersey and illegitimate son of Benjamin Franklin. There were many families of divided allegiance in the War of Independence, with brother pitted against brother and father against son, and the Franklin family provided the best-known case of all. Benjamin Franklin never forgave his son for his steadfast allegiance to the Crown, and they were never reconciled.

Following the occupation of New York in the autumn of 1776 and

Washington's subsequent retreat across the Delaware, the British proceeded to occupy northern New Jersey, though their hold was a tenuous one. Washington was able to strike telling blows against the British early in the winter of 1776-77, following which General Howe withdrew most of his forces to New York.

New Jersey was to become the scene of some of the bitterest partisan warfare of the northern colonies. It was also to suffer greatly from the depredations of British and German troops who looted and pillaged the homes and farms of Loyalists and Patriots alike. This, while leading to considerable antagonism against, and loss of support for, the British, also exacerbated the tensions in a colony where, according to one estimate, potentially active Loyalists made up over a third of a population consisting mostly of farmers. The New Jersey Volunteers raised by Courtland Skinner, a prominent lawyer, became the largest of all Loyalist regiments, with over 2,400 men serving in it before the war was over.

As the British advanced, those with Patriot leanings were zealously pointed out to them by local Loyalists. And when the British withdrew, Patriots took their revenge on the now undefended Loyalists. It added up to a picture typical of a civil war, where, as one clergyman put it, "both parties fought not like real men with sword and gun, but like robbers and incendiaries."[7] To add to the ugliness of this picture, Loyalist raiding parties from New York and, for a while, Philadelphia took to ravaging the countryside in the course of settling old scores.

The British had taken the rebel capital, Philadelphia, late in 1777. Even as Burgoyne was bringing his ponderous army southwards in the expectation of meeting British forces northbound from New York, General Howe was landing the bulk of them in Chesapeake Bay. Advancing towards Philadelphia, Howe found his way barred by the Continental Army drawn up on the banks of the Brandywine Creek, and in the battle that ensued one of those wounded was the young British army officer Captain John Graves Simcoe.

The battle on the Brandywine left Washington's forces in disarray and in full retreat, and the British were in Philadelphia by the end of September, just three weeks before Burgoyne came to grief.

Burgoyne's surrender proved to be the turning point of the war. France had been quietly helping the Patriots for some time with clandestine shipments of arms, besides supplying money and military "experts" of one sort or another. With the news of Burgoyne's surrender, the French made up their minds, and early in 1778 they entered the war as formal allies of the rebellious Americans.

In Britain, the loss of Burgoyne's army brought about a crisis that was deepened by the entry of France into the conflict. With the safety of Britain itself in jeopardy, there was renewed clamour for an end to the war in America. It was decided to continue it, but with major emphasis on the south, where it was felt that there was greater prospect of success, and where the plight of the unsupported Loyalists had long been a matter of concern. This decision led to the abandonment of Philadelphia in June 1778, precipitated by rumours that a French fleet was approaching New York, and to the resignation of an already disheartened General Howe, who was succeeded by Sir Henry Clinton, his second-in-command. At the end of the year an expedition was dispatched to capture Savannah, Georgia.

Even hardened campaigners were appalled at the savagery with which the war in the south was fought. As a general in the Continental Army commented, "The Whigs seem determined to extirpate the Tories and the Tories the Whigs.... If a stop cannot be put to these massacres the country will be depopulated in a few months more, as neither Whig nor Tory can live."[8] Earlier in the war there had been an ambitious plan to come to the support of the Loyalists in the south. For various reasons it came to nothing, but not before hopes of a British landing in North Carolina had led to an abortive uprising in which Scots Highlanders took a leading part.

Largely as a result of the Highland clearances, thousands of Highland Scots had emigrated to southern colonies and many were to remain loyal to the Crown. Thus of the fourteen hundred North Carolina Loyalists who assembled in expectation of the arrival of the British early in 1776, two-thirds were Highlanders. (One of those who helped recruit them was Flora Macdonald, last seen helping Bonnie Prince Charlie escape from Scotland after his disastrous defeat at Culloden.) Marching hopefully to meet the British, the poorly armed Loyalists led by a Captain Donald McLeod were routed at Moore's Creek. Some eight hundred Loyalist prisoners were exiled, though in an unusually humane gesture the Patriots set up a committee to care for their dependants. The British turned up two weeks later to find that it was all over; they then sailed on south to mount an unsuccessful attack on a fort outside Charleston, South Carolina, before returning north again, this to the great disappointment of the Loyalists there.

Charleston, with its six thousand whites, was at that time the only city in the southern colonies worthy of the name. Its prosperous businessmen and plantation owners were highly sceptical of the benefits of revolution, and the Patriots in the earlier days of the revolution had had to work fast to consolidate their position. As elsewhere, Loyalists were threatened and some were tarred and feathered; in one ugly case when a black was found guilty of inciting slaves to desert their masters for the British, he was hanged and burned.

In Georgia the radicals had at first made less headway than in any other colony, largely owing to the firmness of the Loyalist governor, James Wright. Georgia was the only colony in which the Stamp Tax was actually paid, though not for long, and it was the only colony that sent no representative to the First Continental Congress. Wright eventually went back to England, while the Georgia back-country became the scene of a frontier war between Patriot partisans and Loyalists operating from British-occupied Florida to the south.

After taking the coastal town of Savannah in December 1778, the British supported by Loyalists marched inland and before long the whole colony appeared to be under their control, so much so that Governor Wright was sent from London to resume his office. In the back-country, however, rebel partisans gained the upper hand, leaving the British and the Loyalists in control of Savannah and little else.

Much the same was to happen in South Carolina. Under the command of Sir Henry Clinton himself, the invasion force consisting of British regulars and Loyalist Provincials from the north landed near Charleston in February 1780. The city was besieged, and in May its 5,500-man garrison of Continentals and militiamen surrendered. To the rebels this was a military disaster of such magnitude that General Washington felt the southern colonies were as good as lost.

With the capitulation of Charleston, resistance throughout South Carolina came to an end. Outposts in the back-country were manned by British and Loyalist troops, and a start was made on raising local Loyalist militia units to help defend the colony. Confident of its safety, Clinton left for New York, which was again under French threat, taking half his army with him. In the event they were too late. The French had put five thousand men ashore on Rhode Island, placing New York in danger from a joint Franco-American attack.

Sir Henry Clinton had hardly left South Carolina, however, when the rebels in the back-country rose again in open rebellion. British and Loyalist outposts came under attack and within a few weeks the situation had passed beyond their control. In the savage partisan war that developed, nearly four thousand men died in local battles and skirmishes which ended with the slaughter of prisoners and the cold-blooded butchery of the wounded.

Clinton had placed the safety of South Carolina in the hands of his second-in-command, Lord Cornwallis, who felt that the best way of ensuring his position was to strike at the rebels in North Carolina. Encouraged by his resounding success in a pitched battle against a large Continental force which ended in their rout, Cornwallis now proceeded to do this, in spite of war raging in the back-country. By March 1781, Cornwallis was near the Virginia border, where he fought and won another battle, though at a cost his dwindling army could ill afford. Then, after a few weeks at the coast to recoup his forces, and without consulting Clinton, he marched north into Virginia, while far to the south of him the Loyalist defenders of the last outpost in the South Carolina back-country were fighting their way to the comparative safety of Charleston.

August saw Cornwallis at Yorktown in Virginia completely at odds with Sir Henry Clinton as to the future conduct of the war. And it was at Yorktown that he was trapped by a Franco-American army that had marched quickly southwards. With sixteen thousand French and American troops to landward and thirty French men-of-war to seaward, Cornwallis finally surrendered on October 21, 1781.

In London the king took the surrender as a personal defeat. He talked of abdicating and returning to his ancestral Hanover. By this time Britain was facing not only France and the rebellious colonists but Spain and Holland as well. There was little public support for the war and in Parliament an Opposition vote to end it failed by just a single vote. With country and Commons against him, George III was forced into accepting a new government pledged to giving the American colonies their independence.

In fact the war was to go on for another two years, and though the Royal Navy kept busy, little happened of any great military consequence. Sir Guy Carleton, slighted by the subservient role he had had to play in the planning and execution of Burgoyne's ill-fated expedition of 1777, had resigned from the governorship of Quebec the following year, to be succeeded by Frederick Haldimand. However, in May 1782, Carleton returned to North America as the British commander-in-chief in New York, and with his arrival, hostilities in North America were brought to a halt.

That summer the first steps towards negotiating a peace were taken in France, with the Americans, to their alarm, soon discovering that the French were still hankering after their old fur-trading grounds in the Ohio Valley, as well as the cod-fisheries off Newfoundland, while the Spanish were laying claim to everything west of the Mississippi.

From earlier diplomatic manoeuvrings, it was clear that the

Americans had some hopes of getting Britain to cede Canada to the infant United States. But Britain came to the bargaining table by no means empty-handed. New York was still firmly held and, providentially, British ships under Admiral Rodney had crippled the French fleet in the West Indies in an action fought early in 1782.

In the Treaty of Paris signed in 1783, Britain relinquished her claims to all lands between the Alleghenies and the Mississippi, leaving the international boundary in eastern Canada much where it is today. Florida went back to Spain, whose claims beyond the Mississippi were also recognized. Louisiana remained French. And as for the United States, they obtained the right to fish off Newfoundland and Nova Scotia, and their independence was at last recognized. The first British empire, for which the Loyalists had sacrificed so much, thus came to an end. With the American experience not forgotten, the later British empire, and the Commonwealth that followed, were to evolve on somewhat different lines.

For the Patriots of the American Revolution the war had settled many matters. Their troubles, it seemed, were over. For the many Loyalists in their graves scattered throughout the colonies, from the back-country of South Carolina to the lonely valleys of northern Pennsylvania, their troubles, unhappily, were over, too. As for the thousands of Loyalists who survived and went into exile, the granting of independence meant the end of a way of life and the beginning, perforce, of another with all its attendant trials.

No one will ever know what became of them all. When Charleston and Savannah were evacuated on Sir Guy Carleton's order in late 1782, the Royal Navy took with it nearly four thousand Loyalists and five thousand slaves. Many Loyalists went to Jamaica, others to the Bahamas, where they founded a cotton industry, ushering in a period of great prosperity for the islands. To this day many Bahamians recall their Loyalist ancestry with pride, and when in 1973 the islands became independent, Abaco made an attempt to become a separate Crown colony.

Perhaps the strangest story of them all is that of the blacks who gained their freedom when they fled to the British and took up arms against the rebels. Most came to Nova Scotia, where they were given the poorest land and were otherwise discriminated against. In 1792, with the help of London philanthropists, nearly twelve hundred of them under Thomas Peters, an ex-sergeant, went to Sierra Leone in West Africa, a colony founded only a few years earlier to provide a home for the many blacks freed when slavery became illegal in Britain.

It was in Britain itself, as we have seen, that perhaps ten thousand

of the Loyalists were to make their final home. But half of them —
some say as many as fifty thousand — came north to Canada from
New York, the last crowded refuge of the dispossessed Loyalists,
which, with the disbanding of the many Loyalist regiments, became
more crowded still.

Most of the Loyalists who settled in Canada came from the colony
of New York itself. Considered to be the great Loyalist stronghold,
New York probably furnished as many Loyalist soldiers as all the
other colonies combined. During the war no other colony passed
such harsh laws against the Loyalists or evolved more efficient
machinery for suppressing them. The Committee and Commission
for Detecting and Defeating Conspiracies, as it was called, heard
over a thousand cases between 1776 and 1779, and many an unre-
pentant Loyalist was sent to gaol or to prison ships moored in the
Hudson River. Hundreds, many of them farmers, lost everything
they owned. Of the nearly three thousand claims for compensation
processed by the British after the war, over a third were submitted
by Loyalists from New York.

The last great exodus of Loyalists began as the peace talks opened
in 1782. It lasted until November 1783, when the last British troop-
ship sailed for home and General Washington entered the city in
triumph. Sir Guy Carleton left the city four days later. It seems that
he and Washington did not meet.

While some thirty-five thousand Loyalists were taking ship for
Nova Scotia, from which the new province of New Brunswick was
to be carved out for them and by them, hundreds of others were
travelling overland, coming through the Hudson Valley and Lake
Champlain, or following the Mohawk Valley westward to reach
Lake Ontario at Oswego or Sackets Harbor, there to make their
way onwards by boat. Others emerged at what is now Ogdensburg
on the St. Lawrence or travelled around the south shore of Lake
Ontario to Niagara. A series of sad processions with all they owned
carried on their backs, or, if they were lucky, in wagons or strapped
to pack mules or ponies.

They joined those who were already on British soil. Soldiers and
Loyalist refugees had been coming north almost since the start of the
war. Some had headed for Niagara, but most had made their way to
Montreal or Quebec, where, by 1778, their numbers and their destitute state were causing concern. That these problems were solved so
expeditiously was due to Sir Frederick Haldimand, who succeeded
Carleton as governor of Quebec. Haldimand was Swiss by birth and
was to return to his birthplace to die. A faithful servant to the British
Crown since he had joined the British army in 1756 as a soldier of

fortune, he had served as a lieutenant-colonel in the Royal Americans throughout the Seven Years War. After the war, among other things, he was the senior officer commanding the southern colonies for six years, with his headquarters in Florida. Haldimand was then no stranger to America and had a lively appreciation of the problems of the colonists and, later, of the Loyalists, which under instructions from the home government he set himself to solve with a mixture of sympathy and firmness.

In 1778 Haldimand selected Sorel, which lay on the St. Lawrence between Montreal and Quebec, as the best place for a major refugee camp, and there with the winters in mind he built barracks. For five years the camp at Sorel saw much coming and going, with many a happy reunion and many a tragedy when wives and families waited in vain for fathers who had been killed in action.

In 1782, however, when the trickle of Loyalists became a flood, the problem of relocating the refugees suddenly became acute. At first there was no question of settling them on lands west of the Ottawa River which were recognized as belonging to the Indians. At this point, however, Haldimand was grappling with another problem. The new international boundary had left the homelands of the loyal Iroquois in the United States, where they had no wish to stay, and Haldimand had been instructed to find them new lands that were to their liking. It was thus with the Indians in mind that Haldimand first dispatched surveyors early in 1783 to take a look at the land along the St. Lawrence and the north shore of Lake Ontario.

The preliminary reports were most favourable, and Haldimand was still pondering these when he learned that Carleton in New York was sending two hundred families under Captains Grass and VanAlstine who wished to settle near Cataraqui, where Kingston now stands. There was a small British outpost at Cataraqui built near the site of its larger French predecessor, Fort Frontenac, abandoned long since. It was here, as a prisoner of the French, that Captain Grass had got to know the country round about.

The Indians had always been looked upon as allies, not subjects, of the Crown, and private land-deals were strictly forbidden by the British government. Accordingly, to meet the needs of the Loyalists, the government purchased from the Mississaugas a tract of land lying between what is now Gananoque westwards to the Trent River, which flows into Lake Ontario at the west end of present-day Prince Edward County. In the summer of 1783 a Major John Ross arrived at Cataraqui with 450 officers and men with instructions to prepare for the arrival of Captain Grass's party. In erecting the first buildings, Major Ross founded what was to become the city of Kingston.

Meanwhile, the authorities, anxious to learn more about the settlement potential of the land along the St. Lawrence, dispatched Captain Justus Sherwood with instructions to work his way up the river and the Lake Ontario shore as far as the Bay of Quinte, that long, and in places narrow, strip of water between Prince Edward County and the mainland. Captain Sherwood called it the Bay of Kenty; Lieutenant Johns, one of his two junior officers, called it the Bay Cantey. With names taken from the Indians or in some cases from the French, the final English form was a matter of luck as much as anything.

Captain Sherwood set out on September 19, 1783: "Left Mountreal with Lt.Johns & two men of the King's Rangers Ensn Bottum and 7 men of the Loyal Rangers proceeded up the St.Lawrence in a boat."[9]

It seems it was the fate of Lieutenant Johns and Ensign Bottum to do most of the legwork on the trip, though to be fair Captain Sherwood must have had his work cut out handling his boat through the long series of rapids that in those days made the St. Lawrence a nightmare for travellers.

Reporting back on the evening of September 24, Messrs. Johns and Bottum brought good news. In Sherwood's words, "the Land is all the way of the best Quallity they ever saw, it being a black deep Mould entirely free from stones, Ledges, or Swamps, the Timber is very thin but grows exceeding large and tall, it is a mixture of Beach, Maple, Elm, Basswood, Buttonut, White Oak, Hickory and some Pine. The land is exceedingly pleasant all along the shore. . . ."[10]

The party got back to Montreal towards the end of November, when Captain Sherwood handed in his report with a covering letter in which, we are glad to see, his junior officers received a Mention in Dispatches. "[I] beg leave to observe that Lt.Johns & Ensn. Bottum have very much Exerted themselves in Exploring the Country. . . ."[11]

By now Haldimand had received precise instructions from the home government as to how the Loyalist settlements were to be established. They were to be an extension of the French seigneurial system used in Quebec; that is to say, the settlers were essentially to remain as tenants of the Crown. There was no question of their owning their land outright, a great disappointment to the Loyalists.

Heads of families were to be granted 100 acres plus another 50 for each member of the family. A single man would receive 50 acres. Ex-soldiers were on a different scale. Private soldiers got 50 acres, with an extra 50 for each person in the family; non-commissioned officers, 200 acres; warrant officers and lieutenants, 500 acres; captains, 700 acres; and those of more senior rank, 1,000 acres. The acreages allotted to officers were another source of dissatisfaction. When the 84th Regiment or Royal Highland Emigrants had been raised earlier in the war, their officers were promised — and given — much larger amounts of land: 2,000 acres for lieutenants, 3,000 for captains, and 5,000 for field officers. This discrepancy between the Royal Highland Emigrants and the rest remained until 1788 when Sir Guy Carleton, then Lord Dorchester, raised all land grants to a higher level.

The land was to be given free, and the government would arrange and pay for transporting the Loyalists from Sorel and other camps on the St. Lawrence. Survey costs would also be borne by the government. The settlers were to be furnished with tents, tools, blankets, material for clothing, and government rations, most of which came from the well-stocked army commissariats in Britain. The allocation of necessities was, like the grants of land, arranged according to a fairly rigid scale. Thus each family received an axe, a hoe, a spade, nails, and, apparently, a pair of door hinges — a stroke of genius on somebody's part. Saws and woodworking and agricultural implements such as sickles, scythes, and ploughs had to be shared between several families, as did cows if such could be obtained.

The rations consisted mostly of army fare — "His Majesty's rotten pork and weevily biscuit", as one Loyalist put it — along with flour, salt, and butter. The transport, distribution, and fair division of these rations, which was to go on for several years, was to provide Haldimand with many a headache.

The settlers were also to be furnished with seed, and its procurement presented another problem, which was partially solved, ironically enough, by obtaining supplies from the Mohawk Valley in New York, which only a year or so before was being regularly devastated by Loyalist raiders.

Intensive surveying of the land to be settled started early in 1783 with two series of townships laid out, each so many by so many miles, along the north bank of the St. Lawrence in what are now the counties of Glengarry, Stormont, Dundas, Grenville, and parts of Leeds, with a second series from what is now Kingston west to the Bay of Quinte. Later the standard township was to be ten by ten, or nine by twelve miles along navigable waters.

The allocation of land within the townships was far from haphazard. The first five townships in the first series were allotted to the First Battalion of Johnson's Royal Yorkers, with the first township going to Catholic Highlanders, the second to Scottish Presbyterians, and so on, with Anglicans getting the fifth. Allocation of the other townships was on the same basis, men of the same regiment or group staying together. Captain Grass's party from New York went where they wanted to be, in the first township of the second series, which was called Kingston when the townships were first given names in 1788. The party under Captain VanAlstine went to what became Adolphustown in today's county of Lennox and Addington. A township in the future Prince Edward County, Marysburgh, was reserved for British and German regulars, the latter to form one of the first German-speaking communities in Ontario.

It all appears very ordered, too ordered perhaps. But once on the spot, having drawn lots for their land — officers got first crack at the choicer parcels along the waterfront — there was a good deal of swapping, and in the natural course of things it was not long before families sold out and moved, perhaps to other townships or out of the area entirely.

Superintended by Sir John Johnson, the movement of the Loyalists from their camps down-river began with the spring break-up in 1784. By July, Sir John was able to report to Governor Haldimand that a total of 3,776 had been moved into the new townships — 1,568 men, 626 women, and, such was the fecundity of the times, 1,494 children. Included in the total, interestingly enough, were ninety servants.

Providing for the Loyalists and organizing their settlement were amongst the last things Haldimand did in Canada. Earlier there had been a plan to place the defence of Quebec in the hands of Carleton, who was junior to Haldimand in rank. Deeply hurt at this apparent lack of confidence in his military abilities, Haldimand wrote his superiors in London pathetically referring to his forty-three faithful years of service and to his possible replacement by Carleton as "a Mortification which has operated as effectually as if the cause had really taken place." He asked permission to quit Canada.

Haldimand was persuaded to remain temporarily. With his health failing and relations between him and his council deteriorating, he finally sailed for England in November 1784. Before he left, he reported that 6,152 Loyalists had been settled in their new homes.

With the Loyalists taking up land along the Lake Ontario shore in the vicinity of Niagara in the west, and on the St. Lawrence and around the Bay of Quinte in the east, what later settlers were to call the "front" started to form. For the farmers on the back concessions and for those who eventually came to settle inland, the front signified those first concessions lining the Lake Ontario shore and the St. Lawrence where the first towns started to grow, where they took produce to sell and bought their supplies, and where they heard news of the outside world.

The front meant the very opposite of frontier, which in the American sense never existed in Ontario. There was no relentless advance of settlers into a wilderness populated by hostile Indians. The hinterland of Ontario, though certainly a wilderness, came to be settled in an irregular patchwork fashion, with settlements springing up along the easily travelled rivers and waterways that led into the interior.

It was the discontent of the Loyalist settlers in the east that led to the formation of Upper Canada. They disliked the system of government then prevailing in the province of Quebec. They objected to the French system of land-holding. They wanted land to call their own and the type of legal system they were conversant with. In short, they wanted all those British institutions for which they had fought through seven years of bitter war. Their voice was heard and in 1791 the province of Quebec was divided into Upper and Lower Canada. In 1841 the two Canadas were reunited, with Upper Canada becoming Canada West. Then, twenty-six years later at the time of Confederation in 1867, Canada West became the Ontario we know today.

The Loyalists and other Americans who came after them were eventually to spread all over Upper Canada. About a quarter of the century farmers in this book can trace their ancestry to forebears from the American colonies. But it is to the Loyalists who first broke ground in what was to become Upper Canada that we owe a special debt. These were men and women who had their own views on the nature of independence. As William Wragg, a prominent southern Loyalist, put it when he was being interrogated by revolutionaries in South Carolina: "He must be a very weak or a very wicked man and know little of me, who thinks me capable of surrendering my judgement, my honour, and my conscience upon any considerations whatever."[12]

Refusing to abjure his allegiance to his king, William Wragg was eventually banished from his native South Carolina and died in a shipwreck on his way to exile in England. There is a memorial to him in Westminster Abbey, one of the few Americans who have been so honoured.

The Farlinger Family
Matilda Township
Dundas County

The first Farlinger to reach North America arrived in 1710. Little is known about him except that he travelled to England in 1709 from the Rhine Palatinate (a state of the old German Empire) and that he came to the New World the following year as a mercenary soldier with the army of Queen Anne. It seems he was an officer; at any rate, he had brought his family with him, and when the war was over the Farlingers settled in what was then the colony of New York.

John, a grandson of the original Farlinger, was living near Johnstown, New York, when the American Revolution broke out, and like many Loyalists from the Mohawk Valley he hastened to join Sir John Johnson's Royal Yorkers, serving with that regiment through the war and losing his home and all his possessions as a result. Like many Loyalists he was to be compensated by the British government, though only to the extent of £152. As a Royal Yorker, John Farlinger took up land near Cornwall in 1784, settling there with his wife and four children. Later, the family moved to Quebec, where a grandson, Alexander, was born in 1824.

Alexander Farlinger started his business life in Montreal but moved to Morrisburg in 1854 when he married Isabella Findlay Kyle, the daughter of an Irishman from County Derry. The marriage created a joint estate of some twenty thousand acres.

Among many business ventures, Alexander became the owner and captain of the Royal Mail steamship *Lord Elgin* and during his lifetime he amassed a considerable fortune, "guided no doubt by the joint principles of Presbyterianism and Toryism" as a note on the family's history puts it. On February 10, 1870, he organized a banquet for no less a person than John Sandfield Macdonald, first premier of Ontario, and his toryism was strong enough to ensure the intimate friendship of Sir John A. Macdonald. The Farlingers have a chair that Sir John A. used when he visited them, and the Farlinger barouche in which Sir John travelled is in the museum at Upper Canada Village. The Tory party has had the family's support for over a century.

Two Farlinger families live on the St. Lawrence River near Morrisburg. Charlie Farlinger with his wife, Joan, and their four children live in The Blue House, an old stagecoach inn on the farm bought by Captain Alexander in 1859. Charlie's parents, the Allen Farlingers, live next door in Earnscliffe, a brick house on land bought later. The St. Lawrence River is not more than a few hundred yards away.

Ships from all over the world make their stately progress up and down stream using a navigational marker located behind the barn.

Their presence is a reminder of the opening of the St. Lawrence Seaway in 1959. Construction of the Seaway had been approved five years earlier, and when it was completed twenty thousand acres of the historic Ontario "front" were under water, as were a number of small communities such as Aultsville, besides half of Morrisburg and almost the whole of Iroquois. Some eight thousand home-owners were affected, many of whom would go on living in their homes once they had been relocated above the flood-line free of charge by Ontario Hydro. Buildings of historic value were also moved and became the nucleus of Upper Canada Village.

The Farlinger farms were expropriated briefly during construction of the Seaway and then returned. The family was lucky to get them back; few farms were left along the river bank. The Farlingers lost five acres from the front of the farms facing the river, including an old experimental apple orchard, while more land was expropriated at the back in order to allow the relocation of a road and a railway. This and the building of Highway 401, which coincided with construction of the Seaway, resulted in the loss of eighty-five acres.

Another loss to the Seaway was Allen Farlinger's barn, a development which prompted him to sell his herd of Ayrshires in 1956 and go into beef cattle. The Farlingers kept beef cattle until 1970, when Charlie bought into Holsteins, rebuilding a barn near The Blue House to accommodate them. He now has "upwards of ninety cattle".

Charlie Farlinger is enthusiastic about developing a good herd of Holsteins using artificial insemination. In doing this, he practises line-breeding. "I've got in my herd now three lines that are working well together. If you are fortunate enough to get the right lines, then you can improve your herd quickly."

To get the right lines, it is necessary to pick the right bulls for your cows and the choice is perhaps a mixture of luck and good judgment. "One of the bulls I use is Seiling Rockman. He's dead and gone now. I bought quite a lot of his semen six or seven years ago and paid about six dollars a vial for it. Now it could cost me a hundred dollars. It keeps indefinitely at very low temperatures and I order it in when I need it."

The artificial-insemination centres offer a wide range of bulls, and they can take risks that would ruin an individual farmer. For example, a centre might buy a bull for $100,000 and in a very short time send him to the meat packers because he didn't show the qualities desired. "There's only about one in twenty-four bulls that prove out and then there may be one in three or four that catch on. No single farmer could compete with that."

The various artificial-insemination centres in Canada are members of Semex Canada, which is the industry association responsible for exporting semen to forty-seven countries. It produces a catalogue in four languages and has directors all over the world. Over a million dairy cows are now bred artificially in Canada each year, most of them Holsteins — and Canadian Holsteins are considered the world's best. Charlie Farlinger is proud of the record of Dundas County, which he says has some of the best Holstein operations in the province, a number run by century farmers.

On Allen Farlinger's farm there have always been apples. The world-famous McIntosh Red Apple was discovered by John McIntosh, a Loyalist who emigrated from New York State to Upper Canada in 1796. He settled on a farm at Dundela in Matilda Township a few miles north of the Farlinger farms in 1811 and there found the apple seedlings from which his descendants propagated the fruit.

Another Farlinger, Charlie's uncle Alexander, known as "Bud", was, like his namesake the Captain, born to succeed. After taking a degree in philosophy and politics at Queen's University more than fifty years ago, he made a fortune in real estate in Toronto, founding a development company that bears his name.

As a note on the Farlinger history puts it, "the family has been part of the fabric of North American history for more than 250 years. Its contribution to the development of the New World, begun in the reign of Queen Anne, continues actively in the reign of Queen Elizabeth II. . . . Care and prudence have been a part of the Farlinger tradition. So have daring and imagination . . . qualities of resourcefulness needed by pioneers of any generation."

The Dafoe Family
Osnabruck Township
Stormont County

Of all the disasters that may overtake a farmer, none can be more devastating than a barn fire. To see buildings, animals, and machinery destroyed in a blaze is an experience from which some farmers never recover. Barn fires were common in the past when farmers did the chores by lantern-light, and American troops burned barns with enthusiasm during the War of 1812.

Glenn and Audrey Dafoe, who live at Ingleside, near Upper Canada Village, with their two sons, Stephen and David, lost their barn in 1966. A neighbour saw the fire at five-thirty in the morning. Normally, the Dafoes would have been up by then for the milking, but it was February and they had dried off some of the cows, deliberately halting the flow of milk, so the number they were milking was down. By the time they got to the fire, twenty cattle and eight hundred hens had died of suffocation.

Arson was suspected: a number of barns in the area burned that winter. The Dafoes had just remodelled the barn and they were renovating the house. "But for six weeks we hadn't the heart to continue. . . . We just wanted to pack it in."

The Dafoe family name has been spelled six different ways over the years: Dufor, Dufour, DeVoor, Devoe, Defoe, and Dafoe. They were Walloons — Protestants who fled from Europe to New Amsterdam in 1657. During the Revolutionary War, Johan Defoe was captured at Bennington and for nine months was a prisoner in the notorious Simsbury coppermine in Connecticut, where men were kept sixty feet underground in cold and filth. He escaped, and for the rest of the war was a spy for the British. Johan's son, Conrad, fought in the King's Royal Regiment of New York and was given land near Aultsville, a village inundated as a result of the St. Lawrence Seaway. The Dafoes have been in North America for ten generations and on their present farm for five.

The Dafoes have two farms at Ingleside, one dating from 1854. The big white house in which they live was built between 1904 and 1907. It is an imposing house in the Edwardian style, decorated with beautiful ornamental ironwork. Its construction was financed with a loan from a Dr. Jamieson of Osnabruck Township and the mortgage was drawn for $1,760. The material for the house, including the ironwork, came from the Fay and Rombough Sash and Door Company of Aultsville. "The turned fence posts on our front lawn were installed in 1908," Glenn Dafoe says. "They were logs from the original log house and they were turned on a huge wood lathe in the Fay and Rombough factory. Since there is as much wood in the ground as there is above it, each post is estimated to have been about ten feet long."

Across the road is a mid-nineteenth-century stone farmhouse, once coveted by Upper Canada Village. It replaced the log house from which the fence posts were made.

"From day one it was mixed farming," Glenn explains. "In my grandfather's family there were five boys. I recall my great-uncle saying that it didn't take long for them to cut a field of hay because they would cut five swathes across the field with scythes, then five back. Then they raked the hay up with wooden bull rakes. After it had dried, they tied it in bundles.

"I can remember as a youngster that grain used to be thrashed with a flail. They grew timothy grass for hay and flailed it before they fed it to the cattle. Then they put the chaff through the fanning mill and used the seed for next year's crop." There was an old flail hanging on the wall of the barn, but it, like so much else, was lost when the barn burned.

"There's maybe thirty-five acres of rough pasture on the farm, and when I was growing up we kept thirty to forty sheep. I never detested any animal on the farm like I did those sheep! The theory was that sheep could live where nothing else would, but nothing could be further from the truth! They will stay in the rough pasture only until they find grazing somewhere else; and they'll find it, come hell or high water. But those sheep were part of my grandmother's dowry and so they had to stay.

"And every year, however well you took care of the sheep, there'd be ticks in the fleeces. In June they had to be shorn. The fleeces were tied up with paper twine and put in big burlap bags, eight or ten at a time, and shipped to Montreal. The locks that were dirty were thrown into a tub of water and washed. The wool was then hand-carded and shipped to Alexandria to be spun into yarn. I never knew what it was to be without a pair of handmade socks until I married."

Circumstances and not choice have made Glenn Dafoe a part-time farmer. When he left school he had the opportunity to go to university, but instead he decided to train as a carpenter. He chose carpentry because the construction industry was paying good money at the time; he liked being outside and he liked using his hands. His idea was to work in construction only until he could farm full time.

Things did not work out that way. There was the barn fire, and an injury to his back that has worried him ever since and has made full-time farming impossible. Like many other farmers, he works off the farm, and Audrey works, too, demonstrating rug-hooking and quilting at Upper Canada Village during the summer.

"We thought of selling up after the fire. . . . A sale is a fine thing for people who are looking for bargains. Did you stop to think, though, that for the person that's selling, there's a piece of that person's heart that goes with every item sold?" So, perhaps because of interest, or affection, he bought his father's herd of Holsteins and dairied up until 1970.

The Dafoes were lucky to get help with the dairying from a family of Dutch boys who lived near by, but the boys grew older and moved away. Because of Glenn's back injury, Audrey had to handle the milker. It was then that the Dafoes became interested in changing to beef, and to Charolais in particular.

Charolais are large, white beef cattle and one of the oldest beef breeds known today. Named after the Charolles region in the heart of France, they were already a distinct breed in 1760 and by the 1800s they were being selected for beef. The first Charolais cattle came to Canada from the States in 1955 and 1956. Since 1965, some sixteen hundred Charolais cattle have been imported from France.

Glenn Dafoe liked what he saw of the Charolais. They are a hardy breed capable of staying out all winter if given a minimum of shelter from the wind. "I don't call them an 'exotic' breed any more, but they were the first breed of animals to offer an up-breeding program, where by cross-breeding and up-breeding your females you can grade up to the purebreds. This was one of the encouraging things about Charolais that made me select the breed. At that time, too, they were definitely proving to be a faster-gaining animal. But then, I have to admit, this hasn't been nearly as lucrative as we had anticipated. An up-breeding program looks good, provided you get females. But if you don't and you get a male calf, even if you sell it at weaning age, it's not enough return on the cow for twelve months' work. In our first cross-breed crop we didn't get too many heifers, so I realized that it might be ten years before I got any pure-breds. We started buying foundation stock, but of course that was when the Charolais market had peaked. We bought in when prices were at their best. The records showed that the potential for profit was there, provided the market stayed where it was, but it's been downhill ever since." As a temporary solution to the depressed market, the Dafoes have been selling dressed meat.

Glenn talks about other predicaments that farmers find themselves in today. "If you travel down the concession roads you will see land that is being purchased by people who want to build a place in the country.The next thing you find is that you've got twenty residential properties and maybe two or three farms in the midst of what was once all agricultural land. Then suddenly the people in this residential area, as it has now become, get very alarmed about the odour from the nearby farms, and they start lobbying the local municipal government. The municipal government is going to look at where the tax base is, and after all if there are twenty residential properties, they are going to recover more revenue from them than from the farms. So I understand that there are areas where the farmers, if they are spreading manure, have only so many hours to plough it down. It can't be spread on new seeding and top-dressed. It isn't an easy problem to solve. . . . It's unfortunate what is taking place. The young person who wants to start up in farming or who needs to buy more land, just can't afford to pay those [residential] prices."

There are problems in the marketing system, too. "If the so-called middle man is not ripping off both the producer and the consumer — and I have my own opinions about that — then things are passing through too many hands. Think about the cattle that I send to Ottawa. The trucker has to make a living. Then there's the auctioneer's sales commission. Then the person who bought the animal for Burns or Canada Packers or whoever. Then the company gets its share and the retailer his. So there's a lot of people handling that commodity before it arrives at your table." Not to mention the costs of elaborate packaging and advertising.

Will the farm continue in the family? Both David and Stephen, the Dafoes' teenaged sons, are interested. Glenn says, "I can't bring myself to sit here and do nothing with the land. I can't visualize it just lying dormant. My original idea in getting the Charolais was that if, later, the boys did want to farm, we'd have an inventory of cattle they could go ahead with. But I have no illusions about building up an empire here in anticipation of one or other of them taking it over. I just don't think it would be fair, unless there's real enthusiasm, to take any young fellow between the ages of seventeen and twenty and saddle him with a fifteen- to twenty-thousand-dollar mortgage and tell him to go to it. If he's willing to do it on his own and he's willing to make the sacrifices, then I'll take my hat off to him and I'll help him."

The Shaver Family
Osnabruck Township
Stormont County

A mile or so from the St. Lawrence east of Morrisburg stands a dignified grey-stone house with a smoke-house in the back garden and an uninterrupted view across the fields from long windows. Neither Mrs. Henry Shaver, nor her son, Maurice Shaver, knows the date of its construction, though they think it was 1867. The house replaced a log building down by the creek and the stone for it was taken from shallow quarries in a field at the back of the farm.

Inside, the house retains much of its original woodwork. All the wood came from the local bush and the frames for the windows are pine. There are two arches in the living-room, and when Mrs. Shaver was first married fifty-four years ago, heavy red curtains were drawn across them to shut the room off for warmth, rather in the manner of a four-poster bed. Over the stairway hangs the gun of the first Canadian Shaver, or Sheffer, a Loyalist from the Mohawk Valley.

The Shavers' farm, on which the earliest deed is dated 1810, was given to Henry Sheffer for his services in the War of 1812. Part of the original holding was sold by his grandson, George Edgar Shaver, to the Wales Cheese and Butter Manufacturing Company in 1904, but the most critical period in the farm's history came during the 1950s when the St. Lawrence Seaway was flooded. "It was a struggle to keep the farm," Mrs. Shaver says; "Ontario Hydro were bound to have it. They had a big map and all the farms that were to be bought were marked with stars. Ours was one of them. They really didn't need all of it, just a piece for the railroad and the highway. They came here at the rate of one or two a week and pestered us to death for five or six years. Generations of Shavers have lived here. Shavers came here and broke up the land . . . and we weren't going to sell it. Finally, my husband went to Toronto and got it settled up."

The farm is far enough from the St. Lawrence River to be relatively unaffected by the flooding, although the water levels have risen and the creek is now like a small lake.

At first there were Shorthorns on the farm, then Holsteins. In 1939 almost all of the Holsteins contracted tuberculosis and had to be destroyed. Henry Shaver replaced them with Ayrshires. Maurice Shaver at one time thought of returning to Holsteins, but he likes the Ayrshires. "They used to say you could keep four Ayrshires where you could keep three Holsteins. They'd pick up a living where a Holstein would die. Now they've improved the Holsteins — and the Ayrshires, too, of course. About fifteen years ago artificial insemination came in and we improved our herd at a very reasonable cost because we had access to the best bulls in the country. For a small herd, that's quite something and I'd never change from Ayrshires now."

With improvement, the animals of both breeds have grown considerably larger. The Shaver barn was fixed over for the Holsteins (a much heavier animal) and the old wooden stanchions were taken out. Now Ayrshires have increased so much in size that the barn is almost too small for them.

The old barn was moved up from the creek years ago and rebuilt.

It is perhaps fifty years older than the house. The wood in it is all rock-elm. Hand-hewn timbers pegged and morticed. "You'd marvel at the frame of the barn. There's timber there fifteen to sixteen inches square."

Beautiful though the house and barn are, they are not what interest Maurice Shaver most. "When I think of a farm, I always think of the land. If you've got good land, you've got a good farm. You can't live off the buildings."

The Shaver land is gravelly loam and that means stones. Five generations of Shavers have picked them off. "There used to be two stone walls, massive stones in them. Some limestone and some hard-heads. Nothing smaller than the TV set and most of them two or three times bigger. They'd been drilled and you could see where they'd put the pegs in to lift them with a stone-lifter. I've heard the older people tell how they would get the stones out on top in the summer or the fall, but of course they couldn't draw them with the horses. In the winter, when it would freeze up, the horses were sharp-shod. Then they could put two teams on those stones and I guess they could shift about anything if they got the right day. That's when they would get the stones off the field. And if they couldn't do that, they'd dynamite them." The farm still grows stones, but these days a bulldozer does the work.

Maurice Shaver has a small egg-delivery round in addition to the Ayrshires, and he raises beef cattle for a hobby. "I really like to watch them grow and I'm interested in different breeds. I've got steers with four or five different maternal and paternal breeds behind them and it's very interesting to me to see how they do. And they're a conversation piece, too. People come into the barn to look at them.

"I go in for almost anything in cross-breeds — Charolais, Hereford, Angus. From what I observe, Charolais-Hereford is the best cross. . . . I keep about ten. But I'm just playing at it. I'm in and out, and there's a scant dollar to be made in it, too."

Maurice Shaver has a "beef" of another kind. Canada geese fly in from the nearby bird sanctuary on the St. Lawrence River three or four hundred at a time and settle on his fields. In spring they eat his young corn and his clover and leave their droppings on the pasture. The cows won't graze there afterwards. This year geese nested near the creek and fifty goslings hatched out. They will all return to nest in the same place next year and so the population builds up. It is an unresolved conflict between the farmer and the conservationist, and so far no solution has been found.

Maurice Shaver is active in the local branch of the Ontario Federation of Agriculture and is interested in agricultural problems throughout the province as well as in Stormont County. "All my predecessors here have been excellent farmers and excellent men with the land. They built up the land. There was always a lot of manure and they used the best conservation practices. There is land adjoining the farm that in my time grew the best crops in the township, if not in the county. Today there are ash trees on it and scrub. What will happen to that land in fifty years' time I don't know. . . .

"There are new farmers that have moved into the country from overseas during the past few years, mostly good, but some bad. The bad ones may put a small down payment on the farm, cut down the trees, sell off the old fences, strip the barn, grow as many crops as they can, and move on, leaving the land derelict. It doesn't take long for the scrub to move in and for the work of generations to be lost."

This is not likely to happen to the Shaver farm. The bush has been replanted, the fields are tended, and the year's crop of little Ayrshires grazing out in the field are "just a sight".

CHAPTER TWO

Prince Edward County

King George III of England, as well as being subject to periodic bouts of insanity, was a model of all the domestic virtues and fathered a brood of fourteen children. Their names and titles crop up all over Ontario: Fredericksburgh, York, Edwardsburgh, Cambridge, Adolphustown, Cumberland, Clarence, Ernestown, Cornwall, and Williamsburgh, to mention only the townships named in honour of his sons, the Royal Dukes, whom the Duke of Wellington described with customary directness as "the damnedest millstones that were ever hanged around the neck of any Government".[1]

The Duke was being less than fair. Granted, the Duke of Cumberland was lascivious, vicious, hideous, and almost blind, "The Devil in Ernest", and the Duke of York was coarse, drunken, and perpetually in debt. But the Duke of Cambridge was good and dignified, and the Duke of Kent was an amiable man, kind, considerate, and courteous, his hospitality extremely pleasant.

As Prince Edward, the Duke of Kent served in the garrison at Gibraltar. There, in 1790, he pursued his acquaintance with a young woman named Alphonsine Thérèse Bernadine Julie de Mongenêt, Baronne de Fortisson, later described somewhat derisively by Governor Wentworth of Nova Scotia as "Madame of an hundred names and titles"[2] and most often referred to as Mme de St. Laurent.

Prince Edward came with his regiment to Quebec in 1791, bringing Mme de St. Laurent with him. In 1794 he left for the West Indies, but he was to return to Canada twice more, the second time as Duke of Kent and commander-in-chief of the forces in British North America. This last appointment was short-lived as ill-health forced his return to England.

Edward's relationship with Mme de St. Laurent officially ended after twenty-seven years, although he kept in touch with her by letter until his death. In 1818 he married the Princess of Leiningen in order to produce an heir to the British throne. Queen Victoria was his only child. He died in 1820 at the age of fifty-three, it is said from neglecting to change his wet boots.

Prince Edward met the Simcoes in Canada during his first visit to Quebec in the winter of 1791-92, and in August 1792 he went to see them in Newark. He travelled from Quebec to Montreal by a calèche drawn by a French pony, taking a bateau to Kingston and a schooner to Niagara. Mrs. Simcoe wrote in her diary, "The Prince came here the 20th of August. He went to the Ft. at Niagara & when a Salute was fired the Gov. was standing very near the Cannon & from that moment was seized with so violent a pain in his head that he was unable to see the Prince after that day, & kept his Room for a fortnight."[3] Prince Edward visited the Falls and watched a Mohawk dance. On his return he stopped in at Marysburgh, a township named after one of his sisters, on what the French had called "Presqu'île de Quinté" — the Quinte Peninsula. The peninsula was renamed Prince Edward County in his honour, the tenth of the nineteen counties proclaimed by John Graves Simcoe.

Prince Edward County is almost an island, a fact that has governed its subsequent history and development. Joined to the rest of Ontario only by a narrow strip of land, the old Indian portage at Carrying Place, it is a great piece of limestone, gouged out by glaciers that left behind them boulders and gravel, the detritus of the Canadian Shield. Today it is divided into townships of which North and South Marysburgh are the south-easternmost with long, narrow promontories running out into Lake Ontario. Ameliasburgh is the north-western township fronting on the Bay of Quinte. Two families in this chapter, the Heads and the Kerrs, live in the south. The Redners live in Ameliasburgh in the north.

French explorers searching for the legendary North-west Passage to Cathay discovered what was to become Prince Edward County at an early date. Champlain travelled across it in 1615, and in 1668 Sulpician priests established a mission in the Consecon area at the village of Kenté (Quinté), bringing in cattle, sheep, pigs, and poultry with great difficulty from Montreal, then Ville Marie. The mission was abandoned in 1680 and it was not until the end of the Revolutionary War in 1783 that the settlement of the county began in earnest.

The Loyalists that came to settle in Prince Edward County were a mixture of nationalities: Palatinate Germans, French Huguenots, Dutch, Irish, Scottish, English, and some Indians from the Five Nation Confederacy. Among them were discharged soldiers from regular British regiments and soldiers from German principalities whose mercenary services were paid for by George III. Of the nearly six thousand Loyalists who settled in what became Upper Canada, about one thousand came to Prince Edward County.

The first settlement in the county was disastrous. At Fifth Town, in what is now Marysburgh, the settlers were soldiers — English, Irish, Scottish, and German, with a few foreign legionaries from the Brunswick and Hesse Regiment. Some could not speak English. They knew little of farming and nothing of pioneering. Although each Loyalist family had been promised rations for two years and supplies including clothes, implements, tools, lumber, and seed grain, together with a cow and a plough for each two families, some of the supplies did not arrive. Suffering during the first winter was acute. The settlers were miles away from help, and that by water. Archibald MacDonell, who was in charge of the settlement, wrote movingly of their distress to Sir John Johnson as the cold weather began to set in, describing their lack of clothing and blankets to cover them from the heavy rains and "pinching frost".[4]

Not all the settlers of Prince Edward County suffered privations as serious as those of the Fifth Town. Many were accustomed to pioneer life and had the skills necessary for survival. In the so-called "Hungry Year", 1788-89, however, there was a widespread crop failure and the new settlements were on the brink of starvation. There were reports of farms being exchanged for small amounts of flour and of people having nothing to eat but the buds of the basswood tree.

Gradually matters improved. By 1805 Prince Edward County had a reputation for growing good wheat, and in 1808 a gentleman traveller named George Heriot wrote, "The exuberance of the soil around the Bay of Quinté amply rewards the toils of the farmer: it is worked with facility, and produces many crops without the application of manure. The usual produce is twenty-five bushels of wheat, for one acre. The timber consists of oak, elm, hickory, maple, and pines of different species. The bay is narrow through its whole extent, which is upwards of fifty miles, and is navigable for those vessels which are used upon the lake. . . . Great quantities of wild fowl are found in this situation, and excellent fish of different species. . . ."[5]

The Head Family
South Marysburgh Township
Prince Edward County

Century farmers of Irish, Scottish, or Pennsylvania-German background are easy to find. Murray Head is a rarity; his ancestors came to North America from Cardiff, Wales. His family were from Dutchess County in New York, Loyalists who found a new home in Prince Edward County and bought their present farm in 1832.

The land had belonged to a Colonel Clapp, "quite a gentleman", in Murray Head's words. Clapp was a Loyalist from Poughkeepsie, the county seat of Dutchess County, from which he fled in the winter of 1780-81, escaping with his family across the ice of Lake Champlain in a cutter. The Colonel settled at Hay Bay, then moved in his old age to Prince Edward County to engage in the lumber trade in Marysburgh, "the township being to a great part covered in dense forests of pine and oak which was at that day just beginning to find an outlet to Europe through the Quebec market."[6] He built a mill on Black River, Clapp's Mill, later known as the Scott Mill, and this development gave rise to the town of Milford. One of his grandsons married an Irish girl who, when she first came to Canada, is said to have walked the two hundred-odd miles from Lachine to Kingston.

The years from 1860 to 1890 saw unprecedented prosperity in Prince Edward County. Barley, wheat, hops, and peas were in demand and all grew well on the county's dry soil, particularly barley. At a conservative estimate, fifteen million bushels of barley were shipped from the county's ports in those years. This led to a great demand for schooners, barques, and barges to carry away the grain and to the growth of the local ship-building industry. Ships were built in Milford, Murray Head says, before the Black River was made shallow by silt. Some of the pine for the tall masts came from his farm.

"If you take a look around this farm, you'll see the huge stumps. They tell the story. His Majesty's Navy was supplied with great pine trees from this farm. . . . In the middle of my woods there is what's called the Mast Road and it runs right on through to the back country. This was the road they used to bring out the masts for the schooners. . . . I've always wished that through some magic I could see some of the trees that came off those stumps. . . ."

The Head farm straddles the road near Milford, house on one side, barns on the other. It is an attractive complex of trees and buildings, although traffic passes along the road at high speeds. In horse-and-buggy days, this arrangement was probably an asset. "But now I'm not sure," Murray Head says. "It's a little dangerous. Hard on cats and dogs."

The Heads' home is a hundred and three years old and is built of brick. The first settlers' house was located across the road, and fragments of porcelain can be found there. The Heads — Murray, his wife, Leona, and the children, Dean and Glenda — are restoring a room in their house as a museum. In it will be kept the century-old furniture, the spinning wheel, the wooden sap buckets and spiles, the cradles, scythes, and old tools, the books and papers — anything relating to the family's past.

"Some years ago," Murray Head tells us, "our family farm consisted of a few cows, a few hens, some sheep, and an orchard. The sheep were kept in the old orchard, right back of the barn. One year we moved the sheep to another field, but, do you know, they wouldn't stay! There was no way we could keep them out of their old field and they had to be sold."

The Heads now specialize in Holstein cows and apples, the apple varieties being McIntosh, Delicious, and Spy. Murray Head remembers his father recounting the names of thirty different varieties of apples that were grown in his ten-acre orchard. "Fabulous names like Seek-No-Further, Red Astrachan, Wolfe River, Duchess of Olenburg, Yellow Bellflower, Ben Davis, Wagener, Blenheim, Nonsuch, Gravenstein. . . . Today we would have terrible trouble getting rid of thirty different varieties."

What happened to the old apple trees? "Well, there was a bad winter in 1933 and that killed off a lot. It was a blessing in disguise, really, because the orchards were in need of replanting. But I still have two trees of Nonsuch.

"My father told me that sprayers were first used in his orchard around 1900. Up until then you could grow apples, but they weren't the best, they were quite wormy. Finally, my father went down to the village and borrowed fifty dollars to buy enough spray material for the season. This put him on his feet and he was able to grow apples, but it took him two years to pay back the fifty dollars.

"Things were different when my father was a young man. . . . Before Christmas they would bring in two or three bags of oatmeal, and enough oil for the lanterns and house lamps to last the winter. The Saturday before Christmas they would stock up on the other necessities and then they wouldn't go to town again until the first of April. Imagine! To be stuck on this farm only ten miles from the county seat from Christmas until April. They just visited back and forth with the neighbours and had a fine time. . . . Probably happier than we are now."

Reuben Head, Murray's great-great-great-grandfather, was the first of the family in Canada. His children, Dean and Glenda, are the seventh generation. Will Dean continue on the farm? "He's very interested," Murray Head says. "Financially, I hope he'll be able to make it."

The Kerr family
South Marysburgh Township
Prince Edward County

The Donald Kerrs live on the shoreline of Prince Edward Bay, near Black River and west of the island of Waupoos. Lillian Kerr is a direct descendant of Conrad VanDusen, who with his brother, Caspar, arrived with Major VanAlstine's party of Loyalists at Adolphustown in 1784. The VanDusens belonged to a prominent Dutch family that had settled in New Amsterdam, later New York, in the mid-seventeenth century. According to one early history, they exhibited "an especial fondness for accumulating large landed estates",[7] yet when Conrad reached Adolphustown he had with him only two boxes of clothing and some jewellery.

Conrad VanDusen settled on land in Adolphustown, where he kept a tavern near the old court-house. But a story goes that he underwent a religious conversion and that "when the Gospel entered his heart... he deliberately took an axe and cut down his signposts."[8] In 1814 he moved across the stretch of water known as Adolphus Reach, settling in Marysburgh, Prince Edward County.

Conrad was to have fifteen children; his eleventh, Arra Ham VanDusen, was born in 1804. In 1827 Arra Ham married Ann McGrath, who with her sister, Carolyn, had received a grant of land on the First Concession of South Marysburgh Township. Lillian VanDusen Kerr is the great-granddaughter of Arra Ham and Ann; and today she and her husband, Donald Kerr, live on the land granted to Ann and her sister.

Farms on the First Concession of South Marysburgh were surveyed in accordance with the traditional Quebec pattern: holdings with water frontage are long and narrow, shaped like the French seigneurial farms of the St. Lawrence Valley. But there the similarity ends. Prince Edward County, with its many bays, promontories, and inlets, is a surveyor's nightmare. No neat grid of townships, concession roads, and side-roads could be imposed on its irregular outlines, as the number of gores shows — those odd-shaped pieces of land like the gores of a woman's skirt which do not fit into a regular survey pattern. The Kerr farm is no exception to those idiosyncrasies of outline. It includes a fragment of property on the shoreline cut off by a survey line that historically has been a bone of contention with neighbouring landowners.

As with all the houses along this concession line, the original VanDusen house was situated of necessity down by the shore. There were no roads; all transportation was by water or over the ice in winter. Traces of old foundations and pieces of pottery can be found still by the lake. Once the forest behind the house was cut, a second frame home was built on higher land above the road. The existing house, built in the latter part of the nineteenth century, was added onto the old one, incorporating the original fireplace and kitchen.

The existing farmhouse is in the Italianate style at its most imposing, a reflection perhaps of the prosperity that farmers enjoyed during Prince Edward County's "Barley Days". Its hillside location lends added dignity. A flight of steps leads up to the arched front door flanked by magnificent shutters. Who did the building and the woodwork? "My ancestors," Mrs. Kerr says. "They were farmers, but were craftsmen, too." One can only marvel at the versatility that produced such exceptional workmanship.

Until recently, the Kerrs kept dairy cows, but the restrictions on shipping milk in cans imposed in the fall of 1977 put an end to their dairy operation. They plan to keep the cows — "some of them are old friends" — and to sell the heifers when they are ready.

Nor do the Kerrs keep sheep any longer. Lillian Kerr loved the sheep when they had them, especially the lambs, but there are problems with wolves in the county. There are no mixed feelings about sheep, it seems. Farmers either love them or loathe them.

With the forest behind and the shoreline in front, there used to be a very close-knit community along the First Concession of South Marysburgh. Lillian Kerr thinks that a sense of community still exists and Donald Kerr keeps up the old practice of sharing machinery with a neighbour. But the school closed seventeen years ago and the century-old United Church at Black River now holds only one service a year, on Christmas Eve. Still, Lillian Kerr cites the increasing appreciation of family history. Descendants of old families are moving back, she says, to live where their ancestors settled, and if not permanently, at least during the summers. Today Prince Edward County, with its jagged coastline and sandy beaches, is a vacationer's summer paradise.

The Redner Family
Ameliasburgh Township
Prince Edward County

The *Historical Atlas of Hastings and Prince Edward Counties*, published in 1878, contains illustrations of the dignified homes of the counties' leading families. Among them is a drawing of the Redners' house at Rednersville, almost opposite Belleville on the Bay of Quinte. The illustration shows a gabled stone house, with shutters framing its windows and a graceful verandah on which the Redners of that day, their work done, could sit and look out at the blue water of the Bay only a few hundred yards beyond their picket fence. The house is still there, easily recognizable from the artist's rendering. It is now the home of Bernard Redner and his wife, Doris.

The Redner, or Ridenour family, can be traced back in Germany to the year 1559. In 1710 some of the family escaped from the German Palatinate to England and were sent by Queen Anne, not to Ireland as they had expected, but to the British colonies in North America. They settled in what is now the state of New York.

The American Revolutionary War split many families, among them the Redners. A Henry Redner remained loyal to the Crown and left with his five sons when the British abandoned New York in 1783. They made their way by sea to Sorel, where they over-wintered. In the summer of 1784, after an arduous trip up the St. Lawrence by bateau, they reached Adolphustown to find a refuge in the wilderness of what was then still part of the province of Quebec.

The family lived in Adolphustown for thirteen years, surviving the Hungry Winter of 1788-89, then crossed over the water to Prince Edward County to take up a grant of three hundred acres on the Bay of Quinte. Here Henry Redner built a log cabin, a beacon for sailors on the Bay, and here he lived and died.

It is said that it took three generations of the Redner family to clear the land, so dense was the bush on the hill behind the house. They cut logs and cordwood in the winter and slowly brought one field at a time under cultivation.

The Redners were active and enterprising people and they were doing more than clearing their fields. They operated two docks in Rednersville: one for shipping grain and the other for shipping dairy products and fruit. They also built the ferry that ran from Rossmore to Belleville. James Redner opened a general store in Rednersville on part of the original land grant and stocked it with goods brought from Montreal by ship. A retail business still occupies the building he constructed.

The nineteenth century was an era of hurry and bustle on the Great Lakes. As a means of transport, boats were faster than horses, especially when the trip to Belleville meant a long detour across the isthmus at Carrying Place. During the boom years of 1860-90, the wagons lined up from dawn to dusk to unload at local wharves. In

1863 there were more than thirteen hundred sailing-ships on the Great Lakes and an appreciable number of side-wheel steamers and tugs. The first steamship, the *Frontenac*, had been built in Ernestown and launched in 1816. The introduction of steam provided the Redners and other farmers of the Bay of Quinte with a new source of revenue: supplying cordwood to fire the ships' engines. One early steamship was referred to jokingly as a "floating sawmill". Bernard Redner says that in his lifetime ten to eleven ships called at the wharves each day and he can recall his mother going to Belleville one morning to buy a pound of butter and being back by noon, "that was the kind of service they had."

The Redners flourished and built themselves a fine house. The lime for it was burned on the farm, the wood was cut from the bush, and they quarried their own stone. Bernard Redner estimates the cost at about two thousand dollars.

It was a well-designed farm home. At the back was a summer kitchen and through it a pantry; beyond, there stood an ice-house stocked in the winter with ice from the Bay, and a wood-store. A walkway led from the house to the drive-shed where the cutters and buggies were kept and to the stable where there were stalls for five horses. In winter a person could slip from the house to the stable to feed or hitch up the horses without going outside. Once in a sleigh, wearing long muskrat or coonskin coats, fur hats, and gloves, and covered by a buffalo rug, the Redners were ready for a spirited ride on the ice of the Bay of Quinte. Those who can remember sleighing speak of the feeling of exhilaration, the sound of sleigh bells, and the beauty of cold, clear nights.

The story of the Redner family is one of self-sufficiency, hard work and success, and, Bernard Redner thinks in retrospect, happiness. Earlier generations had the satisfaction of working to support themselves, without the burden of heavy taxes or the expense of machinery needed on a modern farm. The family lived on beef, lamb, pork, chicken, and, on special occasions, turkey. They put down large barrelfuls of salt pork and Bernard was taught by his grandfather to cure hams in the smoke-house. Hams were taken out of the brine in the spring to be smoked, then tied in cotton bags and hung from a beam until they were needed. There was apple sauce and sauerkraut in ample quantities. Every farmer netted fish in the Bay of Quinte — whitefish and herring — and salted it for the winter, and they speared good-sized muskellunge.

When Bernard Redner took over the farm from his father in 1929 he paid five thousand dollars for it. He milked twenty cows by hand "with the help of an Irishman" and kept sows to produce between thirty and sixty piglets twice a year. Later, he changed to apple farming.

The trees he first planted now need replacing, but it seems unlikely that this will be done. The value of the land makes it an unrealistic proposition. The orchard alone, Bernard Redner says, is worth almost two hundred thousand dollars. Instead of apples, lots are being sold off which will provide a comfortable retirement for the Redners after a lifetime of hard work. On the hill behind the house where the early Redners laboriously cleared the bush, a town will likely emerge.

The old illustration of 1878 shows a man driving a horse and cart up the hill toward the likely site of this future development. Somewhere up there is an archaeologist's treasure trove, a pit in which the old machines and tools from the farm are buried.

CHAPTER THREE

Inland Towards the Shield

Scarcely ten thousand people were living in Upper Canada at the time of its formation in 1791, and more were urgently needed if the new province were to be placed on a secure footing. John Graves Simcoe, Upper Canada's first lieutenant-governor, had a good idea where they might come from:

> There are thousands of the Inhabitants of the United States whose affections are centered in the British Government & the British name; who are positively enemies of Congress & the late division of the Empire, many of their Connection have already taken refuge in Canada & it will be true Wisdom to invite & facilitate the emigration of this description of people. . . .

And invite and facilitate Governor Simcoe did, eventually inducing thousands to desert the new republic and reassert their allegiance to the British Crown. The principal points of entry of this new wave of settlers were Niagara and Detroit, and with their arrival the western end of the province achieved a new prominence.

It was a prominence that apart from anything else Simcoe was to enhance for strategic reasons, for from its earliest days the infant province was under threat from the newly formed United States to the south, and the clash, if it were to come at all, was expected to come in the west. Thus, Simcoe started work on a military road from Burlington Bay to the Thames River, which would allow speedy reinforcements of the western defences of the province. He called the road Dundas Street. In its beginnings the town of York, later Toronto, had a military, or rather a naval, purpose, while Yonge Street was designed to ease communications with Lake Simcoe and thus with Georgian Bay and Lake Huron.

These and other military projects contributed greatly to the speed with which the south-western portion of the province was settled, as did the influx of emigrants from Pennsylvania in particular, who from the 1790s onwards came to swell the settlements along the Lake Ontario shore west of Niagara, at York, and inland along the Grand River. The founding of Colonel Talbot's settlement on Lake Erie in 1803 would become another powerful stimulus to the settlement of the south-western counties, while even further to the west earlier settlements across the river from Detroit and on the Thames River had been growing steadily.

In contrast, while the far-eastern counties such as Glengarry and Stormont were settled quickly, the more forbidding nature of the hinterland in much of the eastern part of the province tended to confine settlements to the front. From Brockville westwards to Port Hope, the towns were booming; in Governor Simcoe's time Kingston boasted fifty houses — one of them of stone — while Prince Edward County had been thriving since the Loyalists first settled there. But inland the country was all but empty and was to remain so until the Napoleonic Wars had ended.

What was to become a titanic struggle between Britain and Napoleonic France broke out in 1793, only ten years after the War of Independence had ended. The contest went on virtually without a break for twenty-two years, and on the entry of the United States into the fray there was created a war in parenthesis as it were, the conflict known to us as the War of 1812. Both wars were in their own way to have a profound effect on the settlement of Upper Canada, as we shall see.

The struggle against revolutionary France came to an end in 1815 when the Battle of Waterloo removed Napoleon from the stage of history for the last time. The soldiers who had fought under the Duke of Wellington and the seamen who had sailed under Nelson and his brother admirals were for the most part from the dregs of society, culled by recruiting sergeants and press-gangs from the taverns and gutters. "I don't know what effect these men will have on the enemy, but by God, they frighten me," the Duke of Wellington is supposed to have said in 1809 as he watched his troops pass by. By the end of the war the quality of those troops was such that Wellington's army was perhaps the finest that Britain had ever put into the field.

Within a year or so after Waterloo, however, their past services forgotten and without pensions or even a medal, some 300,000 soldiers and sailors were discharged by a government preoccupied by a growing economic crisis. With government contracts at an end and with markets shrinking everywhere, the foundries, mills, and factories were closing all over Britain. Thousands were out of work, and ex-servicemen were thrown out on the streets to join them.

With the country in such a state, the British public was seized with an almost feverish desire to emigrate, and for the next few decades Britons were to leave in ever-increasing numbers. Some went to Australia, New Zealand, and South Africa. Many more came to North America, where so great was the allure of the United States that relatively few considered coming to Upper Canada with its winter cold, wilderness, and still sparsely settled land.

The War of 1812 had demonstrated the vulnerability of a province that still had only about 70,000 people in it. It had also shown how dangerous it was to rely on the St. Lawrence as the province's principal life-line. The Americans had been repulsed, as they had been in 1776, but they might try again. With these thoughts in mind and with the numbers of unemployed rising in Britain, the government sponsored its first post-war settlement scheme in Upper Canada. It was proposed to establish "military colonies" on and about the Rideau River system which, with the Ottawa River, provided an alternative route to Lake Ontario. With an emphasis on ex-servicemen as prospective settlers, not only would the region be opened up, but the Rideau River would be protected, while at the same time a reservoir of manpower would be created that could be called upon in an emergency.

The first emigrants under this scheme were some 250 Scots who left Greenock in three transports in June 1815. It took them three months to reach Quebec. Eventually they arrived in Brockville, from where in the fall of the year an advance party made its way some thirty-five miles inland. They established a base camp on the edge of the forbidding granite of the Canadian Shield on what was then known as the Pike River. This they renamed the Tay, while the settlement that grew up there was called Perth.

In the spring of 1816, the "military colonies" started to take on their intended character, as discharged soldiers from the British and regular regiments took up the land granted to them ranging from one hundred acres for private soldiers to twelve hundred for lieutenant-colonels. Occasionally the grants were made *en bloc* to particular military units, such as the Canadian Fencibles or the Glengarry Light Infantry. One was made to members of a military formation with a very odd history indeed. They were the survivors of some German formations that had once fought for Napoleon. Captured by the British, they were offered a chance of fighting the Americans in Upper Canada as an alternative to prison camp. This they did, eventually settling near Perth, though few of them stayed.

It is said that most of them went to take up soldiering again, this time under the American flag.

In general it seems that many of the rankers in the military colonies did not make the most enterprising of settlers, for as one of the early writers tells us, it was not unheard of for a soldier to part with his land for a single bottle of rum. The settlements prospered, however, though they soon lost whatever military character they had, and it was not long before the British government lent its assistance to two more settlement schemes in the same region, again designed to ease the plight of Lowland Scots.

These came to be known as the Lanark settlements. The story goes that a stream that ran through one embryo settlement was dubbed the Clyde by ironic surveyors, and as a further joke a sign was posted on a storage depot which read, "This is Lanark". The name stuck, with the settlement eventually lending its name to the county of which Perth is now the county seat.

The first group of nearly twelve hundred Lanark settlers left Scotland in 1820. Over six thousand applications were received for inclusion in the second group that sailed a year later, but the numbers had to be limited to eighteen hundred. The 1821 settlers left Greenock, Scotland, in May, disembarking at Quebec towards the end of June. A day and a night in a steamboat took them as far as Montreal. From there they went to Lachine to await the Durham boats that would take them up-river to Prescott. After several days' delay, they set off, three families in a boat, for a week's journey that must have been sheer misery. Designed to negotiate rapids and drawn by oxen plodding along the bank, the shallow-drafted Durham boats offered little protection to the traveller. Passengers disembarked at night, some finding shelter in the barns of nearby farms, but most lying in the open fields under nothing but a blanket, and sodden at that.

At Prescott there was a further three-week delay while the authorities grappled with logistical problems. When it is remembered that there were nearly two thousand people in the party and that they had arrived from Scotland in four different ships, one is not so much puzzled at the delays as amazed that they arrived at all.

From Prescott the settlers made their way to Brockville, ten miles or more upstream, and then struck inland to Perth, some thirty-five miles away as the crow flies, a small village that could provide little in the way of shelter. Thence north-east over roads that were little more than trails through the bush for a further fifteen miles until their destination was reached in the vicinity of the present village of

Lanark. Some never saw it. There had been deaths from sickness and a drowning at Prescott, and one of the many accidents that befell the wagons on the way inland took the life of a small boy.

Arrangements for the Lanark settlers had been made by Lord Bathurst, whose name crops up all over Ontario, and the British Commonwealth for that matter, which is not surprising as he was in charge of colonial affairs from 1812 to 1828. Various Scottish emigration societies were responsible for getting the settlers to Quebec, but from there on the government took over, with each settler granted one hundred acres and with seed and implements furnished at cost. They also received a cash advance of three pounds on arrival, a like sum three months later, and a further two pounds at the end of six months. That this money had to be repaid spoke of a certain optimism on the part of the government that would scarcely have been justified by the quality of the land which the settlers found waiting for them. Rugged and swampy, with fertile soil scattered in isolated pockets, it was land that would have been a serious challenge to those with far greater skills than the settlers then possessed. In time, however, the settlements prospered. As for the loans, it seems that the government had to write off most of them.

Two years after the second group of settlers had arrived in Lanark, perhaps the most bizarre settlement in the history of Upper Canada was established near Arnprior, not far from the Ottawa River. Its sponsor was Archibald MacNab, a bankrupt Highland laird, who for the purposes of his settlement acquired all the land in the township that still bears his name. Managing to trick his Highland settlers into believing that the community was to be run on the feudal lines that still obtained in some parts of Scotland, The Mac-Nab, as he styled himself, soon — and quite illegally — reduced his unfortunate Highlanders to the status of rent-paying tenants.

This state of affairs was to go on for many years, with The MacNab becoming a well-known figure in the area, given to what might be termed "progresses" about the province accompanied by his own piper and a gaggle of kinsmen. On the occasion of a St. Andrew's Day dinner at Kingston he was observed wearing "a whole acre of MacNab tartan" for a waistcoat — he was a large man — while one of the many stories about him is that the future Sir Allan MacNab of Dundurn Castle, on seeing "The MacNab" written in a hotel register, signed himself in as "The Other MacNab".

Eventually the plight of his impoverished settlers attracted the notice of the public and the authorities finally came to their aid. The MacNab was bought out after a series of legal battles in the course of which he was declared a public nuisance, among other things.

Afterwards MacNab retired to Hamilton and later returned to Scotland, regretted, one imagines, by few and least of all by the editor of the Toronto *Examiner*, whom he had managed to embroil in a series of lawsuits.

About the same time as the egregious MacNab was setting up his shabby fiefdom, a group of some 570 Irish settlers had arrived to make their homes in the neighbouring township of Pakenham, due south of Arnprior. This was another government-assisted venture aimed at relieving the distress in southern Ireland, which was in an even more pitiable state than the Scottish Lowlands. The establishment of the settlement had been placed in the hands of Peter Robinson, brother of Upper Canada's Attorney-General. From England, where he happened to be at the time, Robinson travelled to Ireland to select the emigrants himself.

A couple of years later, Peter Robinson recruited and brought to Upper Canada a second contingent of settlers from Ireland. They were bound for a quite different area, the land lying between Rice Lake and the granite of the Canadian Shield, there to found a settlement that came to be called Peterborough, after the man who was instrumental in bringing it about.

Narrow and some twenty miles long, Rice Lake lies at an angle to the Lake Ontario shore, some ten miles from it at its western end north of Port Hope, and twice that distance at its eastern end.

The Otonabee River, now part of the Trent canal system, flows into Rice Lake from its source in the lakes on the edge of the Shield, and it was up this river that surveyors made their way in 1818 to lay out the first township in what became the county of Peterborough. The earliest settlers to take up land there were from Cumberland in northern England. The region was to attract numbers of Englishmen, many of them army and naval officers on half-pay, which in those days took the place of a pension.

In 1825 when Peter Robinson's party arrived from Ireland, there were some five hundred settlers north of Rice Lake, though on the site of the future Peterborough there was but one, a man named Scott, and for a while the settlement that grew around him was called Scott's Mills. Robinson's settlers had sailed from Cork early in 1825, with the first of them arriving at Scott's Mills in the fall, following a journey that saw them lodged for several weeks at Kingston before they were brought on to Cobourg, then to Rice Lake by road. They were ferried across Rice Lake in boats brought in for the purpose, to be transported up the Otonabee in flat-bottomed boats that had been built to negotiate the many rapids. On arrival they found five buildings already in place, one of which housed a church as well as the resident doctor. Another was Peter Robinson's office, while Robinson and his assistant, Colonel MacDonell, lived in a third house with the surveyors.

Each of the over four hundred families involved were given a hundred acres, a cow, tools, cooking pots and pans, and basic rations which were distributed for eighteen months after their arrival. Well organized as it was, Robinson's venture was a success, with the Irish eventually settling in several townships. However, from the point of view of the British government, which had to pay for it all, the Peterborough settlement, while successful, was also extremely expensive, as had been those in Lanark. It was decided in London to sponsor no more emigration schemes. In the event, it made little difference, as by the later 1820s settlers in increasing numbers were making their own way across the Atlantic. In 1820, the population of Upper Canada was 100,000 and it was to be double that by 1830.

The Peterborough area continued to attract settlers from England. Among them was a Colonel Samuel Strickland who subsequently became involved with the Canada Company and later produced voluminous memoirs. He came in 1825 and was joined by two sisters, both of whom are well-known literary figures. One became Catherine Parr Traill on her marriage; the other, Susanna Moodie, whose somewhat acid account of her experiences entitled *Roughing It in the Bush* circulated widely in Britain and deterred many from coming to Upper Canada.

Besides its development as something of a social and literary centre, the Peterborough area was to acquire agricultural fame, for it was in the township of Otonabee that a variety of wheat was first grown that was to be the basis of Manitoba's great agricultural industry. So closely is wheat-growing now associated with western Canada that it comes as a surprise to learn that wheat grown for export was the principal crop in Upper Canada until the middle of the nineteenth century. "Fall" rather than "spring" wheat was grown because the former gave a flour for which millers would pay higher prices. However, fall wheat could only be grown without risk of losing it to early frost in the western part of the province along the Lake Ontario shore as far east as Cobourg and Prince Edward County. Elsewhere, spring wheat was grown, but this, like all wheat, was — and still is — susceptible to a disease known as black stem rust, which in the third and fourth decades of the nineteenth century caused some disastrous crop failures.

In the early 1840s, a farmer named David Fife in Otonabee Township asked a friend who was visiting Scotland to try to procure a sample of wheat from northern Europe. As it happened, when this friend landed in Glasgow he saw a nearby vessel discharging wheat from Danzig. He obtained a small sample and sent it back to David Fife, who planted it the following spring. Except for five ears, all succumbed to rust, and of these five ears, two were eaten by cattle. Yet from these three remaining ears came the rust-resistant variety of wheat known as Red Fife, which by 1860 was almost the only variety of spring wheat grown in the province. And from Red Fife, ironically enough, came the Manitoba wheat that in the 1880s put an end to the export of wheat from Ontario, although by that time the Ontario farmer was already turning to dairying, to the raising of beef cattle, and to other types of farming.

In 1826 when the village of Peterborough was taking shape, a Lieutenant-Colonel John By of the Royal Engineers arrived in Upper Canada to start work on the Rideau Canal, which, on the advice of the Duke of Wellington himself, was designed to secure the alternative route to Lake Ontario in case of another war with the United States. The plan, making use of rivers and lakes, called for a navigable waterway that was to connect the Ottawa River with Kingston, over ninety miles away as the crow flies. The work, which involved the construction of nearly fifty stone dams, went on for six years. It cost hundreds of lives lost to disease and accidents, and nearly one million pounds, an enormous sum for those days; and at the end of it Colonel By, who, as instructed, had completed the mammoth project in the shortest possible time, was censured by the government for spending too much money. Colonel By, however, has his memorial not just in the canal he built, but in the community of Bytown that grew up at the northern end of the canal, destined to be renamed Ottawa and designated the nation's capital.

The Rideau Canal brought sudden prosperity to the region. Land worth one shilling and threepence an acre in 1824 was worth twenty times that amount when the canal was opened in 1832. There was a local boom in what we now call the construction industry, and with log houses giving place to those of brick and stone there was an urgent need for mortar. And for strong and waterproof mortar, lime is a prime requisite.

Limestone is a common bedrock in Ontario, but only in certain areas is it near enough the surface to be quarried. One such area and the largest of its type in Ontario stretches north-westward from Brockville on the St. Lawrence in a broad, irregular band, and a number of farmers in the region were able to turn into cash what so providentially lay close underfoot. The making and selling of lime became a profitable ancillary business that some farming families were to be involved in through the nineteenth and into the twentieth century, though, as elsewhere in Upper Canada, others burned only enough for their own requirements.

The typical farmer in most of Upper Canada was a man who grew wheat. In the eastern counties, however, farming was to a quite different purpose. Here the farmer acted as supplier to the lumbermen's camps or shanties up on the Shield. He produced their pork, peas, potatoes, and turnips. He raised their horses and oxen and he supplied oats and hay to feed them. When there was a slump in the lumber business, the farmer suffered; in boom times the farmer throve. In the 1840s Bytown was said to be the best market for produce in Upper Canada.

The dependence of farmers on the lumber industry gradually lessened as butter and cheese were produced and exported in increasing quantities. Thus, in 1870 two firms in Renfrew shipped twenty carloads of butter to Britain, while a year later a Perth firm made a single shipment of twenty-eight hundred boxes worth fifty thousand dollars. The export of butter to Britain languished in later years as the Canadian product came up against the fine butters of Europe, with Irish butter commanding the highest price of all. Canadian butter also competed against Australian canned butter, which appeared about 1880, as did Dutch margarine.

Cheese fared better. By about 1850 the eastern counties were producing substantial amounts, with the most coming from Leeds and Glengarry. About this time a Bytown cheesemaker, Bradish Billings, was manufacturing fifteen thousand pounds annually. Cheese-making both for local consumption and for export came to be a tradition in the eastern counties, though as in the rest of Ontario today there are few independent producers left.

For most of the nineteenth century the bulk of milk produced went to make butter and cheese. What is now known as the "fluid milk industry" did not emerge until the 1880s when towns and cities grew too large to be supplied by a farmer and his boy casually making deliveries. And as the demand for fluid milk grew, so did the importance of breeding high-yielding animals.

It was the Holstein breed of dairy cattle that eventually achieved dominance in Ontario, the familiar black-and-white animals seen across the province today. The official name of the breed is Holstein-Friesian; it originated in Holland, and it has a history that can be traced back to Roman times. The first animal reached North America in 1852 when a cow was bought off the master of a Dutch vessel that had sailed into Boston. The cow had been carried to supply milk to the crew of the vessel, which, ironically enough, was carrying a load of rum.

It is thought that the first Holsteins were brought into Ontario in 1881 by Michael Cook of Aultsville, a village that was inundated when the St. Lawrence Seaway was built. Two years later, the first animals were brought directly to Ontario from Holland when the same Michael Cook, in association with a breeder from New York State, imported about a hundred head.

Of the more than 610,000 milk-producing cows in Ontario early in 1979, 570,000, or over ninety per cent, were Holsteins. Probably four-fifths or more of all the dairy animals in Canada are of the same breed. Today the black-and-whites are the pride of the Ontario and the Canadian dairy industry.

The Paul Family
Mount Blow Farm
Ramsay Township
Lanark County

"When you look back on it — and perhaps you don't look back until you are my age — it's clear that each generation had a specific job.

"The first generation came here to the bush and hacked out a clearing and built a shelter. Their greatest ambition was to raise a family and just feed and clothe it. Their children went one step further. They built this house here and cleared a little more land.

"It took them a long time. They just didn't do it all in the first seven or eight years. They had to go very slowly.

"My family were among the 1821 settlers. By 1837 all they had was that field below the house there, a piece of land as small as that. Seven acres, that was all they had cleared in sixteen years.

"The Pauls came from Dumbartonshire in Scotland. They disembarked at Prescott and then went overland to Perth, and from Perth to Lanark. But they didn't stop there. They built a raft, put their possessions on board, and rafted down the Clyde and Mississippi, right down to Almonte. And then they came up here."

It was Norman Paul's great-grandfather who made that journey in 1821. He would later become the first assessor of Ramsay Township and take part in an early census, a census that counted not only population, but livestock and buildings as well. The Pauls owned a single horse and an ox in that year.

"My father and my grandfather built the big barn in '97,"

the barn that still stands against the hillside behind the Pauls' houses.

The older of the two houses now at Mount Blow was built in the late 1840s when the first log structure was torn down. Its destruction came as a shock to Norman Paul's great-grandmother, whose home it had been since their arrival in Upper Canada.

"She was visiting her sister in New York and while she was away they tore down her old house and started on the new one. When she came home and walked up the road, she saw the old place torn down. She just sat down on the bank at the side of the road and cried."

Certainly the site of the new house was chosen with great care; its superb location sets Mr. Paul wondering about the man who built it — his grandfather.

"He must have had a certain eye for beauty. . . . Was it perhaps something that went back to the old country?"

As for the earlier dwelling, it was transformed into a pigpen, a fate common to many of the first primitive log-built structures. The logs are still visible, lying at the edge of the bush.

Norman Paul's great-grandmother lived in her new house until 1860, when her son married. Then a second house was built, a few yards from the first, and she moved into that to leave the older house for her son and his bride. When one of their sons (Norman Paul's father) married in his turn and with the old lady still occupying the newer house, the first house was extended to form, in effect, two houses with sliding doors separating the living quarters. The newlyweds lived in one, their parents in the other, so that the two houses sheltered three generations of Pauls.

The two houses at Mount Blow still shelter three generations and three families. Mr. and Mrs. Norman Paul live in one part of the older house, while their son Frank, his wife Eleanor, and their children live in the other. The second house is occupied by the eldest son, Jim, his wife, Betty, and their family.

Altogether there are thirteen Pauls at Mount Blow today. With the hustle and bustle of this number of men, women, and children, the two houses facing each other across the yard and flanked by the farm buildings give the impression of a small but lively village — an effect heightened by the old ash-house that stands like a monument in the middle of the yard. If village it is, it is a busy one, centring on the herd of some seventy-five pure-bred Holsteins.

"I took everything over here in 1925," explains Norman. "I bought my father out lock, stock, and barrel; all he had left were his clothes and the use of his house as long as he lived. . . . I sold a great herd of Holsteins in 1928, sold 'em all down. Just one cow left. Then I went out, bought a foundation, and I started in again with pure-bred Holsteins. The depression came along. Took me ten years to get back to a full herd. . . . I guess I'm classed as one of the ancient breeders of Eastern Ontario."

Norman Paul is being modest. He was a director of the Holstein-Friesian Association of Canada between 1936 and 1944, and in 1958 he was awarded the Master Breeder's Shield. He holds a Certificate of Recognition presented to him for his services to the national and county Holstein organizations. More recently he was singled out as Farmer of the Year by the Eastern Ontario Soils and Crop Association, with an Award of Merit that recognizes his contribution to agriculture.

"I never did anything sensational or anything startling, but I always kept a good outfit. I took over the farm in 1925, and when I quit in 1963 the farm was producing pretty near fifty per cent more than it was when I began. And I did it without commercial fertilizer.

"As soon as I took over the farm I put it on a five-year rotation: three years in sod, two years ploughed up. I never broke that rotation until we started to spray the corn with atrazine. And that meant we had to run corn for two years because we couldn't put grain in after the atrazine." (Atrazine is a herbicide and may leave residues harmful to succeeding crops.)

"There are some who are growing corn on the same land year after year. And you can see the land changing. There are no little hair rootlets left. Oh, they're still growing a good crop of corn — they've been using a lot of commercial fertilizer. But they're not growing as much as they did ten years ago."

Norman Paul goes on to talk of the connection between continuous ownership and wise land use.

"The better century farms have had somebody coming along for the past ten years. They've kept up the land. There's some farms where there's an older couple, but no one coming along after them. If you went and spent money on those farms you'd just be throwing it away. With no one coming along you don't have the same emotional tie."

Mr. Paul considers himself lucky. In 1950 he made his son Jim a full partner, selling him fifty per cent of the operation. In 1963, the younger son, Frank, was ready to marry and he accepted his father's offer to sell him the remaining fifty per cent of the operation. The sons have been in partnership ever since.

The land around Mount Blow is still well-wooded and from their woodlots the Pauls have taken lumber, pulpwood, and, of course, firewood for the three families. It has always been a family affair. Norman Paul has no use for careless contractors.

But it was the limestone that in its time contributed most to the prosperity of the family. The Pauls carried on a commercial lime business that was handed on through three generations and did not come to an end until 1908. Luckily the Pauls found themselves on a limestone of unusual purity that yielded high-quality white lime. So high in fact that Mr. Paul's grandfather won a medal for a sample he exhibited at the Colonial and Indian Exhibition held in London, England, in 1886. That year was a peak year for the Pauls' lime business, which in its time supplied lime to builders as far away as Merrickville over thirty miles distant.

Norman Paul maintains a lively interest in the history of lime-making and is an acknowledged expert on the subject. In an area two and a half miles square around Mount Blow he has located the sites of no fewer than fourteen lime-kilns, two of them on Mount Blow itself. One of them still exists.

Why Mount Blow? Nobody knows for sure. The farm, though on a hillside, is not unusually wind-swept. Perhaps the name has some connection with the acres of lilacs that have gone wild on the slopes. At least that is what the man who drew the mail back in the twenties thought, and no one has yet come up with a better theory.

The Snedden Family
Mississippi Farms
Ramsay Township
Lanark County

Taking the road north from Carleton Place to Arnprior in 1846, a discriminating traveller stopped at the Sneddens' inn and reported later that "Snedden's Hotel is kept in as good a style as any country inn in the Province." In 1861 it was described by another traveller in glowing terms: "Who," asked this enthusiastic man," in this part of Victoria's domain has not heard of Snedden's as a stopping place? Ask any teamster on the Upper Ottawa and he will satisfy you of its capabilities of rendering the traveller oblivious to the comforts of his home."

Could any ad-man improve on that today, one wonders? As far as comfort went, though, it depended on who you were. If you were a teamster you slept in a bedroll on the barroom floor on the ground level. The dining-room was on the second floor, to which all the food was carried up from a cook-house in the yard at the back.

The white frame house dates from 1840, when an earlier building of logs burned down. Its spaciousness and proportions are in keeping with its one-time commercial function. The doors are of particular interest, with some showing "cross and open-bible" panelling. A curious lack of consistency in the design of the doors bears out the story that the house was "cracked up" in a hurry — in order, one might assume, not to miss the coming season's wave of thirsty teamsters.

The inn had its share of brawls. Some time in the mid-1800s, David Snedden pushed a drunken teamster through the front door and out onto the highway. The fellow hurled himself back to find the door slammed in his face. Whether he kicked the door or merely collided with it is not known, but the front door has a crack in it to this day.

One of the regular patrons of Snedden's Hotel was the notorious MacNab, whose settlement near Arnprior made him one of the area's legendary figures. It seems that this august gentleman had the habit of dropping in for drinks and then offering to pay for them with bills of such large denominations that it was beyond the capacity of the hotel's till to change them.

The hotel went out of business some time in the mid-1800s and thereafter became what it is today, the principal residence of the Snedden family.

The Sneddens came from Cambuslang, Scotland, in 1819. Brothers David and Alexander were the first to emigrate, and their parents joined them later. They followed a blazed trail up the Mississippi River and found the sizeable rapids they were looking for not far from the present farm. Here Alexander built a sawmill, and later another sawmill, a grist-mill, a tannery, and a brewery. He became heavily involved in the lumber business, acquiring hundreds of acres in surrounding townships, and he built a timber slide, charging other lumbermen a fee to run their timber past the rapids. A village grew up round the mills, first known as Norway Pine Falls, then as Snedden's Mills, later as Rosebank, and finally as Blakeney, its present name. At the same time as the mills were under construction, the Sneddens were clearing land for which a Crown Patent was granted in 1837, and which became the nucleus of the present farm. In addition to his business enterprises and his contributions to the farm, it must have been Alexander who first saw the possibilities in catering to the needs of teamsters and who brought Snedden's stopping-place into being.

David Snedden, Alexander's son, who acted as bouncer the night the door was cracked, married a relative, Mary Snedden of Glasgow. The large oil painting that hangs in the present house is of Mary and her sisters. As well as the painting, Mary brought with her from Scotland other items of value including a large needlepoint screen and a ship model in a glass case. That such precious and fragile objects formed part of her possessions suggests a certain confidence that she was coming to a large and well-appointed home in Upper Canada.

Alex W. Snedden, David Snedden's grandson, now runs the farm in partnership with his sons, Earle and Sandy. In 1940 the farm name, Mississippi, was chosen for the Sneddens' Holstein herd, a herd that has since become noted for its excellence, and for which Alex W. Snedden has received a Master Breeder's Shield.

Earle and Marilyn Snedden and their four children live in the old inn, the building having weathered the years with dignity. The shed at the back that used to house fourteen teams of horses has gone, but the outside cook-house and bake-oven are still there, reminders of what must have been an awkward housekeeping practice during the bitter winters on these Ontario uplands.

The Mood Family
Asphodel Township
Peterborough County

Rice Lake, so called because of the wild rice that once grew there, lies south-west of Peterborough. When an early traveller visited in 1816, he found that as many as ten thousand bushels of rice were harvested annually from the lake and that the Indians were happy to sell three bushels for a dollar.

William and Mary Mood live on the north side of Rice Lake on Lot 1, Concession 1, Asphodel Township, in the county of Peterborough. The story of the Mood family in Upper Canada begins with Mary Mood's great-grandfather, Richard Birdsall, of whom Frances Stewart wrote in 1823:

> One very wet day I saw two men walk past my window; one had a blanket about his shoulders, a pair of snowshoes in his hands, and a small fur cap. The other was dressed in ragged sailor's clothes. I took the foremost for an Indian as they generally wear blankets about them, but to our surprise we found this was Mr. Birdsall, a very smart young Englishman who is surveyor of the township in this district, and his assistant; they had with them

five other men as chain-bearers, etc. I found that they had all been living in the woods for the months of March and April, which accounted for the ragged and weatherbeaten appearance of the whole party.[1]

Richard Birdsall was born in Yorkshire in 1799. He received a sound education and, it is thought, some training in the survey methods used by the British Admiralty. In 1818, he emigrated to Canada, and in 1820, at the age of twenty-one, he became an accredited land surveyor in the Newcastle District, afterwards the counties of Northumberland, Durham, Haliburton, Victoria, and Peterborough.

In 1821, Richard, who was described as "upright as a wand", six feet two and handsome, married Elizabeth Burnham and for two hundred and fifty pounds bought nine hundred and twenty acres of land north of Rice Lake from his father-in-law, Zaccheus Burnham.

A visitor to the Birdsalls' house on Rice Lake in 1822 found Elizabeth Birdsall and the baby sick with the ague and Richard housekeeping, looking after the invalids, milking the cows, and providing food for the visitors. "This, I must confess, staggered me a little, but I saw no appearance of dejection in him," the caller remarked.[2]

Richard and Elizabeth had four small daughters in rapid succession. By 1827 they had built a fine new house, but in that year Elizabeth died from a fall in the cellar — walled up after the accident and not reopened for a century.

The Moods' elder son lives in the house that Richard Birdsall built "plank on plank" in 1827. William and Mary Mood live in another house — a Victorian brick home built closer to the lake in 1875 — and their other son is renovating yet another old family house, the Mill House on the lake.

It was Richard Birdsall who named the township where the Moods live. The trilliums that he found there reminded him of the asphodel, "the immortal flower of Elysium". The Moods are situated in Asphodel Township only by a matter of feet, because it was from the back of the house that Richard ran the first survey line that divided Asphodel Township on the east from Otonabee Township on the west. Richard Birdsall was also the man who laid out the town plot of Peterborough in 1825. Mary Mood has a letter from the first doctor in Peterborough, Dr. Hutchinson, asking Richard to take on a promising young man and teach him surveying. The young man was named Fleming, later Sir Sandford Fleming.

Modern surveying can be arduous work and it was even more so then. Following their lines, surveyors tramped through forest, marsh, and mud. In summer they often toiled knee-deep in water, pestered by black flies and mosquitoes. Some are known to have fallen through the ice and drowned. Richard Birdsall was a prodigious walker even for a man in his profession, once covering eleven miles before breakfast and, on another occasion, walking forty miles in one day. It seems it was not until the 1830s that he started using a horse — in 1834 only six residents in the Township of Asphodel owned horses.

Nine years after the death of Elizabeth, Richard Birdsall remarried, and fathered two more daughters and two sons. In 1831 he became a captain in the Northumberland Militia under Colonel Peter Robinson, and in 1837 he led the Asphodel Contingent when it was called out in the Mackenzie Rebellion. He became a Justice of the Peace and Land Agent for the Canada Company. On one winter's trip on behalf of the Company, he crossed thirty-one townships and interviewed one hundred and forty-six settlers. With a farm to run as well, it is no wonder that Mary Mood says his life must have been full, if hectic.

In the winter of 1852 he set off for Cavan on a bitterly cold morning. He became ill with ague — pneumonia, in Mary Mood's opinion — and died the following night. He was fifty-two years of age. Some of his contemporaries attributed his death to the fact that he had drunk two glasses of cold water first thing that morning.

Today the Moods run about a hundred head of Polled Herefords on Richard Birdsall's farm. Bill Mood is a graduate of the Ontario Agricultural College at Guelph and he took an early retirement from teaching science at local schools to concentrate on farming full time.

Mary Mood says that when she was a child the family had Shorthorns. But her father and her grandfather wanted a more placid breed of cattle, so they went in for polled or hornless Herefords. "They were instrumental in introducing Polled Herefords and now almost all Hereford herds are polled." The Moods have their own bulls and sell their progeny as breeding stock.

In the Moods' living-room there is a table made from a regimental drum once belonging to the Royal Dublin Fusiliers; the battle honours inscribed on it speak of military glory in the days of the British Empire: Plassey, Seringapatam, Lucknow, Amboyna, Aden, Punjab, Gujerat, the Relief of Ladysmith.

It was a proud regiment raised by Charles II in 1661, and Bill Mood's father served in it. The Moods have not forgotten or forgiven a "snivelling blathering little Welshman named Lloyd George" who disbanded it in 1922. At least such are the words on a note attached to the drum mourning the demise of this fine regiment.

Mary Mood's cousin, Everett Elmhirst, and his wife live a mile or so up the road. Commander James Elmhirst, the younger son of a titled family, served under Lord Nelson in the Battle of the Nile and came to Canada with his servants, dogs, and horses in 1819. He took up a thousand acres of land on what is now the second line of Otonabee Township, part of which still remains in the Elmhirst family. Everett Elmhirst's farm is not part of the original grant, but on or near it he has found traces of far earlier settlers. On the edge of Rice Lake in 1938 he found bone ornaments and the skeleton of an eighteen-month-old child who, archaeologists have confirmed, died two thousand five hundred years ago. He also uncovered a portion of a conch shell from the Caribbean, copper from the north of Lake Superior, soapstone from the Arctic, and stone from British Columbia. These discoveries place Rice Lake on a trade route used by ancient peoples long centuries before Richard Birdsall made his first survey.

The Robson Family
North Monaghan Township
Peterborough County

As you approach Peterborough from the west, the Willaura Herd Farm appears just on the edge of the city. On one side of the highway are its neat farm buildings and open spaces; on the other, in startling contrast, is a strip of motels, restaurants, and garages — the advance guard of an approaching city.

Willaura Herd Farm is the home of Bill and Laura Robson and of their son, Alan, and his wife, Patricia. Bill Robson was born on the farm and has been a farmer all his life. In 1954, when he was in his early thirties, he was struck in the face by a truck rim while changing a tire. Since then he has been blind.

The Robson family have been on this farm since 1838 when they came from Jedburgh in Scotland. Bill Robson's great-grandfather was a carpenter in Peterborough. He built the old Springwood church, and the little Lakewood church three miles north of the farm, and was working on St. Andrews church in Peterborough when he died.

It was Bill Robson's great-great-uncle who bought the farm originally. Thomas Precious, a native of England, had obtained the Crown grant in the time of King George IV: "given under the great seal of the Province of Upper Canada on the 15th day of June in the year 1827." In 1836, Precious sold the land to Edward Cooney for £150 and Cooney made a handsome profit on it when he sold it two years later to William Robson for £256.5.0.

There was an old log house on the property, probably erected by William and John Robson, and the later addition to the house in which we sit talking was built on in 1886 or 1887 when Bill Robson's grandfather was married. "When his uncle died, my grandfather was to keep his Aunt Mary supplied with wood and all as long as she lived. Her quarters were in the front part of the house." At a time when old-age pensions were unheard of, stipulations of this kind were often made in wills, sometimes imposing a burden on a struggling family.

It is indicative of Bill Robson's adjustment to his handicap that the Robsons continued to farm after 1954. "As for carrying on, being well accustomed to the farm and having always lived here was a great help and he just gradually worked back into some of the chores," Laura Robson says. "We owe a great deal to the two boys, who took a real interest in the serious part of the business. We could not have carried on without them." One suspects that Laura Robson's farm background and support were invaluable, too.

Alan Robson now works the farm with his father. His brother, Neal, is a veterinarian in St. Marys. In 1960 the boys were still in public school and members of the 4-H Club when they began coaxing their parents to replace the grade Holsteins on the farm with pure-bred. This they did. The next year the Robsons installed a bulk milk cooler at a seemingly exorbitant cost of about fourteen hundred dollars.

The Robsons are one of some 14,500 producers of milk in Ontario. The milk is sold through the Ontario Milk Marketing Board, described by some as a compulsory co-operative. The Robsons, like other farmers, have a Group 1 milk quota for fluid milk, that which finds its way to the consumer's table. They also have a market sharing quota for milk that goes into manufactured products, on which they receive a lower rate. They are informed annually in April what their quotas for a year are to be.

"It is important for producer and consumers alike, to understand that managing the supply of an agricultural product is not an exact science," the Milk Marketing Board states in its twelfth annual report. "There will be some ups and downs during the year, and from year to year, albeit far less traumatic than under a totally free market system." In 1977, for instance, it was projected that the Canadian market would require one hundred million hundredweight of milk. "As events turned out," the report continues, "conditions for milk production were good, while consumption was less than expected. The combination of these two factors led to a cut in the MSQ [market sharing quota] of two per cent effective September 1, 1977."

For the Robsons, a limit on the amount of milk they were able to ship has meant that they have had to reduce their dairy herd from thirty to twenty-six cows. By the fall of 1977, they had fulfilled their market sharing quota for the year and were left with none until the following April. In addition, a drop in milk consumption in the province led to their being paid off one month at considerably less than their quota. On the other hand, the price paid by the Milk Marketing Board for a hundredweight of milk (now measured in litres) has gone up.

In theory, it should be easy for dairy farmers to keep within their quotas. The average amount of milk a cow yields in a year is known and, in theory, cows can be added to, or subtracted from, a herd. For the farmer, however, with a substantial investment in every animal, it may not be quite as simple as that.

It is fall when we visit and the eighty-five or so acres of corn the Robsons grow is already in the silos — winter feed for the cattle. We go out to have a look at the cows and though it is quite dark Bill Robson walks over to the barn with confidence. After all, as his wife says, he has known this place since he was a child. Barns full of cows are companionable and soothing places. Without hesitation, Bill Robson picks up a fork and tosses hay for them. They snuffle and blow and munch. We look at the bull in his pen in one corner and at a calf that has been bought and is to go eventually to Brazil.

As we turn to leave, Laura Robson switches off the lights in the barn. Bill Robson is still inside and then it is brought home that, light or dark, it's all the same to him — a courageous man who has overcome his disability to an extent one can only wonder at and admire.

CHAPTER FOUR

On the Opeongo Road

*A*ccording to the Ontario Forestry Association's *Honour Roll of Ontario Trees* the largest white pine in Ontario is probably one near Haliburton, which when last measured in 1975 stood 148 feet high. At the height of a man's chest it was then over five and a half feet in diameter. Large though this tree is, it is puny by comparison to some of the giants that fell to the lumberman's axe in the nineteenth century, during which this valuable and once numerous tree was reduced to insignificance as a commercially important species. The eastern white pine, *Pinus strobus*, has been known to grow as tall as 260 feet, with a circumference of over twenty feet. Such a tree felled in, say, 1850 probably started from a seed that drifted to the ground some four hundred years earlier, about the time perhaps when Joan of Arc was burnt as a heretic in Rouen or when a royal decree went out in England that yews must be cultivated in churchyards to ensure a supply of wood for longbows.

White pine and its smaller relative, the red pine, throve on the uplands of the Canadian Shield. On some sites the pines grew in pure stands, but in the main they grew in association with such valuable hardwoods as hard maple, yellow birch, and beech. In the more northerly areas the mixture of species included spruce and balsam fir.

The rugged terrain of the Shield with its dense forest cover was a formidable barrier to the movement of settlers inland, whether they came eastwards from Georgian Bay, northwards from the Lake Ontario shore, or westwards from the lowlands of the eastern counties.

The only practicable route into this *terra incognita* was up the Ottawa River, which flowed through the heart of it and drew its waters from such tributaries as the Bonnechère, on which the future county seat of Renfrew was to grow, and the Petawawa, flowing eastwards from what is now the heart of Algonquin Park.

The lumbering industry that developed on the Shield came to dominate the economy of the eastern counties. The hundreds of cutting camps or shanties associated with that industry gave rise to the market upon which many farmers depended, some totally. Thus the story of farming and settlement in the upper reaches of the Ottawa and on the Shield itself is intimately bound up with that of the lumberman — and it is a story that, but for a few people, had no happy ending.

Wood is heavy and awkward stuff to transport. Thus the attraction of the Ottawa River country was not only its huge area of unexploited forest, but this in combination with the river itself, which would carry the cut timber to its destination so cheaply. In the earlier years of the nineteenth century the immediate destination of the wood was probably Quebec City, from where it was shipped to England. Since wresting Canada from the French in 1763, Britain had had an eye on the country's timber resources. Where to find the wood to build ships of the Royal Navy, upon which the safety of the realm depended, had always been a worry. The traditional source of timber was Sweden, and as far back as the 1660s we see the indefatigable Samuel Pepys, Clerk of the Acts of the King's Ships, weighing the technical merits of masts from New England against those of the ones he was ordering from Sweden.

During the Napoleonic Wars, with supplies from Sweden uncertain — indeed non-existent at those times when the Baltic was closed to British shipping — the need for timber became desperate. In the eight years from 1793 to 1801 the Navy had grown from 15,000 men to a surprising 133,000 men. In spite of losses, the numbers of frigates and ships of the line had increased from 268 to 479. Apart from the demands of the fighting services, there were those of the merchant marine. Through the war years, as the blockade of Napoleon's Europe tightened, an increasing proportion of the world's goods was carried on British ships. Britain's exports had more than doubled; its imports nearly so. A traveller crossing to Sweden from England once saw a thousand British ships in a single convoy, and in 1814 it was said that one could count as many as two thousand ships in the four-mile stretch of the Thames that formed the Port of London. A forest, but of masts and spars.

Quite apart from the wood to build ships, there were houses to be constructed for a population that had started to soar. With an apparently insatiable market, an abundant wood source, and a convenient river to carry it away, it is no wonder that the lumber trade along the Ottawa became in a short time a mammoth and all-consuming enterprise.

It was not an unregulated enterprise, but on the other hand it was never under firm government control. When Britain acquired what was then called the province of Quebec, successive governors were instructed to set aside stands of oak and pine for the use of the Royal Navy. Selected areas were to be withheld from settlement until the timber had been cut by contractors acting for the Crown, and further, it was urged that the forests be surveyed with a view to selecting the best areas for long-term protection. This last forward-looking measure — which sadly was not carried out — anticipated modern land-use planning by two hundred years.

Needless to say, the idea of timber reserves, and the preservation of trees generally, did not go down well with the early settlers, who were primarily concerned with clearing the forests to make way for agriculture. Moreover, by burning wood, or at least hardwood, they could produce potash, which was in great commercial demand. Making and selling potash was one of the few ways that a settler could get an instant cash return for his labour.

Some settlers simply sold ashes to a neighbouring "ashery" or "potashery", while others did not get beyond leaching the ashes to produce lye, from which soap could be made, or boiling off the leachate to produce what were called black salts. The next stage, which required skill and experience, was melting and cooling the salts to produce a purified product that was used in the manufacture of glass, in the cloth and dyeing industries, and for fertilizer and explosives. In 1851 Upper and Lower Canada had 237 asheries. By 1871 this number had increased to 519, but by 1905 there were only three producers. It took an acre of good hardwood to produce a barrel of pure potash, which might fetch between $80 and $120.

In southern Ontario, then, attempts by the government to reserve timber for the Crown met with little success. In the Ottawa Valley, however, where forestry operations were soon taking place in areas beyond the reach of settlers, cutting went forward under a licensing system of a sort, and at an increasing pace.

The Ottawa River divided Upper Canada from Lower Canada, and it was on the northern or Lower Canada side that lumbering began with the first raft of timber sent down-river by Philemon Wright in 1806. Wright came from Massachusetts and he first visited the Ottawa area in 1796. Impressed by its possibilities, he returned in 1800 with a party of thirty settlers, and by 1804 a tannery, a grist-mill, and a hemp- and sawmill had been built. The settlement, known as Wright's Mills, was later renamed Hull.

The early overseas trade was mostly in squared timber, with the squaring done in the bush by a man wielding a broad or hewing axe.

Squared wood made the best use of a ship's limited cargo space. The rafts themselves were sometimes enormous, containing up to five thousand pieces and carefully made in three layers, with the hardwood sandwiched between two layers of the more buoyant pine. It was not until the middle of the century that growing markets for sawn material, both domestic and foreign, brought the sawmills into greater prominence.

Meanwhile, with the forest virtually cleared on both banks of the lower Ottawa, the lumbermen moved up-river. By 1830 they were operating in the vicinity of Deep River, over a hundred miles west of Bytown. Before another twenty years had passed the lumbermen were near the headwaters of all the tributaries of the Ottawa, and in 1845 the inhabitants of upper Peterborough County were astounded by the appearance of some loggers who had come into the area *from the north*.

The industry was by now employing a great number of men. For example, one operator, John Egan, had in the winter of 1854-55 nearly 4,000 men working for him in the bush, as well as 200 oxen and 1,700 horses. These were distributed over probably more than a hundred shanties. To bring in supplies there were a further 800 horses with their teamsters. During one six-year period, John Egan's average annual requirements were: 6,000 barrels of pork and 10,000 barrels of flour for the men, and 60,000 bushels of oats and 1,200 tons of hay for the horses and oxen. Also needed were potatoes, beans and turnips, while at the same time there was a constant demand for fresh horses and oxen to replace those exhausted by brutal working conditions.

This then was the market for the farmers of the Ottawa Valley. With their farm operations closely tailored to the needs of the lumbermen, the fortunes of the farmers rose when timber was fetching a good price and fell when — as often happened — there was a recession in the lumber trade. Such occurred in the late 1840s. Over-cutting had led to a glut of timber, but what made things worse was a failure of the British market. Curiously enough, this failure was connected with the development of railways in Britain. Curious, because a year or two later it was another railway, American this time, that reaching north to the St. Lawrence opened up new markets and brought a sudden rise in fortune to at least some of the farmers in the eastern counties.

The railways came to Britain suddenly. In 1830 long-distance travel was by horse-drawn coach. Ten years later there were 500 miles of railway track; three years later still, 2,400 miles. The country went railway mad. Thousands were enchanted by the delightful

sensation of speeding so effortlessly through the countryside, even
though, as third-class passengers, they sat in open trucks in a cloud
of sulphurous smoke from the puffing engine's tall chimney.

Unfortunately, in the late 1840s over-investment in projected
railways that were never built led to a financial crash. This brought
housing construction to a halt and the demand for lumber fell. On
the other side of the Atlantic, the lumbermen on the Ottawa, eyeing
their stockpiles in Quebec City, curtailed their operations. And the
farmers, low men on the totem pole, were left without a market for
their produce.

The cost of freighting supplies up the Ottawa was so high that as
time went by the lumbermen encouraged agricultural settlements
closer to their shanties. Some lumbermen started their own farms.
John Egan had one; so had Philemon Wright, who later became
interested enough in agriculture to import Devon cattle to cross with
his native animals.

Among settlers with sights set on a quick cash return from their
crops, there was little thought given to the long-term potential of the
land taken up. Proximity to a shanty was what counted. This, in an
area where much of the land was sub-marginal from the agricultural
standpoint, led inevitably to the abandonment of numerous
farmsteads, if they could be called that. Many were just bush clearings where hay and perhaps some potatoes were grown. Such
settlers were more vulnerable than the farmers down-river, especially as many of them were so involved in shantying themselves
that it was difficult to say whether they were farmers turned lumbermen or vice versa.

It was the need for a more stable labour force and local, and
therefore cheaper, sources of food that prompted the lumbering
interests to pressure the government for a settlement scheme in the
Ottawa-Huron Tract, roughly that land on the Shield between the
Ottawa River and Georgian Bay.

In 1855 the government responded with a decision to build "colonization roads" into and across the region while offering free land
grants that would lure emigrants from Europe. In fact, the government had already started work on two roads in Renfrew County,
both following routes already partly established by the lumbermen.
One went from Arnprior to Pembroke; the other from near Renfrew
on the Ottawa River to Lake Opeongo in the heart of the pine
country. The former is still known as the Government Road, while
the latter is familiarly referred to as the Opeongo Road. Two of the
century farmers in this chapter are located on the Opeongo Road.

In time, five roads were built across the Ottawa-Huron Tract to
form a rough grid system. But by the early 1860s things were already

starting to go awry. Complaints began to come in from the lumbering companies about settlers trespassing on company limits and cutting where they should not be cutting. There were bogus settlers who took up land merely to cut the timber that was on it and, having cut it, decamped to do the same thing elsewhere. Then there was the question of the roads' upkeep. Many were roughly cleared trails just wide enough for a wagon and on these the bush soon started to re-establish itself. The settlers wanted roads they could use all year; the lumbermen were interested only in roads they needed for winter hauling. Attempts to keep the roads open by the settlers themselves failed simply because there were not enough of them. For in spite of an advertising campaign that was conducted in German, French, and Norwegian, as well as in English, only a few settlers came, such as the Polish emigrants who founded a settlement in 1864 near Wilno between Barry's Bay and Golden Lake. But in general, the scheme to populate the Ottawa-Huron Tract was a failure.

It was a bad time to try to lure people to the province. In the late 1850s the American west was opening up, and at about the same time as Europeans were being cajoled into settling in the Ottawa-Huron Tract, American agents were busy in Kingston persuading Canadians that they would be better off in Illinois. Many agreed and for a while the exodus to the States was a matter of acute government concern.

Quite apart from the failure to attract settlers, the colonization roads had in them the seeds of their own failure. The lumbermen found that once the roads were built, it was cheaper to bring in supplies in bulk than to purchase them piecemeal from the settlements scattered up and down the roads.

With the lumbermen no longer buying from them, or perhaps gone for good, many settlers abandoned their holdings and left. When Manitoba was opened up for settlement later in the century, interest in the Ottawa-Huron Tract died once and for all. It was the end of the last major settlement scheme in Ontario.

As for the lumbermen on the Ottawa, their great days passed with the virtual elimination of the eastern white pine as one of the world's finest timber trees. Perhaps it might be said that it all ended in 1893 when the government of Ontario, badgered for nearly a decade by an enlightened official of the Crown Lands Office named Alexander Kirkwood, finally established Algonquin Park.

In Renfrew County there are still farmers on the Shield. But for the most part agriculture is now confined to the more fertile clays of the bottomlands that fringe the Ottawa River and to the better soils of the uplands that mark the edge of the Shield. On these uplands large numbers of beef cattle range, and in this area there is a continuing trend for the more enduring and successful farmers to take over the land from those who have given up.

It is said that the days of quick cash returns from the long-dead shanty market have not yet been forgotten in Renfrew County and that there are still some farmers who against all reason and the best of agricultural advice still hanker after a good cash crop.

Davidson Family
Grattan Township
Renfrew County

The Davidsons are among the enduring and successful families in Renfrew County who survived the decline of the shanty market. They have lived at Davidson's Corners, some twenty-five miles west of the town of Renfrew, since 1849. They took up land on the old Opeongo Trail when it was only an Indian track being used as a lumbermen's road, and they were already settled in the heyday of the lumbering period when John Egan employed four thousand men in the bush in the winter of 1854-55.

Allan Davidson was out on his tractor when we called, and we had some trouble finding him. Somewhere in the distance we could hear the sound of his machine and we made our way towards it, walking the length of a newly mown field where the purple flowers of joe-pye weed mingled with the cut grass. On our right was a belt of trees, on the left, a wooded hillside rising steeply to the skyline. The field was a long, narrow strip of cleared land on the edge of the bush. When we found Allan Davidson he obligingly drove back to the house, his old dog running behind, and sat down with us in the kitchen to talk.

Allan lives here with his wife, Justine, and his son, James. The Davidsons came originally from Scotland, but they left "with a price on their heads" to settle in Ireland, he says. Later they left Ireland for Canada, and although he is a third-generation Canadian, Allan speaks with the brogue of his Irish ancestors.

The house we sit in was built during the 1940s, but outside it is the striking complex of log buildings that attracts visitors by the bus-load. It includes an ox stable, a horse stable, a barn, a house, and a summer kitchen. Allan Davidson has looked after the buildings well. "They had flat roofs, but I put on the peaky ones," he says. "I thought if the old people could build the buildings, surely I could keep them up."

He has also looked after the possessions he inherited from his father and his grandfather and has added to them, so that now he has a remarkable collection of early artefacts from the lumbering, farming, and railroading past. His description of these is a lesson in social history: "These old metal knives and forks came from France in the early days," he says. "Here's a marker for marking squared timber. It has 'J. R. Booth' written on it. I worked in the shanties for J. R. Booth. Might even have seen him.

"Here's an old washboard and an old rope-maker. A battleaxe from Germany . . . another kind of French axe, the oldest thing in this country.

"These bullet moulds belonged to my grandfather. He fought in the Riel Rebellion and I have his muzzle loader. . . . These are shanty dishes. Tin. Hand-made. They didn't have presses to make them. . . .

"This is a potash cooler — the flat-bottomed one. Two coolers made a barrel of potash. A cooper in Eganville made the barrels. Used the lye on ships so that the barnacles wouldn't get at them."

And on and on. Perhaps one of the most interesting of his possessions is a prized bear gun made in the United States in 1857. An ingenious self-firing contraption, made to be baited and hung in a tree, it fired into the bear's mouth when the bait was taken.

The Davidsons had been on their hundred acres for fifteen years when they received the deed for it in 1864. The deed was issued in Quebec and signed by John Simpson. Extracts from it read sonorously. "John Davidson of the Township of Grattan, Yeoman, An actual settler," was granted the land "saving nevertheless, to Us, Our Heirs and Successors, all Mines of Gold and Silver that shall or may be hereafter found on any part of the said Parcel or Tract of land . . . and saving and reserving to Us, our Heirs and Successors, all White Pine Trees that shall or may now or hereafter grow or be growing on any part of the said Parcel or Tract of land. . . . In the year of Our Lord one thousand eight hundred and sixty four in the twenty seventh year of Our Reign." The monarch was Queen Victoria, forty-five years old, the mother of nine children, and a widow.

The original hundred-acre grant has been expanded to almost one thousand. Allan Davidson runs beef cattle and raises some pigs, and the farm has fine timber on it. In living memory none has been cut besides the twelve cords or so that the family uses in winter. "I have a lot of people here every week looking for me to sell the timber. But why should I sell it? If I put the money in the bank it would only go down that much even if I do draw the interest. . . . And the timber's growing. Maybe the bank could go flat, but I'd still have the timber."

Behind the Davidson farm are twenty miles of rough bush and lake country in Griffith Township in the direction of a place named, incongruously, Khartum. "We bought a farm back there and planted out about twenty thousand pine. . . . My boy will take it over. He works as a welder, but he comes home to the farm every night. Always comes home and helps us or helps a neighbour.

"The farm? Well, it's the best place to live now. There's a lot of people moving out from the cities. We even have hippies out here. Good lads, couldn't meet better lads, well educated. . . . Indians used to come by selling baskets and stuff like that. All nice people. The ones up at Golden Lake, you couldn't meet better people and I've worked with a lot of them."

The shadows are beginning to lengthen when we leave. With the steep hills covered by dark bush, the fields surrounded by trees, and the weathered log buildings, it is easy to imagine this farm as it must have looked during the last century, a remote clearing on the Opeongo Road.

Dick Family
Grattan Township
Renfrew County

"*I* buy cattle in the spring, small ones. They're sold to a feed lot in the fall. That finishes them up. Then I do quite a bit of buying at cattle sales for other people and I buy cattle from the neighbours. . . . All my life I've bought and sold and trucked and traded — a sort of gypsy outfit you might say."

While many farmers have deserted the inhospitable bush and granite country of the Renfrew County uplands, Ken Dick, who is speaking, has not. He is a highly successful cattleman and lives with his wife, Inez, on a farm near Balaclava in the Scotch Bush area of Renfrew County. In our search for the Dick farm, a turning takes us down a narrow track between dusty underbrush. A fork to the left and suddenly there's a century farm sign. Beyond this and over a cattle grid lies open ground where the turf is short and dry between low mounds of granite bedrock. Long lines of rail fences edge the clearings.

The Dicks' farm is on a knoll, a collection of log buildings set off by freshly painted scarlet and white fences. The old house has been smartly renovated and the white chinking in the log buildings looks almost new. In such spick-and-span surroundings, only our dusty station wagon is grimy and out of place.

The Dick family came from Scotland in 1840. "The first Dick, my great-grandfather, was a miller," Ken Dick explains. "He came up the Bonnechère River as far as Fourth Chute and shantied here for a while; then he went west. He sold the land to my grandfather for a dollar, plus so many hens, a couple of pigs, a team of horses, and five sheep. I have the deed with all that in it. . . . It was my grandfather who built all these log buildings. He was a good corner man and he chopped all the corners with an axe. He also put up the log fences. I have miles of log fences and I maintain them all. . . .

"My mother died when I was five years old and I came to stay here with my grandparents. . . . I walked to school from here, one and a half or two miles through the bush. I got my education on snowshoes in the winter, you might say. Yes, every day was a good day for school. Rain, snow, or freezing."

The school to which Ken Dick went is the little brick school in the Scotch Bush settlement, the Protestant Separate School, Grattan, No. 1. It is one of only two Protestant separate schools in the province of Ontario, and remains a country school in the old style, with children from various grades taught by one teacher. Ken Dick's grandfather established it, and Ken has fought hard to keep it open. "It's not doing too well right now," he says, "but I think this is the best way to teach children, even yet.

"I quit school when I was fourteen. Following April, my grandfather died. He left me the farm, the stock, and the machinery and I've been farming ever since.

"My grandfather was in beef cattle. He was the first man to raise Durham cattle, but they got down pretty small up here. My father, though, he never raised cattle, he bought and sold them, and that's what I've done all my life. There were six boys in my family and we're all in the beef business. We've all made a success of it. I planned to have my son in the business, too. He was coming along dandy, but his health is not too good. . . ."

During the summers Ken Dick is away for three days each week at the sale barns in Cobden, Galeta, and Perth. He runs some 300 beef cattle, though he has had as many as 800. To do this, he bought other farms in addition to the one inherited from his grandfather. "I had five other farms: that's six altogether. I sold one last year and two this spring. But I still have two more really good farms besides this one. I don't farm them at all; just use them for pasture. Then I've five or six farms rented besides, and sometimes seven or eight. . . .

"I've done pretty well here. I'm practically retired and I have been for the past ten years. I aimed at making enough to retire by the time I was fifty so that we could go to Florida for the winters, and I've done that. I don't care if they give me the old-age pension or not."

Inez Dick is equally positive in her outlook. "When we were married and I came here," she recalls, "we didn't have that much, let me tell you. We didn't even have a cow and we had to work hard. Now we have a new car every year and a new truck every two years. . . . We've been thirty-five years married, and we've made it together.

"Ken has been in the cattle business all his life and he seems to know just what to buy. Of course, you never know. Maybe we'll have a bad year this year. Even so, Ken wouldn't want to move from here, and so far we've come out on top."

The Quilty Family
Admaston Township
Renfrew County

*I*t is a very hot afternoon in the course of a hot, dry summer, perhaps not the best moment to drop by. The farmer has been out on the parched fields cutting hay. He is disturbed by the dog barking as we ring at the door.

The farmer is Leonard Quilty. He and his wife, Irene, live in a white house among a cluster of log buildings set back from the road on the old Opeongo Trail some miles from the town of Renfrew. We sit in the new extension to talk of the history of the family and the farm. A quiet conversation, tempered by the heat.

The first Quilty, Thomas, was born in Limerick in Ireland in 1808 and came to Renfrew from Perth with his wife and baby daughter. All three are buried in the cemetery of the Catholic church at Mount St. Patrick, a church which Leonard Quilty says is one of the most beautiful in the whole Ottawa Valley. Leonard's mother's family, from whom the farm was inherited, left Louth near the Ulster border during the years of the potato famines and came from Castleford up the Opeongo Trail. "They made an awful mistake when they came to this country. They followed the maple trees because they thought they were a sign of good soil." But the good soil was north and west of the town of Renfrew in what was then swamp land, unusable until it was drained years later. The maples, however, yielded potash for the early settlers and old ash-pits are still found on the farm.

The Quilty house is like a series of Chinese boxes — a house within a house within a house. There stands a log house, covered by clapboard, then by brick siding, and now by aluminum. For years the water supply was brought up from a well. "It was a ritual to hitch up a horse to the stone boat and drag up a couple of barrels from the field." To supply Michael Quilty's family of nine children this must have been quite a chore, especially in winter. Michael was Leonard's father.

Farming for the Quilty family was, at first, the traditional mixed farming of the early settlers: hogs, sheep, and cattle, with horses to do the work; later a flock of hens. Leonard's mother sent wool to a carding-mill at Killaloe and a black sheep was always kept to vary its colour. The wool was washed on the same spot about a hundred feet away from the well and traces of grease are still there.

It was good sheep country and the disappearance of sheep was almost a disaster for the area. Sheep farming failed because of lack of markets and because of the numbers of wolves and hybrid dogs — inevitable perhaps in an area of hills and forests. The dog/wolf cross is still a problem. The animal is sometimes larger than a timber wolf and much more vicious, occasionally attacking cattle as well as sheep.

The Quiltys used to farm extensively, but now they have a small beef operation. "We keep going because we have a good range of machinery and do a fair amount of custom work. No, we don't grow corn. We keep the farm in alfalfa but this year it hasn't been so good. Whether it is the weather or a lack of bees or what, I don't know." Nor has it been a good year for trefoil. And usually there's enough hay to sell, but this year it's down by about a third.

We might have ended our afternoon's conversation without hearing the other half of the story. Leonard Quilty was not about to tell it without his wife's encouragement, and to have missed it would have been a pity. It is the account of the family's involvement in their community.

Leonard's father, Michael, before he was married around 1900, worked as a lumberman cutting squared timber. The family still has his broad axe. Later when he returned to farming, he walked from farm to farm to set up the first rural mail delivery service. "He had to get so many mail-boxes to the mile to qualify. He ended up with all but two, so he bought two boxes for a couple of old fellows around here."

Michael's next project — the introduction of the telephone — was undertaken in 1918. Local businessmen put up the money for a company called the Renfrew and Shamrock Telephone Association and the Quilty family maintained the twenty-two miles of lines and repaired its sixteen phones until it was taken over by Bell Telephone Company of Canada in 1954. Michael Quilty also helped organize the county road system by which the Opeongo Trail was designated as a county road. In addition he was a councillor for Admaston Township for twenty-two years, reeve for eleven years, and a member of the school board for sixteen years.

Leonard Quilty is now, like his father, the Reeve of Admaston Township and has served on the school board for sixteen years. Thirty years ago he was instrumental in bringing hydro-electricity to the area. In 1962 and 1963 he was the Liberal provincial member of Parliament for Renfrew South. Irene Quilty was teaching music in the Renfrew separate schools at the time, as she still does, and of this experience she says simply, "we survived." Their two boys were young but they were able to help. Leonard was back from Toronto at weekends and a neighbour looked after the farm.

Leonard Quilty says that in running for public office he still gets votes because of his father's record of thirty years ago. Father and son, the Quiltys have amassed between them some sixty-five years of public service. Leonard's community work with various organizations has been equally significant. It is for this that he thinks he was awarded the Papal Honour of St. Sylvester by the Pope in 1963, "although you never know how you get these things." Typically, the St. Sylvester citation is not displayed in the Quilty house, but is found, after some searching, carefully put away in an atlas to keep it flat.

One of the Quiltys' two sons is in the Ontario Provincial Police, the other at Conestoga College. Will they return to the farm one day? Perhaps one of them may. They have both inherited a sense of responsibility from their father and their grandfather, Irene Quilty thinks. Leonard Quilty is a quiet man himself, an embodiment of the family motto, "By reason, not anger". A verse on his favourite mug sums up his attitude:

> Let the wealthy and great
> Roll in splendour and state
> I envy them not I declare it.
> I eat my own lamb
> My own chickens and ham
> I shear my own fleece and I wear it.
> I have lawns I have bowers
> I have fruits I have flowers
> The lark is my morning alarmer,
> So my jolly boys now
> Here's God speed the plough
> Long life and success to the farmer.

CHAPTER FIVE

The Irish of the Eastern Counties

*N*ever robust at the best of times, the economy of Ireland was brought to near disaster by the revolution in the American colonies. The manufacture of linen from flax was Ireland's only industry and the seed for the flax came from America, as did the potash used to bleach the linen, potash laboriously made by methods that the American settlers were later to introduce to Upper Canada. The outbreak of war in the American colonies brought these all-important imports to an end, and not for the first or the last time in her long, sad history, Ireland sank into economic depression.

Nor could the flax seed or potash be brought from America in Irish ships. Such commerce was forbidden by Britain's Navigation Acts, as was the manufacture in Ireland of any articles that might compete with English-made products. Sheep could be raised, for example, but woollen mills were prohibited. The Irish, like the Americans, were in that same economic strait-jacket designed to increase the wealth of England at the expense of her overseas possessions. And Ireland had been to all intents and purposes an English colony since the twelfth century.

Scarcely a hundred years after William of Normandy won the Battle of Hastings in 1066 and went on to conquer England, an Irish earl asked Henry II for help in pressing his claim to the High Kingship of Ireland. Henry agreed to help, and in 1169 a largely Welsh army led by Anglo-Norman knights under the Earl of Pembroke landed in Ireland. One of the knights was Richard Talbot, the ancestor of Colonel Thomas Talbot, who over six hundred years later was to found a settlement on Lake Erie.

The Earl of Pembroke had some thoughts of keeping Ireland for himself, but in the end he offered it to Henry, who formally annexed it to the English Crown in 1172. Seven centuries and more were to pass before Ireland, or most of it, achieved its independence, and even today its troubles are not over.

In the century following that initial invasion, the Anglo-Normans came into possession of half the country, though the area over which the King's Writ prevailed varied from district to district. Around the capital, Dublin, for example, was the Pale, a word having the same root as "paling", meaning a fence. Inside the Pale all were subject to the English; outside were the unconquered Irish — whence comes the expression "beyond the pale" with its unfortunate connotation of something reprehensible and unsavoury.

The enmities between England and Ireland were rooted in religious differences. During the Reformation England became Protestant while Ireland remained Catholic, and the political consequences of this schism became apparent as early as 1595 when Catholic Spain sent one hundred ships and an army of ten thousand men in an abortive attempt to support a rebellion in Ulster.

It was to subdue the Catholic Royalists who supported Charles II that Oliver Cromwell went to Ireland in 1649, there to act with such ruthlessness that his name is abhorred in that country to this day. And it was to the Irish that James II turned in his bid to regain the English throne and restore England to Catholicism — only to be defeated with his army by William of Orange at the Battle of the Boyne, fought, as every Irishman remembers, on July 1, 1690. The tragedy of Ireland was that she lay too close to England for England's comfort.

Subjected to laws that forbade those of the Roman faith to hold any Crown or civic office, practise law or business, purchase land, or even send their children to school, the Catholic Irish watched as much of their country was parcelled out to Protestant settlers in schemes deliberately designed to help keep Ireland under the thumb of the English. Such schemes were initiated in the days of Elizabeth I, to be continued by her successor, James I, who encouraged the Presbyterian Scots to take up land in northern Ireland — which is why many who later emigrated to Upper Canada from Ulster were in fact of Scots origin. Later in the mid-1600s thousands of Cromwell's soldiers were settled in Ireland following their discharge, rather in the manner of Upper Canada's Perth Military Colonies founded for a somewhat similar purpose. Later still in the days of Queen Anne, numbers of Protestant refugees from mainland Europe were resettled by the British government in Ireland. Thus one century farm family from the Rhine Palatinate lived for two hundred years in Ireland before emigrating to North America. And in 1655 there was a scheme for resettling Sligo, a town in north-west Ireland, with New Englanders. Some did in fact emigrate in reverse, as it were, though it seems they did not think too much of the climate.

By the end of the 1700s, of the six million people in Ireland, one million were Protestants, who, though alien, held all the power in the land. They, and English landlords, owned most of the country: more than three-quarters of it, in fact. Over the centuries the native Irish had been reduced to landless tenants who, with the exception of those in Ulster, had few rights before the law. The majority of these people were living in conditions of such squalor and misery that it would be difficult to envisage a lower standard of living. There were very few towns. Dwellings for the most part consisted of low huts bolstered by stones, built on bare earth and roofed with turf, with no chimney to carry away the smoke from the fireplace. In the absence of furniture of any kind, humans slept on the floor with their animals. And over all hung the shadow of the landlord.

Time after time the Irish had in desperation rebelled against their oppressors, only to be subdued with that especial ferocity engendered by religious differences. Then, in the late 1700s, with the failure of the Irish economy that resulted from the revolt in the American colonies, yet another crisis started to build up in Ireland. William Pitt (the Elder), with his belief in free trade, had proposed economic union with Ireland, but nothing came of it. The condition of the Irish continued to deteriorate, until in the 1790s, with Britain embroiled in the war against Napoleon, they rose in a rebellion with the complicity of the French. This revolt was finally put down in 1798 after an excess of brutality that could only add to the bitter hatred of the Catholic Irish for the English.

By this time, another factor was contributing to the plight of the Irish. For reasons yet to be explained, the population of Britain and Ireland started to soar during the Napoleonic Wars and in the years following. In 1811 the census gave a total of about 12.5 million. In 1831 it was 16.5 million, and by 1851, in spite of emigration, it was nearly 21 million, almost double what it had been forty years earlier. For Ireland this meant desperate overcrowding with land divided, subdivided, and subdivided again. In 1841, forty-five per cent of the land holdings were found to be less than five acres.

Survival was made possible on such small holdings only by the cultivation of potatoes, an acre and a half of which, it was reckoned, could keep a family of six for a year. The Irish poor had been subsisting on a diet of potatoes and skim milk for generations. There had always been crop failures followed by famine, but in the early years of the nineteenth century these started to occur with increasing frequency, which, with the rise in population and the depression following the Napoleonic Wars, plunged the Irish into even greater misery.

Following the rebellion of the 1790s, Ireland had been formally incorporated into the United Kingdom in order to keep it under firmer control. Thus, the British government after 1801 became fully responsible for Irish affairs and to do that government justice, the state of Ireland became of increasing concern to it, as witness the government-sponsored settlement schemes that brought Peter Robinson's settlers to Upper Canada. In the first few decades of the nineteenth century over one hundred commissions and some sixty special committees had been set up to report on the state of the country. All predicted disaster unless the Irish economy could be put on its feet, something done about unemployment, and the Irish standard of living raised.

Meanwhile, the Irish poor were falling victim to the "consolidating" landlords who evicted them in order to merge their holdings into units that made for more efficient farming. One such landlord was the third Earl of Lucan, whose obtuseness was later to lead to that gallant tragedy of the Crimean War known as the Charge of the Light Brigade. He eventually evicted ten thousand people from his estates in County Mayo. Whole villages were razed and the inhabitants turned on to the roads without food, shelter, or hope. Those who refused to leave their huts had them pulled down over their heads by "crow-bar brigades". To give him his due, Lord Lucan had a vision of a more prosperous Ireland and poured large sums of money into improving his properties and farms. He built barns and houses, drained land, and bought machinery. But in his opinion there were far too many people in Ireland. They stood in the way of progress and must be got rid of.

In a grim way Lord Lucan's wishes were to be realized through the agency of a pathogen which is now known as *Phytophthora infestans* or "Late Blight". It was Late Blight that led to the deaths of a million people.

It is now understood that this fungus flourishes in humid conditions, that it can overwinter in a diseased potato tuber, that in the spring fungal spores may be air-borne to infect other plants, and that, through the use of blight-resistant varieties and other measures including the use of fungicides, the disease can be effectively controlled. In 1845 none of this was known, and although what we would now describe as expert consultants were called in, they could help little.

All had seemed well until July 1845. Then the weather turned cool with persistent rain, cold, and fog. Disquieting reports of blighted potato fields started to come in from southern England, Holland,

and France. Then the news was received that the fields around Dublin were affected. The British government, however, continued to hope, and as further news of the disease came in, tended to discount it — intelligence out of Ireland was proverbially unreliable. Then the crop was dug. Not every field was affected; but it was bad enough.

The British Prime Minister, Sir Robert Peel, without waiting for Cabinet or Treasury approval, ordered $100,000-worth of Indian corn from the United States. A relief commission was set up in Ireland to organize local relief schemes, raise subscriptions to buy food, and start make-work programs. The Indian corn when it arrived turned out to be flint-corn, inedible unless it was pulverized. Reducing the corn to meal in the huge amounts needed, transporting it, and setting up food depots, involved a tremendous organizational effort which was mounted with the help of the army. Then a totally unforeseen difficulty arose. When the corn-meal was ready it was found that the Irish would not eat it and they could not be brought to do so until they were on the verge of starvation.

Then, in the following year, 1846, came total and irretrievable disaster. The potato crop was a complete write-off. Overnight it seemed that there was nothing but blackened potato fields from one end of Ireland to the other, while to heighten the atmosphere of cataclysm it was a season of violent thunderstorms and torrential rain. Typhus broke out, as did another fatal disease, relapsing fever. To cap it all, Ireland passed, as did the rest of Europe, into a winter of appalling severity.

Up to the summer of 1847 the efforts of the British government on behalf of the Irish had been sincere and whole-hearted, though the measures taken as the disease and famine spread could only partly allay the sufferings of the people. Over eight million pounds had been spent on relief, the equivalent of forty million dollars at the rate of exchange then prevailing and of much more than that in today's money.

Then, with a change in the government and yet another and singularly ill-timed attempt at rebellion, there came a fundamental change in policy that was to be the ruin of Ireland. Henceforward the destitute were to be dealt with under the Poor Laws, which meant that relief could only be obtained through local authorities, whose only source of income was taxes levied on landowners. In short, the Irish were to look after themselves. The make-work programs were to cease, as was the free distribution of soup — a form of relief pioneered by the Quakers.

To meet their taxes, landlords evicted tenants unable to pay their rent. Thousands were thrown on relief and the land was abandoned. And then came two final, crushing blows. In 1848 the potato crop failed yet again and at the end of that year there was a further epidemic — this time of Asiatic cholera. By 1849, Ireland lay in ruins. Towns were deserted, warehouses empty and shuttered; trade was at an end; beggars were everywhere; even the landlords, now owning thousands of acres of useless land, had to eat rabbits to keep themselves alive.

And yet when Queen Victoria paid a four-day visit to Dublin in August 1849, she received a tumultuous welcome from immense crowds and when she sailed away they watched and waited until the last trace of smoke from the funnels of the *Victoria and Albert* had vanished below the horizon.

It has been estimated that one and a half million died in Ireland from starvation and disease in the great famine — very roughly one out of every six people. The overall loss to Ireland, though, was something in the order of about two and a half million. For nearly a million Irish had emigrated: to England, the United States, and Canada.

There is a curious connection between the transportation of emigrants to North America and the growth of the lumber industry in the Ottawa Valley. With the closing of the Baltic in 1807, England started to look to North America for her timber and it was this that put the lumber industry on the high road to prosperity. In 1801 there were fewer than one hundred ships plying between Britain and Canada: by 1845 there were two thousand. There was a problem, however. The small population of eastern Canada required little in the way of imports and many ships carrying timber to England had to make an unprofitable return in ballast. Until they started to carry emigrants.

To an increasing extent, eastbound timber came to be subsidized by westbound passengers. From the economic point of view, everyone benefited. Timber in Britain became cheaper and fares to North America were reduced. In 1816 it cost perhaps £12 to cross the Atlantic. By the 1840s the steerage passenger rarely paid more than £3.10s. Competition for passengers became extremely keen. An American ship-owner stated in 1848 that in the preceding year emigrant fares had brought in as much as five million dollars.

Emigrant traffic was by no means unregulated by the British government. The first acts specifically relating to emigration had been passed in the 1820s. At the time of the famine, the Passenger

Act of 1842 was in force. Each passenger was to be given a weekly ration of seven pounds of bread, biscuit, flour, meal, or rice — or the equivalent in potatoes. This was to make sure that the passengers did not starve on the way. Emigrants were expected to provide their own "sea-store". The numbers of steerage passengers were to be restricted and each passenger was to be allowed ten square feet of deck space.

In reality, the provisions of the Passenger Acts were so loose as to be virtually unenforceable, opening the way to every sort of fraud, chicanery, and double-dealing, not to mention downright brutality: in all of which the Irish emigrant was the helpless victim.

Starving and ragged, and later diseased as well, the Irish emigrants flocked to the ports in their thousands. The recognized place of departure for the Irish was Liverpool, where the travellers fell victim to unprincipled lodging-house keepers and passage brokers. But in 1847, for example, eighty-five thousand left from the ports and harbours of Ireland itself to which vessels of every description flocked in the hopes of making easy money.

Among them were the so-called "coffin ships" such as the *Elizabeth and Sarah*, which sailed from County Mayo in 1846, taking eight weeks to reach Quebec. The ship was only 330 tons and was over eighty years old. Legally limited to 155 passengers, she carried 276, and for these there were only thirty-two berths. She had insufficient water, no food had ever been issued, and there were no sanitary arrangements of any kind. Forty-two died on the way, including the master.

It was not until the Passenger Act of 1842 was amended for the third time that it was forbidden to berth single men and women together. The berths in most cases were six feet square and this space had to be shared by four people. Cooking might be done, if it were done at all, in a small room which, in one ship carrying four hundred passengers, was only large enough for six people to stand in. Most had to do with uncooked food, while the women and the infirm who had no one to fend for them had difficulty getting any food at all. In many ships there were no lavatories, and in any case rarely more than one for every hundred people. Between decks the head-room was usually not greater than six feet and in these cramped and filthy quarters the emigrant could expect to spend anywhere from five to seven weeks. That is, if he or she survived. Deaths and burials at sea were so frequent that it has been said that if it were possible to erect a memorial for each one, the passage of the emigrant ships across the Atlantic would be marked by a forest of crosses.

And when the emigrants arrived in Canada, many were to experience the tragedy, horror, and heroism associated with Grosse Île, the quarantine station in the St. Lawrence, where thousands died of typhus, and from where the epidemic spread to Quebec, Montreal, Kingston, and Toronto to cause the deaths of many thousands more.

Central to the drama of Grosse Île was a doctor named George Douglas. Son of a Methodist minister, he was born in Carlisle in the north of England in 1809. In 1822 he joined his brother, James, who was a doctor in the state of New York and from whom he learned medicine. In 1826 James fled to Canada for an unusual — and possibly unique — reason: he was threatened with prosecution for dissecting cadavers, then illegal in New York State. James settled in Quebec and there George was given his own licence to practise medicine in 1827.

At the time, cholera, originally from India, was regularly being brought to Canada by emigrants from the British Isles, and in 1832 two quarantine stations were set up under the control of the army, one at Gaspé and the other at Grosse Île, a beautiful, three-mile-long island some thirty miles downstream from Quebec City. Following experience at the Gaspé station, Dr. George Douglas became chief medical assistant at Grosse Île and then, in 1836, superintendent with a salary of twenty-five shillings a day. Three years later he married and established a farm on Grosse Île — something that he afterwards must have deeply regretted.

The first emigrants to reach Quebec after the first partial failure of the potato crop seemed relatively well-to-do. In April 1846 the *Lord Sydenham* brought seven hundred passengers from Limerick, all well provided for and apparently bound for the United States. Then, as more ships arrived, the condition of the emigrants worsened as the flight from Ireland gained momentum. Most had embarked without any sea-stores and had had to rely on provisions being doled out on board; arriving literally penniless, they had to be given sixpence to help cover the fare to Montreal.

In the spring of 1847 officials at Quebec watched the ice clearing from the river with uneasiness. News of the second complete failure of the potato crop had reached Quebec, but the magnitude of the flight from Ireland took the officials there by surprise, as it had everyone else. In February, Dr. Douglas asked for three thousand pounds for extra facilities on Grosse Île to deal with what was likely to be an unusually busy season. He was allotted less than three hundred pounds, together with a small steamer to bring the emigrants up to Quebec City, and a sailing vessel — providing he could rent one for the season for less than fifty pounds.

There was an unusually late opening to the shipping season that year with ice persisting until late April. In the first week of May, Dr. Douglas opened the hospital on Grosse Île, installing fifty new beds. The hospital could now accommodate two hundred. With Dr. Douglas were his usual staff of three: a nurse, an orderly, and a steward.

On May 17, the first ship came up-river. This was the *Syria* from Liverpool with 243 passengers. There had been nine deaths at sea, and over fifty were ill. The typhus epidemic had spread to Canada. In the week following, further ships arrived, and by May 21, Dr. Douglas had 430 cases of typhus on his hands. By May 28, there were 856 cases of typhus and dysentery on the island, with a further 470 on the ships requiring treatment. Awaiting inspection were another thirty-six ships with a total of thirteen thousands passengers. The responsibility for inspecting these lay with Dr. Douglas alone.

Meanwhile, Dr. Douglas had been loaned a marquee and 266 tents by the Army, though not the men to put them up — the risk of infection was considered too great. And so exhausted were Dr. Douglas and his minuscule staff by this time that they were unable to get any tents pitched before the end of May. Then he managed to get four of the marquees up with sixty-four beds in each. By now there were many dead awaiting burial. What graves could be dug were shallow because of the rocky nature of the ground and it was not long before the rats from the waiting ships began to discover the bodies. And it was not until July that earth could be brought in to dump on the makeshift graveyards, which in some places were two coffins deep and only a few yards from the hospital tents.

Early in June the rest of the tents were up, while others had been contrived using sails from the waiting ships. A start was made on building shanties. June 10 saw eighteen hundred patients on the island; hundreds more were still in the ships, and more ships were expected. By this time, other doctors and medical attendants had joined Dr. Douglas's staff. Earlier, a Dr. Benson from one of the ships had volunteered to help. Six days later he was dead.

By the middle of June only three of the twenty-six doctors working on the island had escaped infection, one of them being Dr. Douglas himself, though it seems at one time he had the fever but recovered.

In mid-June a spell of rainy weather turned the hospital area into a swamp besides making it impossible to dry out the quantities of hospital bedding that had accumulated. Sanitation was nonexistent. It became increasingly difficult to induce servants to stay on the island or to obtain nurses to help look after the sick. By July the number of sick on the island had risen to 2,500, while from the waiting ships a never-ending procession of boats carried the dead to be buried ashore or the sick to the hospital. A witness described how the latter, in the absence of a pier, were tumbled on to the beach to crawl up it as best they could.

And so through July, August, and September the ships kept coming with dead in their holds and tales of hasty burials at sea as the disease had spread inexorably through passengers and crew. Even the hardened Dr. Douglas remarked on the appalling condition of the survivors of the *Virginius*, which had taken nine weeks to make the crossing. Only six of the crew were alive on arrival and the ship could only be moored with the help of passengers.

According to official records almost 5,300 Canada-bound emigrants died at sea during the summer of 1847. Meanwhile, Grosse Île had long since ceased to function as a quarantine station. The supposedly healthy had been leaving the island since May to make their way to Quebec and Montreal, some to go to Kingston and Toronto. As early as June 8, Dr. Douglas had taken time to dash off a hasty letter to the authorities in Quebec warning them of the danger of a widespread epidemic and suggesting that there should be accommodation for at least two thousand sick at Quebec and Montreal. In the event, Quebec got off lightly. In July there were between eight and nine hundred under treatment, with deaths running at about forty a week. In Montreal possibly more died than on Grosse Île, while of those emigrants who moved on, 1,400 died in Kingston.

The final death-toll can only be guessed at. The number who left Britain for British North America in 1847 has been placed at just on 110,000. Probably one person in six, or very roughly 18,000, died somewhere along the way. And who knows what happened to the thousands who travelled on into the States or into the remoter parts of Canada? It has been suggested that, weakened as they were by starvation and disease, only about half could have survived the rigours of their first Canadian winter.

The quarantine station at Grosse Île was closed at the beginning of November 1847, and in late December Dr. Douglas sent in his report on his year's work. He had inspected 442 ships. Some 8,700 cases had been treated, including ninety-two of smallpox and twenty-five with unspecified diseases. All the rest had had typhus or dysentery. A total of 3,238 had died: 1,361 men; 969 women; 908 children. Of those who had tended the sick on Grosse Île, four doctors were dead, as were six priests and clergymen, and thirty-four others — nurses, orderlies, servants, policemen, and those who had to cart away and bury the dead.

In mid-July 1847, with the quarantine station already choking with sick and dying, the government, rather belatedly one would think, had set up a committee to look into the state of affairs on Grosse Île. Among those who gave evidence were priests who had visited or who had worked on the island. One of them, after criticizing the arrangements in the hospital, went on to complain that money was being stolen from the patients by the attendants and accused Dr. Douglas of making use of government boatmen to work on his farm.

The exhausted doctor admitted that undoubtedly some patients had had money stolen from them. As for the boatmen, he had paid at least two of them more than they had got from the government. Coming to Dr. Douglas's defence, another priest praised his efforts; while another commented on his outstanding zeal and devotion to duty, although at times so weary that he had been unable to walk. The Bishop of Montreal wrote a letter in which he elaborated on Dr. Douglas's praiseworthy capabilities. As for the stories about Dr. Douglas selling milk from his own farm, he knew nothing of that, though he did know that Dr. Douglas had sent free milk out to the ships to help feed motherless infants.

Gossip concerning his alleged misconduct in 1847 dogged Dr. Douglas to the end of his days. Later, in an effort to lay these stories to rest, he was to write a dignified letter to the government defending his management of the quarantine station, saying that he knew nothing was to be gained by protesting his innocence, yet it was hard for him to stand so mistakenly accused when he had done so much.

Dr. Douglas continued to superintend the quarantine station on Grosse Île until it closed in 1861. By this time he was no longer living on the island. Following the death of his first wife in 1852, he tended to spend more and more time in England, where in 1858 he married for the second time. In 1863, his second wife died. In the same year, the quarantine station was reopened and Douglas returned as superintendent. In March 1864 he learned that he was to be replaced. On June 1, depressed and ill, he went to his house on the mainland and that evening stabbed himself. He died the next day.

There is a monument on Grosse Île to all those who died there. It was erected by Dr. Douglas and his fellow doctors. To Dr. Douglas himself, it seems there is no monument.

In the context of the great famine and what happened on Grosse Île, the presence in Ontario today of those Irish families, Catholic and Protestant alike, who came over in those dark days represents a heroic survival. However, the Irish emigrations of the 1840s and

1850s should not overshadow the contribution made by others of their race to Upper Canada. Many who had settled earlier in the American colonies fought as Loyalists, and there were Irishmen in the ranks of the Royal Highland Emigrants when that regiment was defending Quebec against the American invaders in the dark winter of 1765. No one man did more to settle Upper Canada than Colonel Thomas Talbot, whose settlement on Lake Erie was founded as early as 1803. There were a number of Irish in the Perth Military Settlements and it was the Irish who founded Peterborough.

A high proportion of those who came to Canada in the years following the Napoleonic Wars went on to the United States. But many remained, some to build the Rideau Canal, others to work in the shanties on the Canadian Shield, still others to farm. Unlike the Scots, who tended to stick together, the Irish were to scatter all over Upper Canada as the years rolled by. Eventually they became the most numerous of all the province's founding races.

The Moreland Family
Limehill Farm
Storrington Township
Frontenac County

*J*ane Reid, later Jane Moreland, sailed for Canada in an emigrant ship in 1847. At fourteen years of age she was thus one of the "hundreds of poor people" described by Stephen de Vere, an Irish landowner and philanthropist who sailed steerage on an emigrant ship in the same year to see for himself what conditions were like at sea.

Before the emigrant has been a week at sea he is an altered man. How can it be otherwise? Hundreds of poor people, men, women, and children, of all ages, from the drivelling idiot of ninety to the babe just born, huddled together without light, without air, wallowing in filth and breathing a fetid atmosphere, sick in body, dispirited in heart, the fevered patients lying between the sound, in sleeping places so narrow as almost to deny them the power of indulging, by a change of position, the natural restlessness of the disease; by their agonised ravings disturbing those around, and predisposing them through the effects of the imagination, to imbibe the contagion; living without food or medicine, except as administered by the hand of casual charity, dying without the voice of spiritual consolation, and buried in the deep without the rites of the church.[1]

Jane's parents, James and Peggy Reid, came from Northern Ireland. James Reid had been a gardener on the estate of Lord Templeton in County Antrim before worsening conditions drove him to seek a new life in Canada. For him there was to be no future: he became ill on the voyage over and died at Kingston. He was buried among the other fourteen hundred victims of typhus on the site of the General Hospital. In 1966 the remains were reinterred in Kingston's St. Mary Cemetery.

Peggy Reid and her children were left destitute. Fortunately, they had Irish friends on Amherst Island in the St. Lawrence and there they settled near the village of Stella.

Despite this sad beginning, the Reid family prospered. In 1853, Jane Reid married James Moreland, who had been an apprentice sailor in Northern Ireland before coming to Canada in 1845. James worked in winter as a woodcutter and in the summer on schooners on the Great Lakes. In time he became Captain Moreland, in command of a ship.

In 1865 the Morelands bought a farm some eleven miles north of Kingston near Sunbury and moved there with their young children. Ultimately they were to have a family of eleven. Only a woman of character would have undertaken such a move. With her husband away on the Great Lakes all summer when the bulk of the farm work was done, Jane Moreland had to rely on hired men and the help of her young sons. She grew produce and vegetables which she sold at a stall in the Kingston Market or traded for goods with Kingston merchants. She also took vegetables to sell to private homes in Kingston. By 1876, the Morelands were affluent enough to build a new house.

The site that the Morelands chose for their home was spectacular. On top of a hill, it had a breath-taking view over fields and valleys to Collins Lake. It was a big brick house of many gables, sheltering what Jane Moreland's grandson, Paul Moreland, remembers as a large, happy, talkative family. Conversation was a way of life. He remembers fun, laughter, and hard work. "The children had to milk the cows as soon as they were old enough to squeeze a teat."

Like most pioneer families, the Morelands were self-supporting. They had their own meat, poultry, and eggs, and they made their own butter. Wheat from their fields was ground in the mill at Washburn and the bread baked in the family kitchen. They smoked their own hams. In the spring they extracted lye from the wood ash saved over the winter and boiled it up with fat to make a year's supply of soft, brown soap. The farm's orchards produced fifteen different varieties of apples. In time, a herd of Holstein-Friesian cattle appeared, and the sale of milk to the cheese factory at Sunbury two miles away provided a welcome added income. Only sugar, spices, and salt were bought — and green tea delivered once a year by a driver from Daly's in Napanee. There was a cellar in the house and in it were stored hundreds of jars of jams, jellies, and preserves and a great Cheddar cheese sitting uncovered on a bench.

Outside the house was a back-house, "a three-holer," Paul Moreland remembers, "two large and one small — surrounded by a grove of French lilac trees, the aroma from which in spring somewhat counteracted that emanating from our wooden outhouse. Each bedroom, of course, had the customary ceramic wash-basin and wooden stand and there was a chamber-pot under the bed for night-time use. Its use in the daytime was strictly forbidden."

Neighbours and friends came to visit on Sundays, so Saturdays were busy. All the baking of pies and cakes was done and shoes were cleaned. On Sunday evening, the Bible was read.

There was never any liquor kept in the house, no playing cards and no guns. At one time cider was made, but there was an incident when woodcutters went into the cellar and drank too much of it. Jane Moreland turned the spigots in the cider casks, and the cider press disappeared. In spite of an outlook that in some ways might seem austere, Paul Moreland remembers his grandmother with affection and respect. She was the dominating figure of the house, a person of uncompromising integrity and strength of character.

During the summers, while his wife looked after the farm and her large household, Captain James Moreland sailed the Great Lakes. When he retired in the 1890s he had been a captain for thirty years and "had never lost a ship or a man." He was in command at different times of the *Water Witch*, owned by the Kinghorn family of Kingston, and of the *Arabia*, owned by the Nickle and Kinghorn families.

The barque *Arabia* was launched in Kingston in 1853. In May 1854 she set sail for Glasgow. She worked the English coasting trade for a year, then returned to the Great Lakes in 1855. Until 1881 she sailed almost entirely between Kingston and Chicago. William Nickle and George Matheson Kinghorn of Kingston bought the *Arabia* in 1868 and owned her until 1883. It was probably between 1860 and 1881 that she was commanded by Captain Moreland.

"Mr. William Nickle, Senior, owned a brewery in Kingston and Captain James always had a cargo of the brew to distribute to customers in the lake and river ports," Paul Moreland says. "At the end of each sailing season it was the custom of Captain James to present his accounts for the year to Mr. Nickle, the owner of the vessel. One year Nickle, in scrutinizing the accounts, noted an amount for liquor that he questioned. At the end of the following year, there was another accounting. Mr. Nickle said, 'I note with satisfaction that you have not entered fifty dollars for liquor this year.' 'You are right,' James said, 'but it is there nevertheless, included under a miscellaneous item.' "

Captain James's ship also carried cargoes of grain, salt, and stone. "At one time she carried a cargo of twenty thousand bushels of wheat," Paul Moreland says, "one of the largest that had ever been carried by a lake vessel up to this time." The *Arabia* plied between Kingston and Chicago through the Welland Canal, through which the ships were pulled by horses. Horses raised on the Moreland farm were used for this purpose. Captain James also drew stone from quarries in the United States that was used in the Parliament Buildings in Ottawa.

In 1881, after the captain left her, the *Arabia* entered the Georgian Bay trade, where she encountered a series of spectacular misadventures. In October 1884 the last of them saw her seams split in a severe storm. She "gave a plunge and disappeared with a roar"[2] three miles north of Tobermory.

After the deaths of Jane Moreland and the captain, the Moreland farm was run by one of their sons. It was at this time that the Morelands acquired a person who was to become something of a rarity in Canada — a family retainer. John Broster from Chester in England was with the Moreland family for most of his life, and the family speak fondly of him today. He was up at five in the morning to let out the dog and light the fire. He got the cows in and then "gave a hoot" for the boys to get up and milk them. He was a second father to Arthur Moreland, who as a small boy tagged along after him.

John Reid Moreland and his wife and four children now live in the big brick house. His parents, Arthur and Polly, live in a modern house on the farm. Polly Moreland is a descendant of Adam Barr, an early settler near Inverary.

Behind the family home are the barns that house the Morelands' herd of fifty or more Holstein cows and a great new drive-shed. Two things are unchanged on the Moreland farm: the spectacular beauty of the view and the Moreland hospitality.

In 1976, to commemorate the centenary of the construction of the big house, the Morelands hosted a party for some six hundred guests. Afterwards they were given a commemorative plaque by their friends and it now hangs on the wall of the drive-shed. One hopes it will still be there in a hundred years' time to commemorate a second century.

The Morris Family
Clarence Township
Russell County

The house is a log cabin — a pioneer's cabin from the past, whitewashed on the outside in the French-Canadian style. From the road it looks oddly wall-eyed. When it was built, the front door faced a road running through the bush from the village of Sarsfield to the Ottawa River, a road long forgotten and overgrown. Behind the house and a little to the north is the barn and from it comes the sound of an engine working a milking machine.

Ernie Morris and his son, Raymond, live in the cabin. Ernie's ancestry is Irish, but over the generations the family has taken on a French-Canadian patina — as has their speech — and now only two of Ernie's grandchildren speak English.

Inside the house there is one room downstairs with a small bedroom partitioned off. There is no hydro, but a telephone has just been installed. The floors are crooked; so are the walls. There are dark beams in the ceiling, and a wood stove. When the light fades, Ernie brings out an oil lamp. The match flares as he lights it and in the darkness our faces round the table are illuminated like a modern version of a painting by de la Tour.

Ernie's great-grandfather came from Ireland during the potato famine of the 1840s from the County of Tyrone, "among the green bushes". The voyage over took six weeks. The family settled in the Clarence area, where most of the settlers were Irish. It took many years for them to clear enough land to farm, and for the first few years the Morris family were able to build only a cabin for themselves and a rough shelter for animals. The family burned potash, transporting it and tanbark on a winter road to the Ottawa River, where it was picked up in the spring. They walked about ten miles to Cumberland for supplies and carried their wheat to Rockland to be ground — "an awful piece to go". An encounter with wolves on the way meant a quick scramble up a tree.

There were eight children in Ernie's family and, as was the custom in those days when a new baby was born, the older child was moved out of the parents' room. When Ernie's turn came, he shared a bed with his grandfather and he remembers him with affection. Before the First World War Ernie went to Montana three times, once on a harvest excursion and twice taking horses for sale on a rail journey of nine days. He was in Montana when news came of his grandfather's illness and he came home to look after the old man until he died at the age of eighty-three.

In 1921 Ernie married Maphilda Lacroix, a French-Canadian girl.

"Six kids born in this house, three boys and three girls." Two women came to help Maphilda when the babies arrived and a neighbour would drive to Navan for a doctor. "Fifty years ago you only went to a hospital to die." Maphilda cooked on the wood stove and baked all the bread. The family kept pigs, sheep, and cattle. Lambs and old sheep were sold in the fall and a lamb was killed for the family once a year. There was a goose at Christmas and a generous stack of eggs at Easter, but the mainstay of the family was salt pork. "You put a pig's tail near the bottom of the barrel and when you came to that, you knew you had to kill another. . . . I'm not a fussy man to eat," Ernie adds. "Whatever my wife cooked was good." But since her death he has missed the home-baked bread.

Traces of poverty are apparent on the farm and of the previous generations' struggle to survive. But now it seems Ernie and Raymond live the way they do from choice rather than necessity. Ernie wanted once to put in electricity, but why do it when there were five in the family who could handle the milking? The next year he bought another farm instead. He has expanded the original land grant of fifty acres to two hundred and fifty. There is an income from selling wood from the bush, and the milk is sold to a cheese factory. Perhaps there will be an added windfall by severing a building lot.

Ernie buys his tractors second-hand because many farmers, he says, are working for their machines. He has a complete outfit for making silage on the other farm. He uses sprays on the weeds, but won't spray the old apple orchards. "If the apples weren't wormy, they'd get stolen. The cows eat them now."

Some years ago, Raymond suffered a serious injury when the wheel of a baler fell into a groundhog hole and part of the machinery ran over his leg. Since then Ernie has hired a man with equipment to help bring in the hay.

It is getting late. The clock ticks on the wall and the shadows in the corners of the room deepen. It is time to bring out the tall tales. Ernie and Raymond speak of the *mare bleue*, a local area of peat, swamp, and streams unique in North America where gases unite to give off a blue fog. Ernie remembers years ago getting a ride home with the cheesemaker. "When I got across the fields, there was a big light rise up like a log." The cheesemaker turned back but the light followed along the creek and finally disappeared between the horse and the buggy. Another time Ernie went to town with a team and wagon. Coming home, a ball of light appeared to roll under the wagon. He went to look, armed with a pitchfork, but the light had disappeared. Is it imagination, or do we all feel a little uneasy? In the lamplight, superstitions are less easily dismissed.

Outside, without competition from city lights, the Big Dipper

hangs almost within arm's length in the sky. Ernie is speculating
on the nature of the stars. Whatever age he may be — and he's
not telling — he's a lucky man, with much humour and a lively
mind.

The O'Keefe Family
Cornwall Township
Stormont County

*I*t might be a scene in southern Ireland. The house is at
right angles to the road and some distance from it up a laneway. The
impression is of a long white building on a slope backed by a fringe
of trees. Sadie O'Keefe is a passionate gardener and the cultivated
beds suggest an old-country cottage garden at its most colourful.

Joseph O'Keefe's grandfather, Patrick O'Keefe, came from
Limerick, Ireland, in the 1840s, the decade of the Irish potato
famines. His first home in Upper Canada was a shanty down by the
creek. Joseph and Sadie O'Keefe now live in the second house built
on the farm, a log house covered by white sheathing that makes it
"the warmest house there is". The family never suffered too much
from the cold anyway, Sadie O'Keefe thinks. There was always
plenty of wood to burn, and there were heavy woollen clothes, fur
mitts and gloves, and the ultimate in warmth — buffalo robes.

Sadie O'Keefe's family came from Alexandria near the Quebec
border, and winter was the time when they bundled up and went to
Montreal by sleigh to fetch supplies. If you could keep warm,
travelling in winter was easier. Susanna Moodie waited anxiously
for a heavy snowfall so that sleighs could be sent to take her away for
ever from "roughing it in the bush". There are many tales of execra-
ble roads at other times of the year, of carts disappearing up to their
axles in mud, and of tremendous holes that had to be filled up with
boughs. Anna Jameson, a visitor to Upper Canada in the 1830s, was
almost jolted out of her admirable wits on a journey of twenty-five
miles that took nine hours.

The O'Keefes, like many other farmers, stopped milking cows
when government regulations made the installation of expensive
milking equipment mandatory. The stables behind the house, now
unused, have not been modernized, and in them are found the
original wooden stanchions and a large sleigh used for hauling logs
from the bush in winter. A small, square white building over the
well contains the cement water troughs in which the milk cans were

cooled. The O'Keefes now run some beef cattle. "There are only two dairy farmers left within five or six miles. But those who are still in it are producing a great deal more milk."

Patrick O'Keefe was a drover as well as a farmer. He bought cattle all over Cornwall Township, kept them on the farm until he had enough to sell, and then drove them "to the Canal bank" at Cornwall about ten miles away to catch the cattle boat to Montreal. There are family stories of how the boys in his family of thirteen would have to run, driving the cattle down the unfenced roads, while their father rode behind in a cart or buggy. Barking dogs would run out and scare the cattle, sometimes scattering them in the bush. Sheep were bought, too, and driven forty miles to Prescott, where they were probably sold for the flourishing American market. "Folks were used to walking. Women walked many miles to visit friends or relatives or to go to church. . . . You see, the horses worked all week in the fields at clearing the land, and farmers knew that they had to be given a certain amount of rest," Sadie O'Keefe says. There are many early accounts of people walking long distances, from Pennsylvania to what is now Waterloo County, for example, or from Orangeville to Dundas, carrying a bushel of wheat to be ground — and back with the flour. In 1826 Samuel Strickland walked fifty-eight miles in one day to visit his sick wife. When he got within five miles of his destination, he stopped at a tavern where some men were discussing a funeral to be held the next day — hers.

The village of St. Andrews West is three miles from the O'Keefe farm. It used to be a much busier little town with two general stores, a post office, and an elementary and a high school, as well as the great Catholic church. At one time it could boast of having a doctor. Today this historic village is "impacted" by Highway 138, so it is no longer the "peaceful place of rest" described on the plaque in the burying-ground.

When she was first married, Sadie O'Keefe says with nostalgia, two or three families always dropped in unexpectedly over the week-end. There was much entertaining and always plenty of food in the farm pantries. All that has gone; only relatives visit now. But one of her two sons has built a new house in the field to the south, so another generation will continue to live on the O'Keefe farm. Sadie O'Keefe may be some future historian's delight. She has kept that most valuable of all personal records, a diary, all her life.

We have tea in the farm kitchen looking out over the fields. There is maple syrup on the table, tapped in the bush on the farm and boiled up outdoors in an iron kettle over a wood fire. It tastes faintly and deliciously of wood smoke.

The Thorpe Family
Rockelmdale Farm
Cumberland Township
Russell County

*F*lorence Thorpe is sitting in the kitchen of her farmhouse at Hammond, eighteen miles east of Ottawa. It is a hot afternoon. Outside her husband, John, is bringing in the hay with the help of his son and his grandsons.

At eighty, Florence Thorpe moves and speaks like a woman thirty years younger. Loaves of bread are cooling on the kitchen counter, the product of her morning's baking. "Grandma's home cooking," her grandson says appreciatively.

She was born Florence Kinsella and married John Thorpe fifty-five years ago. Both were from local Irish families, although Thorpe is an English name; perhaps long ago the family was part of an English settlement in Ireland.

At first the Thorpes lived in a log house "under the hill", but in 1924 they moved the log building to the site of the present house. "There was nothing here except a hayfield, John Thorpe says. "I started to put up the barn on the fifth of July. Did all the boarding myself. It was a race to get the barn up and the hay in and you couldn't get any help — they were all out haying. Started to get the hay in on the fifth of August. If you'd done as much work as I have, you'd remember dates too. Got the barn ready just as it started to hail."

"When we first came here we had to draw water in barrels from a spring in the bush. Then Watsons of Cumberland came and drilled a well. . . . It was the driest summer that the Lord ever sent," Florence Thorpe recalls. "There were fires everywhere and I just mind that the sun was blood-red, nearly, with the smoke. No, the fire wasn't around here. It was bush burning miles away. . . but there was no rain."

The Thorpes raised four children during the Depression. "I baked the bread and then made shirts out of the flour bags. For birthdays and holidays I always had a little something extra. But I remember one Easter when I didn't have anything. The children didn't notice it; it was only me that felt bad."

John Thorpe replaced the log house in 1949 with a house of cement blocks, a tribute to the fact that farmers can turn their hands to anything. "First block I'd ever laid was for this house. I'd only seen people laying blocks a couple of times and a man told me I had an awful nerve to do it. But afterwards I built another cement-block house, much the same, for Fergus Minogue at Cumberland. We cut all the wood for our house in our own bush. The flooring is red oak, sent away to be tongued and grooved, and we laid it ourselves. We did all the work except the electrical wiring."

The house is heated by a wood furnace, and although it is only August the wood for the winter has been cut and stored in the cellar ready for use, an insurance against the winter's cold.

John Thorpe runs Herefords on the farm. He has about a hundred head of these white-faced red cattle which were first brought to Canada about the year 1860. He raises calves and sells them locally. Or gives them away, he says, "Took a four-year-old cow that weighed 1,345 pounds to the sale barn. Over 1,300 pounds of meat and they gave me seventeen cents a pound. That's what I got and that's poor business. She didn't pay for the feed.

"I gave up milking Holsteins because I wasn't so young any more. Couldn't hardly get the milk to suit the dairies, they were that particular. It's bare-faced robbery. A year ago they asked people to put in more milk. When they had built up their milk, they turned around and wouldn't pay them for their quotas. Now wasn't that a trick?

"As far as I'm concerned, times are worse now than they were sixty years ago. I'd never seen the day you couldn't sell a cow or a pig or any darned thing you wanted. But now a machine is so dear, you can't afford to buy one. And if you do, you'll never see it paid for."

Cecil Thorpe, John Thorpe's son, used to farm but now sells real estate in Ottawa as well as helping his father farm their three hundred acres.

"A century farm represents a century of toil and it's the only business I know that you can work at for a hundred years and not get anything out of it," says Cecil. "Money and farming are two different things. I like farming much more than working in the city, but there's no money in it.

"Beef is cheaper than it was twenty years ago but costs have gone up five hundred per cent in that time. If you sell an animal, they may tell you that it's worth thirty-five cents a pound. If it weighs a thousand pounds, you get $350. Yet after hanging in a cooler for fourteen days, the carcase is worth $700 to the man who bought it. "You see, a farm is like a wagon on a hill. It never rolls up. It just rolls down. If we moved out today and came back in a year, you wouldn't know this place. It would be like all the others that have gone that way: weeds and bush and grass. The fences broken down. A farm is not like an apartment building. I could buy an apartment building in Ottawa that would bring in a sizeable income from the day I bought it. But for the same investment, a farm wouldn't bring in five cents."

In spite of it all, Cecil Thorpe has some good recollections of the years he was farming full time. He showed corn at agricultural fairs for eight or nine years and one year he and his brother astonished the judges in Ottawa by carrying in a sheaf of corn seventeen foot six inches in length. "We didn't get a prize for it, because the judge figured that it couldn't have been grown in a field." He was wrong.

The Thorpes' grandsons are around to help bring in the hay: imposingly tall, bronzed young men. A son, too, comes from western Canada every year to help with the haying. A farm may be unremunerative in relation to the work and effort put into it during a lifetime, but viewed in human terms, there are compensations. Take the family. On this particular day, there are three generations out helping with the haying. It is the people that keep the farm wagon from rolling down the hill.

Outside the house the old dog is sleeping in the sun. There are guinea fowl behind the barn, and inside, Cecil Thorpe's magnificent Clydesdale horses. "People say when they come here that we have a nice set-up," Florence Thorpe says. "I never think of it that way. It's just my home."

CHAPTER SIX

The Scots of Glengarry County

*N*o other nationality played a greater part in the settlement of Upper Canada than the Scots. They were the first to arrive in any numbers and they exerted an influence on later settlement that persisted long after their numerical predominance declined. They were to settle all over what is now Ontario; to take up land and farm, pursue their trades, and build houses, mills, and factories. Both Highlanders and Lowlanders were to become prominent in business, government, and public affairs. They served the province well — and their descendants are serving it still.

The saga of the Highlanders begins early in the sixth century when they left northern Ireland to settle in Kintyre, the long arm of land on the west coast of Scotland that stretches southwards to within a few miles of the Irish coast. They were a race of Celts known as the Scots and it is they who gave their name to Scotland. They spoke their own brand of Gaelic, which, persisting in the Highlands for over a thousand years, was to become so much gibberish to Lowlanders and Englishmen alike, a barrier to communication that did much to increase their cultural isolation.

There is a vast difference between the romantic version of life in the Highlands that gained currency in Victorian times and the reality, which saw for long centuries men eking out a living in the rough and isolated terrain of northern Scotland, hunting, fishing, keeping a few black cattle, and raiding their neighbours or, when time grew really hard, the Lowlanders. That the Highlander survived at all was largely due to the intense support given him by the fellow-members of his tribe or clan.

The clan system was central to the life of the Highlander. The clan was in effect his family, the chief of the clan its head. To the clansman the chief was his father, his protector, and the source of all justice — which is why the inhumanity of the Highlanders' treatment by their own chiefs in a later century was to cause them such lasting hurt.

In time, various clans laid claim to their own particular parts of the Highlands, claims asserted and defended by the sword. The land itself belonged to the chief. In the course of time a pattern of land-tenure emerged that saw the chief renting his land to his principal supporters or tacksmen, often relatives, who in turn had sub-tenants. Below the sub-tenants came the cotters. Allegiance was to the chief, and when the chief decided on war, all members of the clan, from tacksman to cotter, were expected to fight.

And decide on war the chief often did. The history of the Highlands is one of perpetual clan wars; of feuds; of raids and counter-raids; of slights, real and imaginary, sometimes remembered for generations: a history summed up — by a Scotsman let it be quickly added — as "one long, bloody brawl".

A clansman's loyalty to his clan could be a source of immense strength, a fact often demonstrated in later years when that loyalty was transferred to the king's regiment in which he served. But there was an overriding loyalty, central to the drama that is Scottish history, that was to lead in the end to the destruction of the Highlanders and their way of life, namely the loyalty borne to their royal house, the House of Stewart, a name derived from the old title of High Steward.

Fourteen Stewarts, or Stuarts, were to sit on the throne of Scotland, with the later ones occupying England's throne as well. They were an unlucky lot. One was assassinated, two were killed in battle, another was standing too close to a cannon when it burst, two were alleged to have died from broken hearts, and two were beheaded.

Of the two who were executed — or murdered, depending on your point of view — one was Charles I; the other, Mary Queen of Scots. It was Mary's son who became the first Stewart ruler of both England and Scotland; he was James VI to the latter, James I to the former. He came to the throne in 1603, the year that Champlain first sailed up the St. Lawrence.

With a Stewart on the throne of both countries, the history of Scotland was to become closely entangled with that of England. And out of that entanglement was to come, a century and a half later, the rebellion in the Highlands of 1745 which had as one of its tragic consequences a great exodus of Highlanders from Scotland.

In 1715 an attempt was made by James II's eldest son, James Edward Stuart, to seize the throne that he considered to be rightfully his. Parliament, who wanted no more Catholic kings, thought otherwise. The attempt of the Old Pretender, as he came to be called, failed in a tragic waste of Scots' blood and of that of Englishmen who had rallied to his support. The abortive rebellion led also to measures designed to keep the Highlanders under control. They were required to surrender weapons, and old and rusty ones were given up, with the best of them hidden away. Military roads were pushed into the Highlands and forts established, in an attempt to make the subjugation complete.

By 1745, all this was in the past. Scotland was tasting the first fruits of a national revival. The resurgence of spirit began with farmers who, inspired by such men as Andrew Fletcher, formed the Honourable Society of Improvers of the Knowledge of Agriculture in 1723. Drawing on the example of English agriculturists, all, it seemed, from laird to small-holder, were soon experimenting with such innovations as crop-rotation and Townshend's celebrated turnips, as well as Jethro Tull's seed-drill and new types of English ploughs.

The Highlanders benefited from the agrarian revolution and their black beef cattle were in great demand in the Lowlands and in England to the south. As for the Highland chiefs, the gap between their clansmen and themselves gradually widened as their greater riches allowed more of them to travel and to mix with Lowland society, there to sample the delights that wealth can bring.

It was thus in a Scotland enjoying a revival of national pride that the Old Pretender's son, Charles Edward Stuart, otherwise known as "Bonnie Prince Charlie", landed in 1745 to raise the standard of rebellion; a Scotland where even the Jacobites, supporters of the ancient Stuart line, were becoming self-conscious in their hopes of a Stuart restoration, realizing that they were indulging in a romantic, if exciting, game of make-believe.

Charles Edward was a charming and rather foolish young man, possessing, to the Highlanders' undoing, an infectious enthusiasm that was difficult to resist. Because of it some of the wiser chiefs refused to see him. Even with his royal charm many of the clansmen only followed him under threat of roof-burning by their chiefs. Nevertheless he raised an army and marched down into the Lowlands, routing government forces at Prestonpans and occupying the city of Edinburgh.

Charles then marched south by way of Carlisle and got as far as Derby before the clan chiefs balked at going further. With three English armies now in the field against them, the dispirited Highlanders turned for home, fighting a rearguard action, and routing another government force near Falkirk, before retiring into the mountains of Scotland once more. Early in 1746 they emerged again to make their last desperate stand at Culloden, in the parish of Croy, between Inverness and Nairn.

To the British regulars who faced them at Culloden, the unkempt

Highlanders with their kilts tucked high for freedom of movement, their round shields and their broadswords, and their wild cries must have appeared as outlandish as the Indians they were to meet in North America or the tribesmen they were to encounter in India. Prince Charles had fewer than five thousand men under him, not only ragged and hungry, but desperate for sleep as well, for they had spent the previous night attempting an attack on Nairn that had come to nothing. Against them were arrayed some nine thousand troops, including three regular Lowland regiments, supported by militia, cavalry, and a company of artillery: the whole commanded by the Duke of Cumberland, George II's second son, who, for what he did after the battle, was to be remembered in history books, English as well as Scots, as "Butcher" Cumberland.

The battle did not last long. For over an hour the clansmen stood, waiting for the irresolute prince to give the order to charge, with the guns of the Royal Artillery firing at them from a distance of only a few yards. An appeal to Prince Charles finally produced an order for the clans to advance, but the messenger carrying it was killed, and still the clansmen stood, until, with hundreds already dead, they broke away towards the enemy. The gunners, seeing them coming, changed from solid shot to grape — a lethal all-in-one package of powder, nails, and bits of scrap iron. A few clansmen managed to break into the line of regulars, but most fell before they reached it as the volleys of musket-fire began, while others, with their swords useless against the fringe of bayonets, stood hurling stones at the redcoats, unable to go further and too proud to retreat, until one by one they were shot down.

The low grassy mounds that mark the mass graves of the clansmen at Culloden have an especial sadness, for they symbolize the passing of a Highland way of life. After Culloden, the Highlands would never be the same again; events would be set in train that would lead to the land becoming nothing more than sheep pastures, empty mountains, and deserted glens where men did not live any more. And even now, over 230 years later, the Highlands are home to only a very few.

The memory of Culloden was to become seared into the national consciousness of the Scots, and in many Ontario families of Scots origin it is mentioned still. Some families had relatives fighting on both sides. The Chief of Clan Chisholm, for example, hedged his bets by having two of his sons fight for King George, while another led the clan for Prince Charles. The MacLeods, perhaps remembering their virtual obliteration at the Battle of Worcester under another Charles Stuart, the future Charles II, refrained from committing themselves as a clan in 1745. However, a story goes that one of the MacLeod forebears, one Angus MacLeod of Swordland in Glenelg, rallied to Prince Charles's cause and was killed at Culloden, together with seven of his eight sons. Olgair, the eighth son, had been left at home. Later he and his widowed mother offered to shelter Prince Charles, who was by this time on the run with a price on his head. On the approach of Cumberland's troops, Olgair took the prince and his two companions to hide in a cave, there to watch as Angus MacLeod's widow was dragged from her house and the house itself burned. Later, Olgair MacLeod married and his descendants settled in Glengarry County.

No sooner had the last of the clansmen fled from the battlefield of Culloden with its heaps of dead and dying men and with Prince Charles already gone, than the Duke of Cumberland started to earn his title of "Butcher". Wounded clansmen lying on the battlefield were dispatched as a matter of course, though there were some in Cumberland's army who refused to co-operate in the slaughter. One of them was a young officer, James Wolfe by name, then a brevet-major. Ordered to pistol a "rebel dog" lying wounded at his feet, he refused and offered his commission instead. It seems that someone else was found who was more obliging.

Off the battlefield, the work of killing was taken up by the cavalry, and such was their enthusiasm that not a few who were sabred were those spectators who had come out to watch the battle. Two days after Culloden, following Cumberland's possibly ambiguous order, a visit was paid to the battlefield by what were nothing less than execution squads to make quite sure that none of the clansmen survived.

The total Highland dead has been estimated at something over twelve hundred, but that was only the immediate cost to Scotland of Prince Charles's mindless exploitation of Highland loyalties. For months afterwards as the hunt for his royal person went on, the Highlands were terrorized by the king's troops, Scottish Lowland regiments among them. Houses were pillaged and burned, with suspected rebels treated with a studied brutality that sometimes included summary execution. And, striking at the very heart of their way of life, the Highlanders' precious black cattle were rounded up to be sold in the Lowlands or in northern England.

Of the 3,470 prisoners officially taken, 120 were executed — though of these, 38 were deserters from the army. Four of the Jacobites were peers and these were beheaded; the rest were hanged with all the disgusting ritual traditionally reserved for traitors, including the disembowelling and quartering of a victim perhaps not quite yet dead. Nine hundred and thirty-six prisoners were sentenced to transportation to the colonies, another 222 banished to the colonies for life.

In a series of acts aimed at destroying the Highland clans once and for all, the ancient rights of chiefs were taken away. Those chiefs who had supported Prince Charles lost their lands; the carrying of arms laid Highlanders open to the death penalty; the wearing of plaids, tartans, and kilts or any other traditional Highland dress was forbidden on pain of transportation. It was not until 1782 that a Scotsman could legally wear the kilt, unless he elected to wear the government tartan of a soldier in the service of the king.

A way of life and a culture destroyed, the Highlands started to empty. Some clansmen left to join the new Highland regiments to see service in the West Indies or in Canada. Many that came to Canada remained there when their regiments were disbanded. Others emigrated, joining their kinfolk in the American colonies, whence many Scotsmen had gone in the course of the seventeenth and eighteenth centuries.

But what of Charles Edward Stuart, the Young Pretender and Bonnie Prince? He escaped finally to France, where his presence became unwelcome after France and Britain made peace in 1748. After living in the Netherlands and in Switzerland, he ended up in Italy, where he spent the last forty years of his life. He died a drunkard in Rome in 1782, even as the descendants of the clansmen who had once supported him were establishing those first settlements along the St. Lawrence. As for "Butcher" Cumberland, he left Scotland not long after Culloden to be fêted in London as the saviour of England. They say that the flower "Sweet William" was named in his honour: in Scotland they call a particularly noxious weed "Stinking Billy".

In the years following the '45, Scotland entered into what is often called her "golden age", an astonishing outburst of national energy that was to lead by the end of the century to Edinburgh's becoming one of the cultural centres of Europe, with Scottish industry and technological advances a source of wonder to visitors. It was an age that produced James Boswell, Johnson's biographer, and in its latter years Robert Louis Stevenson, explorers such as Mungo Park and Alexander Mackenzie, to whom Canada owes the exploration of the far north-west and the discovery of the river that bears his name, and painters such as Raeburn, who gave us a picture of The MacNab of Renfrew County in all his pompous glory. It was an age, too, that produced the engineer James Watt, who made the steam engine a practicable proposition; John Macadam, who gave us our smooth roads; and hundreds of others who founded the great Scottish industries around Glasgow and made the Clyde renowned the world over for the quality of the ships built on it.

But all this passed the Highlands by. Following the '45 and the dismantling of the clan system, the heart went out of the people — as did the cash from the chiefs' coffers. As early as the mid-1700s, some chiefs desperate for money were raising their rents so high that their own tacksmen could not afford to pay them. The only solution for many, such as the MacDonells of Glen Garry, was to leave the Highlands altogether. The tacksmen emigrated and took their tenants with them, which accounts in part for the fact that after the American War of Independence no fewer than eighty-four MacDonells were among the Loyalists taking up land in the county they were to name after their native glen.

At about this time, however, the agricultural revolution was beginning to bear fruit in a form that was to solve the clan chiefs' financial worries, bring greater prosperity to the Lowlands, but empty the Highlands still further. It was a man named Robson who first bred Cheviot sheep, an animal named after the rolling hills between England and Scotland where it originated. The Cheviot not only carried a greater weight of mutton and wool but it was unusually hardy, admirably suited to the harsh winters of the Highlands. The sturdy Cheviot sheep were to finish off the work begun by "Butcher" Cumberland.

The idea of renting out sheep-walks to Lowland farmers dates back to the 1760s, but it was not until 1782 that the full implications of such a development were made clear by the wife of the MacDonell chief, a lady whose Gaelic name translates as "Light-headed Marjorie". In renting out her land to Lowland sheep-farmers, she happily agreed to one of their stipulations — namely that five hundred or so MacDonells and MacDonalds be got out of the way of the sheep. "Light-headed Marjorie" obligingly shipped them off to Canada, where they joined their kinsmen in the settlements along the St. Lawrence. In 1785 the good lady was at it again. In that year the ship *Macdonald* sailed with over five hundred more of the clan crammed into its steerage space, suffering conditions that have been described as "sickening hell". Marjorie's work was to be continued by successive chieftains until in 1853 there was scarcely a MacDonell left in Glen Garry. All the rest had been dispatched abroad, most of them to Canada.

The Chisholms of Strathglass were dispersed even more thoroughly. In 1790 the chief would have none of the Lowlanders or their sheep, but when he died his brother proved less scrupulous and in 1801 evicted half his clan at one go. In 1858 there were but six Chisholms left in Strathglass, and yet when their chief came into his majority in 1832, the exiled Chisholms in Canada sent him an address of loyalty, a poignant comment on the traditional ties between clansmen and their chief, remembered by them, if not by him.

Elizabeth Gordon, Countess of Sutherland, Marchioness of Stafford, later first Duchess of Sutherland, and wife of the richest man in England, owned lands amounting to more than seventeen hundred square miles in the north of Scotland. The Duchess was a great believer in land improvement, and in the name of improvement thousands of her tenants lost their homes forever, though at least some of them attempted to take up a new life on the coast, where it was thought that they might learn to fish. Many of them came to Canada, where some settled in the Embro area of Ontario's Oxford County. The Duchess's agents went about their business with a will, pulling down cottagers' roofs over their heads with sheep already milling about them; later, becoming more daring, they got rid of the people by the simple expedient of setting fire to their dwellings within a few minutes of serving writs of eviction. In a single week in 1814, eighty houses in four townships were put to the torch, and barns with them, and there were deaths among the old and the sick. What was thought to be an incipient rebellion by the Clan Gunn was quelled by troops, backed by artillery. In 1819 hundreds of houses were burned, and the year after that when the evictors were met by a protesting crowd, mostly women, they were set upon with truncheons and one woman died with a musket-ball through her chest.

It may be noted, too, that over 70,000 clansmen left to serve in the British army during the Napoleonic Wars. From the Island of Skye alone had come more than 10,000 men and over 600 officers, twenty-one of whom rose to the rank of general. With the war over in 1815, with Britain passing into an economic slump, and with their homelands fast becoming one great sheep-walk where, it seemed, men were not allowed to live any more, many Highlanders looked to Canada as the place where they could begin again.

It has been estimated that by the 1820s something between a half and two-thirds of the entire population of the Highlands had been driven from their homes, most left with no alternative but to emigrate, many of them to Upper Canada, where they joined Lowland compatriots, who earlier had founded the Perth and Lanark settlements, and the Highlanders of Stormont and Glengarry. The Scots came to take up land in the Talbot settlement, in the valley of the Grand River, in the Huron Tract that was being opened up by the Canada Company in the 1830s, and indeed throughout south-western Ontario. In 1967 many of their descendants were to qualify for the century farm sign.

In the Highlands of Scotland the sheep had won. The glens and straths were desolate and empty. In 1854 when the Crimean War broke out and the British army sent recruiters to the Highlands they were greeted with jeers, with men bleating like sheep and barking like sheep-dogs. "Since you preferred sheep to men," they were told, "let sheep defend you."[1]

The MacLeod Family
Lochiel Township
Glengarry County

In the year 1794, Alexander MacLeod settled on Lot 18, Concession 6, of Lochiel Township in Glengarry County. It was an adventurous journey that had brought him to Canada.

A year before, the troubles in Scotland had caused him to give up his possessions in the Highlands and to engage a hundred and fifty settlers to join him in emigration from Glenelg. The settlers embarked with their baggage on June 15, 1793, and set sail. Accounts of the voyage differ. In a petition for land written in 1837,[2] Alexander MacLeod stated that the ship had proceeded nearly half-way across the Atlantic when she encountered a tremendous storm which caused her to spring a leak and forced her to return to Greenock, where a second ship was chartered. This ship too was beset by bad weather and made to turn back.

Another and more colourful account has it that as France had declared war on Britain in February 1793, Captain MacLeod armed the ship with cannon and provided muskets and broadswords for the able-bodied men. When they had been four days at sea they sighted what they thought was a French vessel and, after a long chase, ran it down, only to find that it was a harmless Dutch merchantman. The strain of the chase precipitated a leak and they returned to Greenock. A second vessel was chartered but a fierce gale forced her to put into an Irish port for repairs.

Wherever the truth may lie in these two stories, the emigrants made another start, and after a voyage of eighteen weeks arrived with a foot of ice on the decks at what is now Prince Edward Island. By then it was impossible to sail up the St. Lawrence and they overwintered in Prince Edward Island "among their own country-men". Early in April 1794 a schooner was chartered and the party made its way through the ice of the St. Lawrence to Montreal. "From thence they were accommodated with the King's Brass with a passage to the River Aux Raisin,"[3] Alexander wrote, travelling by bateaux and portaging their baggage past the rapids. Most of them then struck inland and settled on two hundred acres each in the vicinity of Kirkhill, then known as Glenelg, where a historic plaque commemorates the MacLeod Settlement.

Alexander MacLeod fought in the War of 1812 and was honoured by Sir Isaac Brock with a captain's commission in the 2nd Regiment of Glengarry Militia. He had fourteen children and, in keeping with the Gaelic superstition, his seventh son, also an Alexander, was said to possess healing powers and to have performed many cures of the King's Evil, a running sore, and other ailments of the day.

When we visited Captain Alexander's farm, we were greeted by Rod D. K. MacLeod, a descendant of his tenth child, who managed the family farm with the help of his wife, Nora, and his son, George.

All that remains of the first MacLeod homestead built before 1825 is the foundation stone and mortar. The remaining timbers of the second log house near the creek were pulled down in the spring of 1977. The MacLeods' present house was built in 1870 by "the same bunch of Scots who built all the brick houses around here". The soft brick was made in several local brickyards. The house has the original glass in the windows and the old pine sills are covered in white lead, "no sign of rot in them yet". It is a friendly house with many reminders of the family's past history. Outside, over an arch in the garden, is written a Gaelic greeting for the approaching traveller, and Rod MacLeod is quick to point out a large boulder in the yard. It is on this stone that his ancestors prepared and ate their first meal on the new homestead, using the iron kettle in which they had cooked their meals on board ship.

The cows line up at the gate waiting to be milked. In keeping with the Scottish traditions of Glengarry County they are Ayrshires. With their large doe-like eyes and small build, they trip into the stable like a herd of deer. The bull, a pasha among his harem, strolls in with dignity and lies down to chew the cud. Cats emerge from nowhere for their evening milk. The farm dog lies panting on the stable floor. There is the sound of snuffling and blowing as the cows lick up their evening meal ration.

Inside the barn the evening sunlight filters through the cracks between the timbers, and sparrows and barn swallows twitter in the rafters. A mouse runs down the wall. "All the timber in this barn was cut out of the bush by hand," Rod MacLeod tells us. "The ladder there — that was made with an axe. The rafters are balsam. . . . They hold a nail pretty good and they'll last forever unless there's a leak."

The barn holds seven thousand bales of hay, pretty well all alfalfa. "The more protein we can get the less soybean meal we have to feed — that stuff has just about doubled in price in the last year." As a crop, soybeans seem particularly susceptible to the vagaries of the marketing system and in 1977 a third of the world's soybeans were bought by one multimillionaire in an attempt to corner the market.

Years ago, too, the cows were fed turnips. "We had a root-cutter. There was a hopper on the top and one of the more robust kids would put in about a bag of turnips before school and get on the crank. They were good to eat, too. But with the labour shortage we had to give all that up. Today you can only grow crops like corn and alfalfa that can be harvested by machine."

For many years Glengarry County was famed for its cheesemaking. At the turn of the century one of the MacLeod family was a pioneer cheese manufacturer and operated eighteen factories. "We had to get the milk to the factory by nine o'clock. Hitch up a horse and take it." Mrs. MacLeod, who was one of a family of four daughters and did the chores for her father, enjoyed it. "We'd meet all the boys on the road and race the horses back." At the cheese factory, lining up to deliver the milk became a social occasion. There was time for a chat and a friendly visit.

Outside, between the house and the road, the fields have been tile-drained using, one suspects, much the same methods as the Romans. Rod MacLeod appreciated the government scheme for encouraging tile drainage, but he was not optimistic about the future of farming. "We may be frozen out . . . may have to give up the cows. We have a load of pulpwood in the bush cut last winter and no one has come for it yet . . . been laying there for five months. And the price of everything is crazy. We have to watch every step."

One sensed, too, that he was saddened to see some of the fields which his ancestors and others laboured so painfully to clear now untended and returning to bush. The ownership has changed: week-end farmers from Montreal, wealthy city folk looking for a place in the country, different people with different priorities.

The MacLeod family motto is *Hold Fast* and that they have done to this piece of land through six generations and nearly two centuries. The MacLeod Genealogy describes the MacLeods as good-

tempered in their outlook on life, scrupulously dependable in all
their dealings, and possessed of a stubborn independence — or an
independent stubbornness. Qualities that, one suspects, made for
excellent settlers in Ontario's past. In retrospect, these qualities
were evident in the personality of Rod D. K. MacLeod, who, before
his death in the fall of 1977, was a proud heir to the MacLeod family
traditions.

The Kinloch Family
Charlottenburgh Township
Glengarry County

In 1753 the French government persuaded some fifty-
three Christian Iroquois families to settle on St. Regis Island, now
Cornwall Island, in the St. Lawrence River. The Indians claimed all
the surrounding country for themselves, but when the American
War of Independence ended and Loyalist settlers were in need of a
home, the St. Regis Indians were persuaded to sell their territory
to the British Crown. After 1784 they retained only a narrow strip
two miles wide between the St. Lawrence and the Ottawa River,
known as the Indian Lands, together with the islands in the St.
Lawrence itself. However, even the Indian Lands did not remain
long in the exclusive possession of the Indians.

By 1801 there were to the east of the Indian Lands and inland from
Cornwall the beginnings of a village at Martintown, where Lieutenant Malcolm MacMartin had established a sawmill on the Aux
Raisins River — so called because of the prevalence there of wild
grapes. The village grew over the years, and with it the settlers' need
for churches. In 1826, an enterprising and energetic Scot, the Reverend Archibald Connell, arrived to minister to the Presbyterian congregation. He built a church of beech logs on the Indian Lands
known as the Beech Church. Later, with a congregation numbering
some thirteen hundred, mostly from the Highlands of Scotland, he
required a larger building. He set off for Scotland on a fund-raising
expedition and returned, not only with the money, but with a
master carpenter and a master mason. These were the Kinloch
brothers from Midlothian.

The Kinlochs fulfilled the commission building the St. Andrews
stone church and a stone manse at Martintown. One of the brothers,
Alexander or "Sandy", then went to Montreal, where he worked on
St. James's Cathedral, the Bonsecours Market, and the Lachine
Canal. He prospered and brought out his family from Scotland, his

father and one brother dying on the voyage. His family responsibilities put an end to his own romance, for he wrote to his fiancée in Scotland telling her that because of them he could not contemplate marriage.

There is a story that Sandy Kinloch loaned a large sum of money to his partner with which to start a sugar refinery that is now a household name in Canada. Believing that the man was as good as his word, he did not ask for a promissory note or a signature and the money was never repaid. In disillusionment and in straitened circumstances he returned to Martintown, and in 1849 bought a farm of two hundred and thirty acres in the Indian Lands for £57.12.6 from Peter Sinclair, an Indian agent, who had bought it from the Indians in 1806.

On this farm Sandy Kinloch erected two remarkable buildings and an equally remarkable well. The house is of stone with sixteen rooms and five fireplaces. George Kinloch, who lives in it with his wife, Grace, and son, Henry, says that the stone was drawn from Summerstown by horse and sleigh during the winters until the Kinlochs found a source on the farm itself. The lead slates for the roof were brought from Scotland. "The order went out one summer and the slate was delivered the next."

Lime for the mortar was burned on the farm. Sandy Kinloch built the kiln with such skill that no mortar was used in its construction. The kiln was fired for nine days and nine nights without a break and the lime was made, cured underground, and used the following year.

The Kinlochs suspect that the house may have been a copy of the Laird's house in Midlothian. It was a double house and the Kinloch house too is built with two separate entrances in the cellar. Its architecture is, however, much in keeping with an early Quebec style. The house has extended eaves over the verandahs, and its dormer windows are similar to those of *habitant* houses.

It is the stonework of the house that is outstanding. George Kinloch says that his "Uncle Sandy" served an apprenticeship of seven years, and his skill shows. The stones round the doors and windows are beautifully dressed, all shaped by hand with hammers and chisels. His tools were around the farm for years, but have now disappeared. The chimneys have a crook in them as a built-in draft control so that they draw in all weathers.

The Kinlochs built not only a house. A few yards away is another building — a small, square, enigmatic blockhouse or fort. The dangers that might have threatened after 1849 seem obscure, but the fort was intended to counter a real threat. The slits in the walls face in all directions and are enlarged on the inside to ensure maximum movements of a gun barrel and effective cross-fire. There are hand-hewn timbers for floor-boards, and uprights notched so that partitions could be inserted to make small rooms. Everything was thought of to withstand a siege. The blockhouse, if that is what it was, overlooks the valley of the Raisin River. Perhaps it was constructed when heightened international tensions led to renewed fears of invasion from the south.

Down in the field below the blockhouse, almost hidden by grass, is a well. The stones for it are inset without mortar and so close together that there is hardly a crack between them. There are twenty-three spiral steps down to the bottom of the well, each one measuring a foot in height. The water supply has never failed. Through switching or dowsing, an underground stream running straight east and west was located. Like the house and the block-house, the well is a remarkable piece of stonework.

The Kinlochs now have eighty head of Holstein cattle and grow hay, grain, and corn. George Kinloch has been involved with farm organizations for many years and is a delegate from Glengarry County to the Ontario Plowmen's Association, the association that sponsors the annual International Plowing Match. Ploughing matches have been a feature of fall fairs since 1842, and in 1846 one was held at Yonge and St. Clair, now in the heart of the city of Toronto.

The Kinloch farm was described in 1849 as "containing 230 acres more or less" and "running down to the water's edge of the south shore of the Rivière aux Raisins". The family has the original indenture for it dated February 10, 1806, between Peter Sinclair, the Indian agent, and various Indian chiefs of the St. Regis Lands. The Indians put a mark opposite their names, and according to a tradition in the Kinloch family these rusty brown thumb-prints were made in blood.

The MacDonell Family
Beaverview Farm
Charlottenburgh Township
Glengarry County

The great Scottish Clan Donald, "of all the clans . . . by every rule of antiquity, power and numbers fully entitled to be spoken of before any other,"[4] embraces a hundred or more

septs or sub-clans, among them the MacDonells and the Mac-
Donalds, with all their various spellings. In Scotland, the clan's
wide homelands stretch along the western coastline from Lewis
in the north to the Mull of Kintyre in the south. They include
the Western Isles "and the blue water between",[5] and it is a
chief of the clan who claims the proud title Lord of the Isles. Clan
Donald played a central role in Scotland's turbulent history, and
its members were to be equally influential in the early history of
Canada.

Many of the clan were "out" for Bonnie Prince Charlie in the
Rebellion of 1745, and after the defeat at Culloden their homelands
were laid waste and the Chief's castle at Invergarry burned. Later,
the MacDonell chiefs evicted their tenants from their holdings so
that they themselves might benefit from the new wealth that
sheep-rearing was bringing to Scotland. The clearances led to the
migration of thousands of the Clan Donald to North America, leaving next to none in their Scottish homelands. Some of the clan
crossed the Atlantic as soldiers in the service of George III, or more
specifically as members of the 78th Regiment of the Line under the
command of Simon Fraser, whose father, Lord Lovat, had been
executed after Culloden. They participated in the taking of Louisbourg and in the capture of Quebec, and it was a French-speaking
Captain Donald Macdonald who lulled the suspicions of a French
sentry and made possible the seizure of the Plains of Abraham.

Then in 1773, because of worsening conditions in Scotland, more
than six hundred clansmen from Scottish Glen Garry sailed in the
Pearl for the colony of New York, where they made their home on
the Mohawk Valley lands of Sir William Johnson, who, though an
Irishman, was a distant kinsman. It was to prove a temporary
asylum. With the outbreak of the War of Independence, some
slipped away to join in the defence of Quebec against the Americans, while others joined Sir John Johnson's Royal Yorkers or
Butler's Rangers.

At the end of the war in 1783, these Loyalist MacDonells and
MacDonalds were to settle in Canada and were among the discharged soldiers who took up land allotted to them in the Royal
Townships, those first settlements along the St. Lawrence. Here
they were joined by clansmen driven out of Scotland by "Light-
headed Marjorie" and her ilk.

Archibald MacDonell lives on the Summerstown Road, just east
of the city of Cornwall; his family history is closely interwoven with
these events. His farm — Lot 14, Glen, in the Township of
Charlottenburgh — was granted to a Loyalist ancestor from the

Mohawk Valley, John McDonald, whose daughter Flora married "Big Donald", son of another McDonald named Angus Ban, who emigrated directly to Canada from Scotland. This Angus Ban McDonald had lived on a farm called Muinall, or Peninsula, Farm in Knoidart on the west coast of Scotland. According to the census of 1755-56 this farm was stocked with eleven horses, thirty-nine black cattle, thirty sheep, and thirty goats. Nevertheless, Angus Ban and his wife were evicted during the clearances. In 1785 they sailed in the ship *Macdonald* from Greenock to Quebec in company with nineteen cabin passengers and over five hundred clansmen crammed into the steerage space. The McDonalds brought with them their four sons, Donald, John, Finan, and James, all large men and known as the "Big People".

Of these sons, "Big Donald", Archibald MacDonell's ancestor, died in 1825. A second brother, John McDonald, known as "McDonald le Borgne" because he was blind in one eye, became a fur-trader and a partner in the North West Company. For a time he was chief factor in charge of the Upper Red River and later of the Winnipeg district. He then moved to Simcoe County with his wife, Marie Poitras, a woman of French and Indian parentage. There, "he had a good library" and his children played on the floor of a shanty on the Penetanguishene Road with leather-bound volumes of Plutarch and their father's gold coins.[6]

John McDonald and his wife were on their way back to Glengarry when they fell ill. She died at Newmarket on January 15, 1828, and he a month later. Earlier, John McDonald had befriended the explorer Sir John Franklin when he made his famous journey down the Mackenzie River, and it was Lady Jane Franklin who sent out a headstone from England to mark the McDonalds' graves in the old Church of England cemetery at Newmarket.

Finan McDonald was with David Thompson on the Columbia River between 1807 and 1812. During the course of a long career in the North West and Hudson's Bay companies, he established the first fur-trading post in what is now the state of Montana, helped build Kootenay House, and was one of the founders of Spokane, Washington. He married an Indian girl, daughter of a Pend d'Oreille chief, and "took to the Salish way of life with gusto", once joining in a battle with their hereditary enemies, the Blackfoot. He was six feet tall, with broad shoulders, and "to the gentleness of a lamb he united the courage of a lion."[7]

For generations, perhaps for centuries, individuals in the family have married within the clan. Thus, both Archibald MacDonell's wife, Isabel, and his mother, Florence, were McDonalds who married MacDonells, and marriages between men and women of the same last name were commonplace. It is through his mother that Archibald is related to the "Big People", and through her too that his farm was inherited. The MacDonell family has had its full share of distinguished and colourful characters as well.

One was Lieutenant-Colonel John MacDonell, first Speaker of the Legislative Assembly of Upper Canada, to whom Elizabeth Simcoe refers in her diary. The Simcoes visited him in June 1792 when he was building his new home, Glengarry House, near Cornwall, and it was he who gave Francis Simcoe a "little Cannon" for his third birthday. Another was Archibald MacDonell, in charge of the disastrous Fifth Town settlement in Prince Edward County in 1784. He built a blockhouse and a home in what is now called Prinyer's Cove.

Then there was "Spanish John" MacDonell, so called because he had fought as a boy with the Spanish army in the Adriatic in 1774, admitting that in the midst of the volleys of bullets in one action, "his heart was panting very strongly."[8]

Spanish John later lived at St. Andrews West. He wrote: "We are building a pretty snug and decent stone church at River aux Raisins. It is Mr. Roderick's hobby horse. It is expected to be finished this year."[9] This is a reference to the first stone church at St. Andrews West, completed about 1801 and now the oldest stone structure in the province. "Mr. Roderick" was the Reverend Roderick Mac-Donell, chaplain to the Highland Catholic United Empire Loyalists under the auspices of the King in 1785, and first "Catholick Priest" to Upper Canada. He ministered to the Indians of the St. Regis Indian Lands, and there is a local story, probably unfounded, that when he died in 1806 the Indians hid his body and buried it secretly.

At the time of the War of 1812, a John MacDonell was attorney general of Upper Canada and provincial aide-de-camp under General Brock. He died at the battle of Queenston Heights. Nor would any account of the family be complete without a reference to Alexander MacDonell, a priest in the mould of the crusading prelates of the Middle Ages. He raised the Glengarry Fencibles in Scotland in 1794, a Roman Catholic regiment which was recalled from Guernsey in 1798 and sent to Ireland because of the troubles there. When the regiment was disbanded in 1802, Alexander MacDonell obtained grants of land in Canadian Glengarry for several hundred Highland settlers. An ardent Conservative and patriot, friend of Roman Catholic and Protestant alike, he became the first Roman Catholic bishop in Upper Canada in 1819, and the town of Alexandria is named in his honour.

With a family history of this kind, it is not surprising that there is a trunk filled with family documents in a living-room of Archibald MacDonell's house on the Summerstown Road. The construction of this big white house with its long front verandah was financed by money made by Archibald MacDonell's great-grandparents from railway contracts in the Canadian West. Inside and out, it has been much altered, and it now shelters three generations: Archibald MacDonell, his wife, Isabel, their four children, and his mother, Florence MacDonell.

At eighty-two, Florence MacDonell knows much of the history of the family and the farm. Her notes on the construction of the barn, and on later alterations to it and other out-buildings, record a continuing process of accommodation to new farming methods and machinery. The skeleton of the fifty-by-one-hundred-foot barn, she noted, was erected in a single day in 1886, when a crowd of neighbours gathered for a raising bee that had every last rafter in place by nightfall. The timber for the barn had been cut from the bush months before, then laid out in a field, where it was cut to fit by a man nicknamed "Koovish" McDonald, a skilled carpenter although he could neither read nor write. Over four thousand feet of sheathing was needed to cover the rafters, and the peak of the barn was fifty feet above the ground.

The MacDonells now have a dairy herd of some forty Holsteins that was first registered in 1909 or 1910 and may thus be the oldest registered herd in the county. For them the barn was completely renovated in 1976 at a cost of seventeen thousand dollars. The family also has a small pig operation, and in the spring they tap some twelve hundred maple trees, boiling the sap in an old shanty in the bush.

Archibald MacDonell works the farm with his son, Hugh. It is a source of some satisfaction that he has an option to buy back another farm that once belonged to his great-great-grandfather, and he hopes to do this with the assistance of the ARDA program — a government program designed to help enlarge the size of farms under the terms of the Agricultural Rehabilitation and Development Act.

In 1845 no fewer than five MacDonells and MacDonalds held seats in the provincial Parliament, where they represented Stormont, Dundas, Glengarry, Cornwall, and Kingston. Archibald MacDonell has kept up this tradition and has an impressive list of public offices to his credit. He has held positions in the Rural Ontario Municipal Association, the Ontario Milk Marketing Board, the Conservative Association of Glengarry, and the Children's Aid Society — to name only a few. It is appropriate that in Canada's Centennial Year he was named Warden of the United Counties of Dundas, Stormont, and Glengarry, bringing further distinction to a family whose long-standing reputation has been that of "the most prominent of all the Glengarry settlers".[10]

CHAPTER SEVEN

Indian Lands and
Plain People

*A*s the American War of Independence dragged to its close and preliminary peace negotiations began, rumours regarding the future boundary between Canada and the United States began to circulate among the Six Nations Indians which, if true, meant that their homelands in upper New York would come under American jurisdiction. Their leader, Joseph Brant, travelled to England seeking reassurance, only to be fobbed off with evasive answers. Finally, in May of 1783 he went to Quebec to see Governor Haldimand. In a moving appeal he asked Haldimand for the truth.

"Brother Asharekowa and representatives of the King," he said, "the Sachems and war chieftains of the Six Nations of Indians and their allies have heard that the King, their father, has made peace with his children . . . the Americans in rebellion. And when they heard of it, they found they were forgot. . . ."

Brant reminded the governor of the great services to the Crown rendered by the Six Nations in the past, and ended his speech with a final appeal: "Wherefore, Brother, I am sent in behalf of all the King's Indian allies to receive a decisive answer from you, and to know whether they are included in the treaty with the Americans, as faithful allies should be, or not. . . ."[1]

The answer, it transpired, was that they were not included. The treaty that recognized the independence of the United States was to have nothing to say about the territorial rights of the Six Nations Indians, whose lands would now pass into American hands for ever.

Originally, there were five "nations" or tribes in the League of the Iroquois. Immediately to the south of Lake Ontario were the Seneca, the Cayuga, and the Onondaga; to their east lived the Oneida and the Mohawk, with the homelands of the latter extending eastward as far as Lake Champlain and the Hudson River to include the Mohawk Valley which was to figure so prominently in the War of Independence.

e in the 1500s, the five tribes had entered into a form of loose political union; a union, it might be added, that in its sophis- been compared with those formed by the cities and ncient Greece. In 1720, or thereabouts, a sixth tribe, the om Carolina, came north to join the confederacy, there- d to as the League of the Six Nations, or collectively as .

he seventeenth century the Mohawk tribe came into h the French and from then on the animosity between ned, to be bloodily sustained until the British conquest the Seven Years War. It was an animosity of which the to make effective use. The Iroquois first became their in the war against France that broke out in 1689, a war dians on both sides taking part in savage raids and ls that were among the more unpleasant features of that conflict. Early in the eighteenth century, the Anglo-Mohawk alliance was strengthened by the state visit to England of a group of Mohawk sachems or councillors, in the course of which they became the sensation of London society. It seems that their stay was one continuous whirl of banquets and receptions, while their cultural horizons were broadened by attendance at a performance of *Macbeth* at the Haymarket Theatre. They were also taken to see the refugee camps on Blackheath where destitute Germans from the Palatinate, of whom more later, were being looked after pending their resettlement in Ireland and the American colonies.

More to the point, however, was the audience given by Queen Anne. In the course of their loyal address, the Mohawks requested that a missionary be sent to them. The British went one better, building a chapel in the Mohawk Valley complete with carpet, royal coat-of-arms, and organ. With the chapel came a gift from Queen Anne that is treasured by the Mohawk to this day: an eight-piece set of communion silver.

The Mohawks' visit to England proved to be a great success, and the loyalty of the Six Nations Indians to the British Crown was sustained through the next two wars against the French. In the course of them, however, the ancient League of the Iroquois started to break down, its final collapse brought about by the American Revolution. Some Indians decided to remain neutral; others sided with the Americans. That the Mohawk, with whom the Six Nations had now become identified, remained loyal to the British was largely due to Sir William Johnson.

Since his appointment as Superintendent of Indian Affairs in the mid-1700s, Sir William's residence near Albany, New York, had become the focus of all that was Mohawk. Following the death of his first and possibly only legal wife, the daughter of a German missionary by whom he had three children, Sir William took Indian women as his second and third wives. The first died young. The second was Molly Brant, who was known as Miss Molly or the Brown Lady Johnson.

Joseph Brant, who would emerge as the pre-eminent leader of the Six Nations Indians, was Molly Brant's brother. One of several young Indians whom Sir William had sent off to school in Connecticut, Joseph was described by his teacher as a modest young man with a "serious turn" to him.

Sir William Johnson died not long before the American colonists broke into open rebellion, and was succeeded in his official position by his nephew, Sir Guy. With war imminent, Sir Guy came north to the British in 1775, to be followed by Joseph Brant and his loyal Mohawks. Sir John Johnson, Sir William's son, stayed behind to look after the family estates. Then he, too, fled north to Montreal, there to raise the King's Royal Regiment of New York, as we have already seen. Later, Sir John took over Sir Guy's job, becoming the third Johnson to superintend the affairs of the Six Nations Indians, which in the years following the end of the war became very tangled indeed.

In 1783, however, the immediate problem facing the British, and one which Governor Haldimand, in the absence of any instructions from London, had to solve himself, was the settlement of the loyal Iroquois on lands that met their approval. Apart from anything else, the bloody uprising of discontented Indians under Pontiac following the Seven Years War was still a vivid memory.

In the event, the Iroquois split up. About a hundred under John Deseronto went to settle on the north shore of the Bay of Quinte, where their descendants live to this day at the place named after their leader. The rest of the Iroquois went with Brant to the valley of the Grand River. As for their chapel in the Mohawk Valley, it had been destroyed in the war, its ruined walls finally disappearing in 1820 when the Erie Canal was built.

The land on which Joseph Brant wished to settle his followers belonged to the Mississauga Indians, as did a large part of what is now southern Ontario at that time. However, the Mississaugas professed themselves happy to see the Six Nations Indians live among them and, as a fraternal gesture, transferred the coveted land for a consideration of £1,180.7.6d., paid by the government. Not much for what was afterwards found to be about 570,000 acres or nearly nine hundred square miles.

Governor Haldimand generously, if rather loosely, defined the tract to be transferred as being "six miles deep from each side of the river beginning at Lake Erie and extending in that proportion to the head of the said river. . . ."[2] Establishing the lateral boundaries of the tract gave little trouble — but where was the "head of the said river"?

The Grand River rises high on the Niagara Escarpment some 180 miles north of Lake Erie. The Mississaugas had not intended to be *that* generous. At the same time, their own definition of the northern boundary of the tract, which was the extension of a line running north-east from Burlington Bay to the River Thames, made little sense, as such a line drawn from Burlington Bay can never reach the Thames, that river being where it is. In the end, Thames or no Thames, the line suggested by the Mississaugas was accepted, giving the Six Nations a twelve-mile-wide strip centring on the Grand that started in the vicinity of the present Elora and ran south to Lake Erie.

So it was to this magnificent tract, with its dense and in some places luxuriant forest of hardwoods, that Joseph Brant led about twelve hundred of his Six Nations Indians, there to establish on the banks of the Grand River the settlement of Brant's Ford, later Brantford. With the help of the government, a school, a sawmill, and a grist-mill were built, as well as a chapel to take the place of the one left behind in the Mohawk Valley.

Meanwhile, with the disbanding of Butler's Rangers and the post-war influx of Loyalists, the settlement at Niagara was expanding. It is claimed that it was to Niagara that the first Loyalist refugees came as early as 1776 when five women and thirty-one children staggered into Fort George. Among them was a Mrs. Secord with her three-year-old son, James. When James grew up he married Laura Ingersoll, who thus became the Laura Secord remembered for her exploits during the War of 1812.

To the original two hundred acres or so of land acquired from the Mississauga Indians at Niagara during the war was added a further two hundred and fifty acres bought from them for a tenth of a penny per acre. From then on the land was settled at an increasing pace, with the earlier Loyalist arrivals joined by the many who flocked in from upper New York and Pennsylvania when the war ended in 1783.

The land on the Lake Ontario shore west of Niagara was soon taken up, with a settlement of some note growing up on the Twenty Mile Creek, so called because it was twenty miles from the Niagara River. Other Loyalists settled on the northern shore of Lake Erie at its eastern end, while still others made their way to join the settlements at Petite Côte in the vicinity of Detroit, and along the lower Thames.

Among the Loyalists were a number of Quaker families who settled in the Niagara Peninsula in 1783. They were the advance guard of what was to become a massive northward migration of Plain People — Quakers, Mennonites, Dunkards, and other religious sects, whose sombre dress and simple way of life was an expression of their religious faith. For many of the Plain People, this was the end of a long journey in both time and space that had started with earlier generations in the dark and intolerant days of the Reformation.

It is a curious fact that even as the Reformation was reducing many thousands of men and women to the status of religious or political refugees, new lands were being discovered beyond the seas that would one day be their refuge.

In 1492, the year that Christopher Columbus made his celebrated voyage across the Atlantic to plant the first European flag — that of Spain — in the New World, Martin Luther was a boy of nine going to school in central Germany. In 1517 Luther nailed his Ninety-Five Theses to the church door in Wittenberg in the act that is usually taken as signalling the start of the Reformation. Less than two decades later, Jacques Cartier caught his first glimpse of the St. Lawrence, by which time the Reformation in Germany was at its height.

The Reformation by no means burst upon a Europe unprepared for it. As early as the mid-1300s John Wycliffe had completed the first translation of the Bible into English, and it was widely read. Wycliffe, sometimes called the "morning-star of the Reformation", had much to say about abuses in the Catholic Church and he had a considerable following. His movement was suppressed in England, but it took root in Bohemia — now part of Czechoslovakia — under the leadership of John Huss, who had King Wenceslaus, the Good King of the Christmas carol, as one of his supporters. Huss was burned as a heretic in 1415, but out of his teachings came the Moravian Church. Four hundred years later, the Moravians were to bring their Indian converts north to Upper Canada to found Moraviantown, near Thamesville, where General Procter met defeat in the War of 1812. By the time that Martin Luther appeared on the scene, the Moravians, in spite of persecution, were already to be numbered in their tens of thousands. Thus the Reformation came to a Europe that already knew religious turmoil. It came moreover to a Europe deeply troubled in other ways.

After centuries of oppression the most down-trodden group of all, the peasants, revolted against their rapacious and tyrannical overlords in what is known as the Peasants' War, which culminated in a battle in 1525 that saw them slaughtered like cattle and their leader executed. While to add another dimension to the secular-cum-religious struggle for power, there was the threat to Christendom posed by the Ottoman Turks.

Coming out of Asia some time in the sixth century, the Ottoman Turks pushed into eastern Europe in the early 1400s. In 1453 they took Constantinople. Egypt and Syria were added to their empire in 1517, as was half of Hungary in 1526. Three years later they were at the gates of Vienna.

Standing in the way of the Turks was the Holy Roman Empire, a loose confederation of German-speaking principalities, states, and so-called free cities, each with its own ruler, but with a single elected emperor ruling all. Considering itself to be the successor of the Christian empire of the Romans, the Holy Roman Empire, it is said, was not strictly speaking an empire, was certainly not Roman, and was anything but holy. Be that as it may, the Holy Roman Empire was the Turks' principal opponent on the mainland of Europe, and the last thing that the Empire wanted as it battled the infidel was dissension in its own ranks, which accounts for the savagery with which apostates of the Roman Catholic faith were dealt with.

While the Lutheran faith spread in some of the German principalities, the people of France were listening to the voice of John Calvin, who was born in Picardy in 1509. Calvin, in rejecting Roman Catholicism, preached the grim doctrine of predestination. From birth you were either damned or you weren't and there was nothing you could do about it except have faith in God's mercy and hope for the best.

In France, Calvin's followers became known as Huguenots, and some half a million of them fled persecution to settle in many countries, including the American colonies, where in the course of time families of Huguenot origin such as the de Lanceys of New York were to number themselves among the Loyalists. A form of Calvinism also took root in Scotland, brought there by the irrepressible John Knox. In bringing the Reformation to Scotland, Knox founded the Presbyterian Church.

In an England that had been officially Protestant ever since Henry VIII prevailed on Parliament to acknowledge him as head of the Church of England, the followers of Calvin became known as Puritans. The sect grew in numbers, with many of its adherents joining in the mass migration to the American colonies that in the early 1600s depopulated many English towns and left whole villages deserted. Other Puritans stayed, to exert with other non-conformist sects a profound influence on the course of English history in the seventeenth century.

Some German princes, too, adopted Calvinism, as did the Netherlands, which had fallen under the overlordship of Spain in the mid-1500s. Following persecution at the hands of the Spanish Inquisition, the northern provinces rebelled, combining to form the United Dutch Republic in 1579 under William the Silent, the great-grandfather of William of Orange, who later became King of England. With the establishment of the Protestant Dutch Republic came a measure of religious tolerance, and Holland became a haven for such persecuted sects as the Quakers and the Mennonites.

The Mennonites were one of the many sects that had their roots in Anabaptism, a faith originating in Switzerland in the early 1500s. The Anabaptist believed that a Christian community could arise only by bringing mature minds to bear upon the truths in the Bible, from which follows a denial of the efficacy of infant baptism and the need for an adult to be baptized anew. Hence the name Anabaptist, the prefix "ana" meaning "anew" or "again".

With their denial of the rights of government to meddle in religious matters, the Anabaptists antagonized both Catholic and Protestant, and, at the hands of both, thousands of Anabaptists were to suffer death for their beliefs. Even Henry VIII, who was not an intolerant man for his times, achieved something of a record when he burned twenty-five Anabaptists in a single day.

With its emphasis on the simple and pious life devoted to the needs of the community and with its insistence that a man's conscience was his own, the Anabaptist movement spread rapidly, appealing as it did to the lowest stratum of society, the despairing peasants. As might be expected in a movement emphasizing the right of the individual to make up his own mind, it wasn't long before the term "Anabaptist" was applied to a multiplicity of sects. One under Joseph Hutter was to adopt a form of communism based on religious principles. Hutter was burned at the stake, but his teachings are followed to this day by the Hutterites.

In 1536 a Dutch Catholic priest called Menno Simons was rebaptized and became an elder in the Anabaptist faith. Around him a group formed that had some measure of cohesion; its members came to be known as Mennonites. The Mennonites were pacifists, abjuring the use of violence even to defend themselves. They also refused to bind themselves by oaths — though civil disobedience was not part of their creed. As far as the civil authorities in sixteenth-century Europe were concerned, however, the Mennonites were Anabaptists and that was that. From 1542 onwards, Menno Simons was a fugitive with a large price on his head, and his followers were relentlessly hunted down to be executed if caught.

Some fled to England, where, as we have seen, they were to find little mercy, though their survival there with others of the Anabaptist faith was to lead to the founding of the Baptist Church. Other Mennonites made their way to remoter and safer corners of Europe — to Bohemia and Moravia, Poland and Prussia. Made unwelcome in Prussia by Frederick the Great in the eighteenth century, the Mennonites were invited by Catherine the Great of Russia to settle on lands north of the Black Sea, an area that came to be called the Ukraine. And it was from the Ukraine that Mennonites were to come to Canada in the nineteenth century, most to settle in Manitoba, some to stay in Ontario and make their homes in Waterloo County.

In 1618 a series of wars started that convulsed the Holy Roman Empire. They went on for thirty years — until 1649 — and so for want of a better name were lumped together and called the Thirty Years War. They started when Protestant Bohemia revolted against the Catholic Emperor and soon several of the German states were drawn into the conflict. As so often happens, what had been a religious quarrel turned very quickly into a political one, and before the war was over, Denmark, Sweden, and France as well as Spain and the Netherlands had all become involved in it.

The Thirty Years War devastated Germany. Countless towns and cities were ruined, with the countryside reduced over huge areas to a blackened waste. Of greater consequence to Germany was the loss in terms of human life: a staggering total of seven million people out of a total population of about twenty million.

In the opening stages of the war, a German state called the Rhine Palatinate had been in the thick of it — both geographically and politically. Lying on the Middle Rhine, roughly half-way between Holland and Switzerland, the Palatinate, with Calvinism as its state religion, had become a place of refuge for Huguenots from France and Calvinists from those provinces of the Netherlands still under Catholic rulers. However, with the outbreak of war it was a refuge no longer and the exodus from the Palatinate began. Many of the Palatinate Germans went to Holland, from where they made their way to the colonies that the English and the Dutch were founding in America. Others went to England and to Ireland. The ancestors of a century farmer near Owen Sound left their home on the German-Dutch border in the early 1600s to go to Ireland, where England was encouraging the settlement of Protestants, and in Ireland the family remained for two hundred years before coming to Canada during the years of the Irish famines.

The Palatinate, in fact, made a remarkable recovery after the Thirty Years War. However, in 1688 it was invaded by the French, who laid the country waste with such thoroughness that the extent of the destruction is often singled out for comment by historians. Not only were fortifications and military supplies burned by the French, but six cities were put to the torch, together with hundreds of towns and villages. Crops of any and all description were burned, the vineyards systematically destroyed. With their homeland in ruins, the last and greatest exodus of the Palatinate Germans began.

Their plight aroused great concern in England, as they had been allies in the war against France. And it was with Palatines in mind that a bill was passed in 1708 that offered naturalization to all foreign Protestants. About the same time, the British government circulated literature in the Palatinate and the Rhine Valley promoting the American colonies. As a result of these two measures, perhaps as many as twenty thousand Palatinate Germans started to pour into England.

Caring for them posed an enormous problem, for most were destitute. Many were housed temporarily in a camp on Blackheath, then outside London, and it was there that they were visited by the Mohawks who were paying their memorable visit to England. Some of the Palatinate Germans chose to stay in England; some were conveyed to Ireland; still others to the Carolinas. The remainder, numbering several thousands, were settled in New York, where a century or so later many of their descendants became Loyalists fighting for the king.

The first Mennonites had arrived in Pennsylvania some thirty years before the mass resettlement of Palatinate Germans, and the story of their coming is linked with that of the Quakers or Society of Friends. This sect had its roots in fifteenth-century Spain, where a movement began within the Roman Catholic Church that stressed meditation, passive acceptance, and withdrawal from the world. The movement spread to England, where in 1643 George Fox, a nineteen-year-old shoemaker's apprentice, heeded a divine call to start his ministry. Fox soon built up a following, as evidenced by the unhappy fact that within ten years or so there were nearly a thousand Quakers in prison. The movement spread quickly through the British Isles and it was in Ireland that a young William Penn, son of an admiral, went to gaol for the first time for being a

Quaker. In 1677 he and Fox went on a preaching tour through Holland and Germany, where Penn made contacts that resulted in the great German migrations to Pennsylvania.

William Penn had already had something to do with sending Quakers to western New Jersey, when in settlement of a sixteen-thousand-pound debt owed by Charles II to his father, now dead, he was granted a deed to the land that William was to name in memory of the old admiral. That was in 1761, and the next year he sailed for America with about a hundred settlers to establish his model commonwealth, to be based on Quaker principles and with Philadelphia, the "city of brotherly love", as its capital.

Much as Queen Anne was later to do, Penn distributed literature in Holland and north-west Germany advertising his colony, with especial emphasis on the religious freedom to be found there. To the many uprooted people, Penn's promise of religious tolerance offered an end to long years of persecution. And so the emigrants came, some making their way down the Rhine from as far away as Switzerland to take ship in Holland, Pennsylvania-bound. Within a year of founding Philadelphia, the first Germans were settling in; among the first were Mennonites from the Lower Rhine.

By the time of the American Revolution there were 100,000 Germans in Pennsylvania — one-third of the total population of the colony — and by then their way of life and their culture, often erroneously referred to as "Pennsylvania Dutch", was firmly established. The "Plain People" among them were pacifists, and as such their position *vis-à-vis* the Patriot authorities during the Revolution was an equivocal one. The Patriots recognized the non-combatant status of the Plain People, reaffirming an earlier British act which exempted them from bearing arms, though other types of war service had to be performed in lieu. However, this concession on the part of the Patriots did not prevent the Plain People's lack of co-operation in matters military from leading to confiscation of property, gaol terms, and death threats.

Then, in 1777, the Pennsylvania Assembly required everyone without exception to take an oath of allegiance to the new Republic. And this the Mennonite, loyal citizen though he might be, could not do, for he had one ultimate loyalty, and that was to God.

After the war there were other causes of discontent, besides a shortage of good land in Pennsylvania. Then in 1792 came Governor Simcoe's invitation to take up land in Upper Canada, with the promise of an exemption from military service for those whose religion forbade it. And so the Plain People came north in increasing numbers. Since 1786 there had been a Mennonite community on the

Twenty, a creek twenty miles from the Niagara River between the Niagara Escarpment and Lake Ontario. Some joined it, as did the ancestor of one of the century farmers in this book; others went on to search for new and fertile land.

It was in the autumn of 1799 that two Mennonites from Pennsylvania, Joseph Sherk and Samuel Betzner, arrived with their families. With winter coming on, Sherk and his family found a place to live near Niagara Falls, but Sam Betzner pressed on to Ancaster, then nothing more than a few houses in the wilderness, an outpost of the settlements hugging the Lake Ontario shore. To the west was the all-but-empty valley of the Grand River, home of the Six Nations Indians.

It seems that it was at Ancaster where he spent the winter that Samuel Betzner learned that some Indian land along the Grand River had been sold, and fine, rich land it was, from all accounts. Perhaps there was more to be purchased.

The sale that Sam Betzner had heard about had taken place the year before, and it had brought to an end a long wrangle between Joseph Brant and the government that had its roots in the problematical right of the Six Nations Indians to dispose of their land as they saw fit.

Brant took the view that the land was theirs to sell or even give away if they wished, and in fact he had been doing just this since 1787 when he first issued deeds to various people who wanted land. This perturbed the authorities and also tended to alienate those among the Mohawk who held to the Indian's traditional view that land was not just another commodity to be bought and sold. Brant disagreed. There was a lot of land and very few Indians. The fur trade was dying out, at least in the region of the Grand River. The Six Nations must become farmers and they could only do this successfully with the help of white settlers with their mills and their up-to-date know-how. This reasoning was all very well, but it seems clear that Brant was by no means averse to making a bit of money for himself.

As the government saw it, the Indians could only sell their land with the approval of the Crown, and when John Graves Simcoe arrived in 1791 matters became deadlocked when he refused Brant permission to sell. He feared that the Six Nations would become prey to speculators, and time was to prove him correct. A patent prepared by Simcoe which gave the Crown first refusal on any sale of Indian land was firmly rejected by Brant on principle, and there matters stood until Simcoe was succeeded by Peter Russell, who Brant found to be a more pliable man and one soon burdened with the worry that Spain and France might launch an attack on the new province, for that long struggle against Napoleonic France had just begun.

Brant, who had gone ahead anyway and was already negotiating with prospective buyers, now hinted that if the fighting spread to North America, the loyalty of the Mohawks should not be taken for granted. It was a clever move. The government gave in and, setting up a board of trustees to make sure none of the money went astray, finally approved of Brant's land deals.

On February 5, 1798, the Six Nations of the Grand River parted with six parcels of land, amounting to 350,000 or so acres, well over half of that magnificent tract given them less than fifteen years before. The price on paper works out at something under thirty cents an acre in today's money. As things turned out, they were not to receive even that for it.

In the spring Samuel Betzner and Joseph Sherk set off to take a look at the Indian lands. In the vicinity of what is now Waterloo they found a tract much to their liking, the property, they learned, of a Colonel Beasley. From this gentleman Betzner purchased 200 acres, and Sherk 261 acres, which he paid for by selling his horse. However, in his anxiety to close the deal, the Colonel, sometimes referred to as the "Squire", neglected to tell them that the land was mortgaged.

Unhappily, this fact was not to come to light for a couple of years, by which time the Betzners and the Sherks had been joined by other Mennonites and their families. The authorities were aware of the Colonel's peculations and stepped in with a scheme whereby the Mennonites could buy the Colonel's holdings for ten thousand pounds, the Colonel agreeing to discharge the mortgage first. This was all very well, but the Mennonites did not have ten thousand pounds, or anything like it.

What followed provides a justly renowned example of communal co-operation among the Mennonites. One of them travelled back to Pennsylvania, where, in response to his personal appeal for help, a Mennonite community subscribed a large part of the sum needed — in cash — at the same time forming what they called the German Company. The money came north partly on horseback, partly in a keg on a carefully guarded wagon, though another version of the story has it that it was sewn into specially made canvas bags. Anyway, it arrived, and the German Company was duly launched, though it was not until 1805 that the Mennonites obtained a clear deed to their land.

Colonel Beasley's sixty thousand acres was divided into 128 farms with 488 acres in each, and a number of smaller parcels. Back home in Pennsylvania, the shareholders drew lots for their holdings and, with no limit to the number of parcels that could be bought, one man acquired twenty-one of them, to give him a total holding of over ten thousand acres.

And so, once again in their long history, the Mennonites were on the move, travelling the more than four hundred miles from Pennsylvania to the Grand River in their remarkable wagons, which have almost become the principal, if inanimate, heroes of the whole enterprise.

The design was based on covered wagons built by English settlers in Pennsylvania; the Mennonites adapted and improved it until a definitive version appeared about 1736 in the valley of the Conestoga River — hence the name given to the vehicle. It was long and wide — the latter to reduce the chance of upset — and the floor was built so that it sagged in the middle, in order that loads should settle inwards and not press on the sides. The white homespun cover curving up and out in a graceful bow was typical of the Conestoga, as was the "lazy-board" sticking out to one side from which the driver controlled his team of horses, as many as six of them if the load were heavy. But perhaps the most interesting feature of all was the fact that the body was made watertight, so that at a pinch — and with a deep river to cross — it became, quite simply, a boat.

The Mennonites thus came north to the valley of the Grand River, establishing the first inland communities in Upper Canada and bringing with them a wealth of agricultural expertise gained through a hundred years or more of farming under North American conditions.

With the Beasley Tract in their hands it was not long before the Mennonites were looking with a speculative eye at another block of Indian land immediately to the north. As with the Beasley Tract, and for that matter every one of the six blocks of Indian land, difficulties arose with respect to ownership. These were overcome finally, and the German Company came into possession of another forty-five thousand acres.

By this time, Ebytown, the village named after the secretary-treasurer of the original German Company — who was also the first bishop of the surrounding Mennonite community — had started to flourish. Later, it would be called Berlin; still later, in the twentieth century, Berlin would be renamed Kitchener.

In 1816 another village that had been founded by the Mennonites was renamed Waterloo to commemorate the Anglo-German victory over Napoleon the year before, a victory that brought the Napoleonic Wars to an end.

The end of the War of 1812 saw the British government averse to further American settlement in Upper Canada and steps were taken to discourage American immigrants. These measures were applauded by extreme Loyalists, but deplored by those who had land to sell. One such was William Dickson, a Scottish lawyer with an office in Niagara, who, after the war ended, bought a tract of Indian land immediately to the south of that being industriously worked by the Plain People.

The land in question, over ninety-four thousand acres of it, had the usual chequered history. In 1798 the parcel had been bought by a man who made no down payment, took out a mortgage on the entire parcel, paid no instalments on the mortgage, then died insolvent in an American prison. Subsequently there were three separate claimants to his land, which was finally awarded to his sister. She sold it to William Dickson.

Balked of American settlers, Dickson advertised his Grand River project in his native Scotland. And to good effect. From 1817 onwards Scots in their hundreds — both Highlanders and Lowlanders — came over to settle in the Dickson Settlement. Like Colonel Talbot, Dickson worked hard to make his settlement the success it was, though his was on a much more limited scale than Talbot's.

Helping William Dickson was a young and energetic Pennsylvanian named Absalom Shade, who devoted his life to the settlement and to its nucleus of Shade's Mills. Shade's Mills grew, and in 1827 was renamed Galt, after John Galt, a Scottish literary man and a friend of William Dickson's who appeared on the Canadian scene in the somewhat surprising role of superintendent of the newly formed Canada Company.

Meanwhile, after the dust of the 1812 war had finally settled in the 1820s, the Mennonite communities in the Grand River Valley were joined by fresh waves of emigrants from Pennsylvania, as well as by Amish settlers coming directly from Europe.

One of the many sects that hived off from the Anabaptist movement in the seventeenth century, the Amish under the leadership of Jacob Amman (hence the name of the sect) practised an extreme conservatism in matters of dress and custom in order to reinforce their faith in a changing and possibly corrupting world. Today in the Elmira and Waterloo districts, members of the "Old Order", with their sombre dress and reluctance to become dependent on modern technology, attract much, and for them surely often embarrassing, attention and perhaps some envy.

The migration of the Amish from Europe was part of a wider movement of Germans seeking to escape from the increasingly militaristic régime of the Prussians, whose dominance of nineteenth-century Germany was to have such tragic consequences. From 1825 onwards, thousands of Germans were to emigrate, and many chose Canada rather than the United States, gravitating towards communities with German connections such as Waterloo County.

The last of the Indian lands were not finally disposed of until the 1830s when part of the northern block passed into the hands of a Captain Gilkison, who planned a settlement that he named Elora. The development of his holdings fell to his sons after his death. The other part of the block was bought by Adam Fergusson, a Scots lawyer, who was largely responsible for settling the area with his own countrymen — mostly Lowland Scots. The present town of Fergus reflects the name of its founder.

With the sale of the last of the six blocks went over half of the Six Nations' holdings on the Grand River. But they were still left with a substantial tract of river land running south of Brant's Ford, essentially to the Lake Erie shore. These lands — and Brant's Ford itself — came under heavy development pressure from 1820 onwards, and further land was sold or surrendered to the Crown.

As time went by, the pattern of land ownership along the lower reaches of the Grand River became so confusing that the government advised the Six Nations to surrender all their remaining lands, with the exception of those they were then occupying, in order that the situation might be regularized to their own benefit. This the Six Nations did in 1841. Today they hold about forty-five thousand acres in their reservation south of Brantford, about one-twelfth of the huge tract that was once theirs — disregarding for the purposes of the present account that before the coming of the white man, all of Ontario, indeed all of North America, belonged to its native peoples.

At Deseronto, about half-way between Belleville and Kingston, live the descendants of the Six Nations Indians who chose that area in preference to the Grand River. Near to the reservation office a Union Jack flies, recalling a loyalty to the Crown that goes back three hundred years. Here in the hands of a specially designated custodian is half of Queen Anne's communion silver. The remainder rests at the Mohawk Chapel in Brantford.

After the War of Independence was over, Joseph Brant had his rewards. For services rendered and because of his rank of captain, he was given a sum of money, as well as a 3,500-acre grant of land — now part of Burlington. Here he came to build a mansion and to maintain an establishment complete with a retinue of black servants. He died in 1807, involved to the last in wrangles that accompanied the sale of the Six Nations lands. At what point and to what degree his concern for the well-being of the Six Nations became a concern for that of Joseph Brant is still a matter of speculation. A controversial figure in his own day, he remains so now.

The Moyer Family
Cherry Avenue Farms
Clinton Township
Lincoln County

"*P*ICK YOUR OWN . . . OVER 15,000 TREES ON 140 ACRES . . ." So began a large, eye-catching advertisement in one of Toronto's leading newspapers in the summer of 1978. The advertisement went on to list the varieties of fruit available each week through August to September. "Refreshments. Tuck Shop. Washrooms. Plenty of parking space for cars and buses." Two maps showed the route to the farm from Toronto and the advertisement concluded, "For ready picked farm fresh fruit visit our fruit stand outside St. Lawrence Market . . . every Saturday 6 a.m.–2 p.m."

Sam and Liivi Moyer, who inserted the advertisement, are owners of Cherry Avenue Farms in the Vineland region of Niagara — a century farm that has been in the Moyer family since 1801.

The first Samuel Moyer was a member of one of the Pennsylvania families of German origin in Lincoln County — the famous fruit- and wine-growing area of southern Ontario, now part of the Regional Municipality of Niagara. He settled with his parents on a hundred acres, chosen it is said because of a large walnut tree growing there, black walnut being taken as an indication of fertile land. It is of interest that the family has no Crown Deed to the farm. The document was burned when Newark, now Niagara-on-the-Lake, was sacked by the Americans during the War of 1812.

In 1819 this Samuel Moyer married a woman named Charlotte Hilts, whose first husband, a member of another well-known local family, had been "shot by the Indians with sixteen bullets at Stoney Creek for insulting a squaw to whom he trying to sell fish," according to the Moyer family history.

The first Mennonite services in Vineland were held in the Moyer house, but Samuel and Charlotte's son, a second Samuel born in 1827, left the church for a time when the congregation refused him entry to their place of worship. He had built a canopy over his buckboard and added a fringe to it, a frivolity unacceptable to the Plain People.

From the mid-1800s until the end of the century, large amounts of wheat were grown in Vineland and the Twenty, and wheat and flour were regularly shipped from Jordan Harbour to destinations as far away as Europe. In the 1870s, Jacob Moyer, a member of the family, built his own grain elevator and a pier into Lake Ontario just west of the Twenty Pond. The Samuel Moyers grew wheat, and kept cattle, hogs, and sheep. Later they had a dairy herd and there are two silos on the farm, incongruous now among the fruit orchards. Then the cattle were phased out and fruit took over; but, says the present Sam Moyer, when he was a teen-ager some twenty-five years ago, "we always kept a hundred to a hundred and fifty feeder cattle during the winter. The cattle provided manure for the orchards that was hard to come by otherwise.

"My father eventually had the entire farm under fruit. He had four trucks on the road and four stores near Owen Sound. Then he changed the varieties and went over to processing types of fruit for canning. When I took over the farm, I changed again to pick-your-own fruit and for ten years we have had a stall at the St. Lawrence Market as well.

"It seems to me that you have to find a formula. . . . To begin with we advertised locally and in Oakville and Burlington with so-so results." Then a columnist from one of the Toronto papers did a write-up on the farm. "It was fantastic. Just hours after the paper came out, five or six cars rolled in."

So now the Moyers run a carefully phrased, half-page advertisement in the same paper during the summer, and on one Sunday in 1978 they had an estimated three thousand visitors.

This success is due not only to advertising, but to hard work, forethought, and very careful planning. The Moyers grow sweet cherries, sour cherries, raspberries, red currants, apricots, plums, pears, and grapes, but by far their largest crop is peaches. They grow twelve different varieties of peach on seventy-five acres of land. The varieties are chosen to ripen in sequence, "because with that number of trees, it would be impossible to harvest them all at once." The Moyers have planted more trees of a variety of peach that will ripen at the end of August or during the first ten days of September because they know that the public's demand for peaches is then at its peak.

As well as doing business right on the farm and at the St. Lawrence Market, the Moyers sell fruit in a farmers' market in Thornhill and to a large retailer in Toronto. But they intend to sell a larger proportion on the farm each year. "The pick-your-own operation is more challenging and interesting," Sam Moyer says, "because you are dealing with people. It's exciting to have people coming and going and you have to be all the more aware of producing a quality product.

"Why do people come? Picking fruit is only fifty per cent of their motivation. They want a family outing that is different. They want to get out in the open air and they want to get some good clean mud on their feet.

"One thing I have noticed. The agricultural industry is not doing its homework properly in conveying to city people what is involved in farming. There are so many misconceptions about farmers. They are seen either as hayseeds or as millionaires, and there is no medium through which the public can be shown what farming is really like."

Dispelling these misconceptions is another aspect of Sam Moyer's operation. Displaying traditional Mennonite skill with his hands — his grandfather built a dog-powered treadle to run a washing-machine — Sam Moyer has built a small train pulled by a tractor. In this train, visitors are taken for tours round the orchards in spring when the cherry and peach blossoms are out, and at other times of the year as well. Sam Moyer shows the visitors what work is going on — pruning, spraying, thinning — and explains what is happening and why. In this way he thinks that they gain a much greater appreciation of what is involved in a farming operation and in growing high-quality fruit.

To cope with the work and the visitors, the Moyers have a staff of about twenty-five people during the spring and summer. In addition, they have a foreman who works all year round, and for the past ten years they have employed two students from Denmark each summer. Talking to the Danish boys presents no problem. They speak English, and Sam Moyer speaks Danish, as well as French and some Portuguese.

The Moyers' farm year starts in the spring. In April the pruning, spraying, and fertilizing begin, and from July onwards work on the farm continues along with the pick-your-own operation. In winter, Sam and Liivi Moyer take stock of their operation and try to establish objectives for the following year. Both have degrees in agriculture, Sam from Cornell University and Liivi, who is of Estonian background, from McGill. In the winter, too, they attend conferences in the United States and prepare their mailing list of some twelve thousand names.

The Moyers have three young sons, Paul, Peter, and Tommy,

who are at Ridley College in St. Catharines. Naturally, their parents hope that one of them may be interested in continuing with the farm.

At today's land prices, Sam Moyer could sell his farm and live comfortably on the invested income. But money is not his main objective. As he puts it, he has no desire to be the richest man in the graveyard. "I like the free-enterprise type of thing . . . but it's getting harder all the time." Perhaps for farmers in general, he thinks, there should be greater compensation for their life's work. They would not then have to sell their land to provide for a secure retirement.

The farm barns are painted in red and white and are as neat as a new pin. One of them is used as a coffee shop and farm stall. Facing them across the ghost of an old road is a rambling L-shaped house, pleasantly irregular in outline, a mixture of styles and periods, partly frame, partly brick. The centre portion, built in 1801, sheltered the first Mennonite services. The inside woodwork and the woodwork in the old horse barn are chestnut and there are solid blocks of this now rare wood built into the walls as insulation. The east wing of the house is the old wash-house and harness room. The wash-house has a large, open brick fireplace and an iron crane on which cauldrons of water were heated for scalding the butchered hogs.

Outside, the driveway is lined with beds of roses, and the whole scene seems as charmingly familiar as a nineteenth-century lithograph by Currier and Ives.

The Haynes Family
Louth Township
Lincoln County

*B*ruce Haynes and his family grow grapes and cherries on a century farm in the fruitlands that lie between the Niagara Escarpment and Lake Ontario, near the village of Jordan — the promised land of the early settlers. Here the Twenty Mile Creek, once called the Jordan River, flows down from the escarpment to empty into the Twenty Pond, and then into Lake Ontario at Jordan Harbour.

In 1783, much of the land in what was to become Louth Township was granted to disbanded soldiers of Butler's Rangers and to settlers of Pennsylvania-German background. Among them was Adam Haynes, who was born in 1747 at Peaswick in the County of Albany, New York. Adam served with the British during the War of Inde-

(above) Once swamp-land, the Raleigh Plains near Chatham produce cash crops on some of the most fertile soil in Ontario. Roger and Winifred Dolson stroll in the fields behind their house.

(below) Glenn Dafoe and his son, David, inspect Charolais cattle on their farm near Morrisburg. Their ancestor, Conrad Dafoe, fought as a Loyalist in Sir John Johnson's "Royal Yorkers" and was granted land at Aultsville, a village now beneath the waters of the St. Lawrence Seaway.

(above) Three generations of the Paul family burned limestone in this kiln, which was last fired in 1908. A sample of the Pauls' lime won a medal at the Colonial and Indian Exhibition of 1886 in London, England.

(opposite, above) Norman Paul, noted farmer and Holstein breeder of Ramsay Township, Lanark County. His forebears emigrated to Upper Canada from Scotland after the Napoleonic Wars.

(opposite, below) A cow in the Snedden family's herd of pure-bred Holsteins gazes curiously at the camera. The herd is registered under the name "Mississippi", the Ontario river on which this Lanark County family settled after they emigrated from Scotland in 1819.

(opposite, above) On the Opeongo Trail in Renfrew County, the log buildings on the Davidson farm are still in use. In the foreground, Allan Davidson stands behind his grandfather's potash cooler. It took an acre of hardwood trees to produce a barrel of potash — a life-saving source of income for many early settlers.

(opposite, below) Successful cattleman of the Renfrew County uplands, Ken Dick of Grattan Township. At the age of fourteen, he inherited a farm, stock, and machinery from his grandfather.

(above) In 1876, James Moreland, captain of the Great Lakes barque Arabia, and his wife, Jane, built a house of many gables, here shown in detail, high on a hill near Sunbury, north of Kingston.

(left) George MacLeod, century farmer of Lochiel Township. In 1793, after an adventurous journey during which they were "accommodated with the King's Brass", MacLeods from Glenelg, Scotland, settled in Glengarry County.

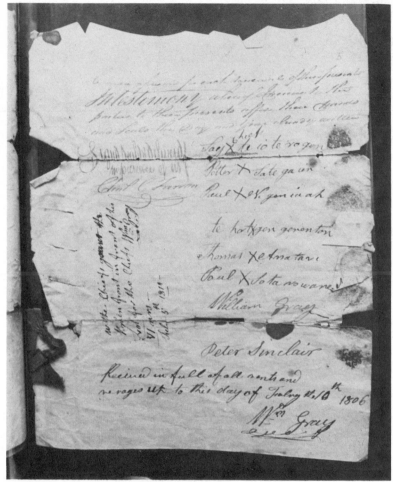

(above) Thumbs of St. Regis Indian chiefs, dipped in blood, are said to have made the rusty brown prints on this deed which records the transfer of land near Martintown, now owned by the Kinloch family, to Peter Sinclair, an Indian agent, in 1806.

(opposite, above) Ernie Morris's Irish ancestors came from "among the green bushes" of County Tyrone to settle in Clarence Township, east of Ottawa. He and his son, Raymond, live in this modest log house, little changed since pioneer times.

(opposite, below) Visitors to Sam Moyer's Cherry Avenue farm near Vineland in the Niagara Peninsula are taken to see the orchards in spring blossom; later in the season they will be back to pick their own fruit. The land has belonged to the Moyer family since 1801.

(above) Built on an old Indian trail in 1829, this neo-classic brick farmhouse overlooks vineyards at Jordan in the Niagara Peninsula. The Haynes family have farmed this land for nearly two hundred years.

(below) Toylike in a flat landscape, the drying kilns on the Dertinger farm at La Salette, Norfolk County, rise out of a sea of tobacco plants.

pendence and at the end of the war he made the long trek round the south shore of Lake Ontario with his wife and several small children, among them a son, four-year-old Lewis.

It was Lewis Haynes who built the Hayneses' house in 1829. This elegant neo-classic brick farmhouse with its beautifully proportioned façade and typical semi-circular windows in the side gables, faces an old Indian trail that wound its way towards the escarpment along the edge of a rocky outcrop. The house can be seen across the vineyards from a road that runs south through Jordan Station and east of the Twenty Pond. The brick for the house was made on the farm and brick fragments still turn up in the vineyards on the site of the old kiln.

Inside the house, the floors are of pine, the oak beams supporting them a foot square. Many of the windows contain the original glass. The inside walls of the house are of plaster over brick, and in the upstairs hall designs were painted on the plaster to simulate wallpaper. In the living-room there is a tin ceiling made in Preston and added later.

The house replaced an older log house and at the back is an "up-ground" cellar built in 1812 with stone walls nearly three feet thick. Above the cellar is a "weave-shop" dating from the time when sheep were plentiful and the Twenty was noted for the skill of its weavers. One of the best-known of these, Samuel Fry, wove coverlets prized for their beauty and the complexity of their designs. His price for a coverlet was one dollar, materials provided by the customer. In the Hayneses' "weave-shop", the girls of Samuel Fry's time — Bruce Haynes's grandaunts — spun wool and wove it into coverlets, now cherished family heirlooms.

Lewis Haynes, like all of those first settlers, kept hogs, sheep, and cattle, and grew wheat. He loaded the wheat into saddle-bags and rode some twenty or so miles to the nearest mill at Newark, now Niagara-on-the-Lake, to have it ground. Or rather, so a puzzling family story goes, he put the wheat in one saddle-bag and balanced it by stones in the other, thus making, one would have thought, a double load for the horse.

Although French colonists planted European grape vines and made wine from Canadian grapes as early as 1636, there is no record of commercial grape cultivation in Upper Canada until 1811, when a small winery was established by Johann Schiller in Cooksville using grapes grown on the banks of the Credit River.

Grapes were not grown in the Niagara Peninsula in appreciable quantities until much later. In the 1850s, farmers there were still apprehensive about the effect of severe frosts, but by the 1860s and

1870s grapes ranked third in importance among Ontario fruits. Bruce Haynes recalls being told that the first vines in the Jordan area were brought from New York State in an eleven-quart basket and planted near Vineland on a farm belonging to a member of the Overholt family around 1887. Grapes were grown on another Haynes farm about 1900 and sold fresh in baskets.

On the Bruce Haynes farm, grapes did not displace the earlier types of farming until the 1950s. Until then, Bruce Haynes grew wheat, much as his ancestors had done, and kept dairy cattle and, later, a herd of Polled Angus. The family had a large apple orchard, and maple syrup was tapped in the bush. What put an end to the mixed farming was the construction of a highway through what are now the vineyards, cutting the farm in half. "You can't drive cattle across a road," Bruce Haynes says. So the cattle were sold and both barns disappeared, the one pulled down, the other accidentally burned.

Now grapes are the main crop on the Haynes farm along with sweet and sour cherries. The Hayneses — it's a family business with three grandsons, Robert, Douglas, and Brian, coming along — now grow eight different varieties of grapes including Concord, Niagara, Catawba, Veeport, de Chaunac, and Maréchal Foch. They produce between two and three hundred tons of grapes a year, part of fifty thousand tons grown annually in Ontario, and they have a ten-year contract to sell their crop to Jordan Wines, a company formed in 1920 by a member of the family, Archibald Haynes.

A highly specialized knowledge of viticulture — the culture of vines — is needed in the commercial production of grapes. Care of the vines includes trellising, fertilizing, spraying, pruning, and the removal of suckers; and the care and treatment of one variety of vine may differ from that of another.

In the past, Ontario's wines were made from the distinctively flavoured native grapes, including Concord and Catawba. But in 1947, French hybrids were brought in as experimental plantings by the Vineland Horticultural Experiment Station. Some of these hybrids were found to be suitable for commercial production and wine is now being made from these grapes. The de Chaunac grape, for instance, was named after Adhémar de Chaunac, a French-born agronomist who devoted his life to improving the quality of Canadian wines. It produces a medium- to light-bodied, fruity dry red wine. The Maréchal Foch grape is an Alsatian hybrid derived from the Pinot Noir, and produces a medium- to full-bodied dry wine "with an aroma reminiscent of a Burgundy".

Labour for harvesting the Hayneses' grape crop used to be a problem, with "off-shore" labour hired much as for the tobacco crop, but about nine years ago, mechanical grape-pickers were introduced. These great machines — costing the farmer between $45,000 and $60,000 — move through the vineyards straddling the trellises of vines. They knock or shake the fruit off into bins and the grapes are then loaded into trucks for transport to the winery. Bruce Haynes owns one of these machines jointly with two neighbours. He harvests his own crop and does custom picking. "The machine won't backfire on you and you can go out and pick in the rain. Monday I was out at five o'clock in the morning and in two hours I had eighteen to twenty tons picked."

No machine has yet been invented that will harvest the sweet and sour cherries. Robert Haynes, Bruce Haynes's grandson, usually hires a gang of about thirty local young people to do the picking. There are so many sweet red cherries that they can't be harvested for eating with the stalks on, "and so they go for maraschinos." The sour cherries are sold for freezing, then bought by a manufacturer of pies and cakes.

On the rich farmland of the Twenty, the Pennsylvania-German settlers created an industrious, self-sufficient community with an astonishing range of small industries and skills. Here there were blacksmiths, carriage shops, shipbuilders, harness works, cabinet-makers, broom-makers, weavers, potters, a brick factory, and an apple-drying plant — all in one small area between the Niagara Escarpment and the Lake. These settlers had indeed found their Jordan, and they repaid the country of their adoption in full measure by the richness of the legacy they bequeathed to those who came after them.

The Gingerich Family
Oaklot Farm
Wilmot Township
Waterloo County

*A*lvin Gingerich's family have lived on Oaklot Farm in Wilmot Township, some miles west of the city of Waterloo, since 1825 when the first Gingerich walked four hundred miles from Baltimore to settle here. The story of how he came to make his journey begins four years earlier in 1821 when a peasant farmer named Christian Nafziger left his home in Bavaria with "little more than his walking stick".

Nafziger travelled down the Rhine River to Amsterdam, where he persuaded a wealthy Mennonite merchant to finance his trip to North America. He landed in New Orleans and took a river boat to Cincinnati, Ohio, then walked some four hundred miles to Lancaster, Pennsylvania, where Mennonites and a few Amish had settled during the previous century at the invitation of William Penn. There, the Amish Mennonites gave him money and an old horse and suggested he look for land in the small Mennonite settlement on the Grand River near what is now the city of Waterloo.

The Mennonites on the Grand River advised Nafziger to apply to the government of Upper Canada for a parcel to be developed as an Amish settlement. The appeal was successful. Sir Peregrine Maitland, the Governor, promised Nafziger fifty acres of free land for every family he could bring, provided they completed certain settlement duties, with an option to buy the remaining hundred and fifty acres of each lot for about $2.50 an acre. A "German Block" was surveyed along the Nith River and the Mennonites of Waterloo Township appointed a committee to help the Amish establish their new settlement.

The offer of free land was important to the Amish, who were often desperately poor. In Europe, Napoleon had instituted compulsory military service for his armies and the Amish Mennonites were conscientious objectors. They had therefore to pay an exemption tax or fine to keep their sons out of the army; with their large families there were often many of them, and the financial drain was crippling during the years when conscription was in force.

Christian Nafziger returned to Europe. But, mindful of the swindle over the Beasley Tract, he — a peasant farmer from Bavaria — stopped at London on the way, and in what must have been a memorable visit to George IV sought and obtained the king's personal ratification of Maitland's promise.

One of the Amish Mennonites who responded to Nafziger's offer of free land in North America was Jacob Gingerich. The Gingerichs were originally Swiss, but because of religious intolerance in Switzerland they had fled about a century earlier to Alsace-Lorraine in north-eastern France, and their culture had become Alsatian-Amish.

Jacob Gingerich, his sister Margaret, and brother-in-law Christian Honderich landed in Baltimore in 1825. It was possible at that time to travel by river boat up the Susquehanna River and through the Finger Lakes, but they had no money. Instead they walked along the old Indian trails, covering the four hundred or more miles between Baltimore and the site of their new home on foot. Jacob was a wagon-maker by trade, and all he had with him were his tools. His sister, Margaret, was pregnant. Her son was born shortly after their arrival — the first white baby born in Wilmot Township.

The Honderichs settled on Lot 16, Bleams Road, where members of the family still live, and Jacob Gingerich settled on Lot 15, calling it Oaklot Farm because of a heavy stand of oak trees suitable for making wagon-wheels. The brothers-in-law built two log cabins and cleared the land between them, and in 1828 Jacob married Veronica Litwiller. Wheat was planted on the cleared land and the first wheat crop was harvested and taken to the mill at Ayr to be ground. There is a story that Veronica heard alarming noises coming from the pigpen and found a bear molesting the pigs. She seized her broom and ushered the unwelcome guest back into the woods, thus saving the family's winter supply of pork.

In 1830 a survey showed that the Gingerichs had completed their settlement duties, and their ownership of the land was guaranteed. According to the first Wilmot assessment roll of 1832, they had sixteen acres of cleared land, two oxen, two cows, and one young "horned beast". By 1840, the farm had grown to forty acres of cleared land, with two horses, two oxen, five cows, and five other cattle. By 1861, they had thirteen cows, and the list also includes "a pleasure carriage".

The family, too, had grown. Jacob and Veronica had eight children between 1829 and 1844. Larger buildings for the farm and family became essential. The first barn, built of rough logs flattened on two sides with the bark left on, was replaced in 1849 by a large bank barn with a fieldstone wall enclosing the first storey. The upper section, used for feed storage, had a hand-hewn log frame of exceptionally fine oak and pine. With few alterations, the barn is still in use today. Smaller buildings were constructed round it for the increasing numbers of hogs, sheep, and poultry. A two-storeyed fieldstone house was built during the 1850s. Surrounding the house were an orchard and a garden, and small buildings, including a wash-house with a room for curing and smoking meat and another for drying fruit and vegetables. There was also a summer kitchen, with a woodshed and carpenter's shop attached.

The 1840s and 1850s were busy decades. Along with the construction of the buildings and a growing variety and number of livestock, crops were increased to include oats, barley, peas, and both winter and spring wheat, while portions of the forest had still to be cleared.

Jacob Gingerich was succeeded on the farm by his son, Rudolf or Rudy, who continued to develop the farm. He cleared more land, built and installed field drains, and erected fences. Rudy was fond of fine horses and in 1880 he built a separate barn for them. While the main farm enterprise was milking cows, he also fed steers and hogs, and had flocks of sheep and poultry. But Rudy was not a good milker. It is said more milk ran off his elbows than into the pail. So he spent chore time looking after the horses, first thing in the morning and last thing at night. His grandson, Alvin Gingerich, says it was like a fever. "That was his life. He aimed to have the finest horses on the road." He bought "Scotch Tops" for his horses, leather ornaments that were put on the hames of the harness for decoration. By tradition, Scottish people had "Scotch Tops" but Amish men did not. Rudy Gingerich was reprimanded for using them, Alvin Gingerich says, and after the reprimand he never used them again, but they are still kept as family souvenirs.

Rudolf's second son, Abraham, possessed two traits that are inherent in the Amish people: inventiveness and skill with his hands. He was interested in a dam and water-wheel on his farm which provided power for grinding feed grain for livestock, and as early as the turn of the century he produced electricity for his house and barn by enlarging the dam and installing a large home-made water-wheel and generator. By 1920, commercial hydro made the water-wheel obsolete, so it was sold and the building that housed it demolished.

Alvin Gingerich is a member of the fourth generation to live on the farm, each generation having held it for approximately forty years. He is married to the former Ruby Wagler and they have four children: Laura, Samuel, Heidi, and Katherine. The Waglers are remembered for the part they played in introducing Holstein-Friesian cattle in Waterloo County in 1883. Christian Wagler exhibited at the Toronto Industrial Exhibition, where his cow, Musette 219, was declared Grand Champion. Again, however, the displeasure of the Amish Church was provoked; he was severely disciplined and never showed his cattle again.

When Alvin Gingerich started farming, he carried on with his father's Durham or Shorthorn cattle, but the herd, he thought, had degenerated during the 1920s and 1930s. When he married Ruby and she inherited some of the Wagler family's Holsteins, he went in for a Red Holstein/Shorthorn cross. The farm still has some of these animals, but Alvin Gingerich now imports and breeds Brown Swiss cattle, a change compatible with his Swiss ancestry.

The Alvin Gingerichs are Progressive Amish Mennonites. They do not wear the traditional dress of the Old Order Amish Mennonites, which very much resembles the old folk-dress of Lorraine, nor do they adhere to the Amish rules proscribing the use of electricity and some machines. Since the time of Rudolf and his son, Abraham, they have been innovative and forward-looking farmers, but in their personal lives they adhere to the faith of their ancestors.

In 1975 there were approximately 3,420 descendants in North America of Jacob and Veronica's six married children. Alvin Gingerich wrote in that year of the adventure, the faith, and the hopes of his pioneering ancestors. He added: "To have been born and raised on the Gingerich homestead in Wilmot Township was not our choice, but one of God's gracious gifts for which we thank Him. . . . Many blessings are ours because of the sacrifices made by our pioneering forefathers. Their trust in God, their search for freedom to worship and serve Him according to a conscience enlightened by His Word and Spirit have inspired us to seek to follow Him, as they did."

CHAPTER EIGHT

Tobacco and Trees in Norfolk County

*N*orfolk County, now part of the Regional Municipality of Haldimand-Norfolk, lies along the north shore of Lake Erie. Towards its western boundary, a narrow spit of land named Long Point stretches out into the lake and here, each spring, whistling swans land on their long flight northwards to their nesting-grounds in the High Arctic. Long Point is the site of a historic Indian portage, first recorded in 1670 by two French Sulpician priests, and Governor Simcoe visited here in September 1795, his wife noting in her diary: "The Gov. returned & is far from well. He was pleased with Long Point, which he called Charlotteville, the Banks of the Lake 150 feet high, on the shores grew weeping willows covered with vines, he gathered some Grapes already sweet."[1]

At the end of the Revolutionary War there was a small settlement of some five families at Long Point and here they were joined by Loyalist families, among them the Culvers.

The Culvers, who were to become one of the county's most noted and numerous families, were said to have emigrated from England in the early days of the American colonies. At the time of the War of Independence, a Jabez Culver served as chaplain in Washington's forces, thus tempering loyalty with caution as his sympathies were, it is said, all on the side of the British. After the war was over he rode north to consult with Governor Simcoe as to possible terms of settlement for his family, and Simcoe offered him six hundred acres for himself, four hundred acres for each son, and two hundred for each daughter.

Accompanied by another family named Sovereign or Sovereen, the Culvers moved north to Norfolk County, bringing with them, by one account, "twenty wagons, forty yoke of oxen, three hundred sheep and a large number of horses, cows, etc." During the journey, "they were frequently attacked by wolves."[2]

Jabez Culver settled in Windham Township but others of the family pushed on to become the first settlers of Townsend Township. "A few trappers who lived with the Indians had made temporary houses there . . . but it was the Culver Family who settled upon . . . the first farm ever tilled in Townsend. The Culver family crossed the Niagara by fording it, and coasted along Lake Erie until the harbor of Dover was reached. They then penetrated the dense forest, following an Indian trail until they reached the spot above-mentioned. Here they pitched their tent; that is to say, they drove stakes into the earth and formed a rough wigwam in which they abode until a log house was built. Traversing the forest in those days was a slow and difficult process. It was the custom to place the young children in baskets which were slung in pairs over the back of a cow. In this fashion did the youthful Culvers make their entry into Townsend,"[3] and there they settled on land that four years later in 1798 was selling for twenty-five cents an acre.

Parts of Norfolk County were heavily timbered; the Culvers had to chop their way through brush-entangled forest when they arrived in the winter of 1793-94. But not all of the county was forest-covered. One traveller wrote after visiting Long Point: "When I first visited this part of the Province, the sudden change which took place in the aspect of nature seemed like magic. The soil became light and sandy, the forests had dwindled away and natural groves and copses met the eye in their stead. The fields were beautifully level, and the uncultivated lands had more the appearance of a pleasure-ground than of a wilderness. The trees being small and few in number, and distributed in beautiful clumps, did not at all suggest the idea of a forest, but added charms to the country and the variety of the prospect." What the traveller, John Howison, was commenting upon were the famous Norfolk sand- or oak-plains that extend westwards into Elgin County.

At the outset the pioneers, as they did elsewhere, practised mixed farming, and cattle were run year-round on the oak-plains, foraging for themselves in winter. But once the trees had been cut and the humus destroyed, productivity on the light and sandy soils declined, and wind eroded the land. Mixed farming was superseded by the cultivation of wheat, corn, rye, and peas in the 1880s, and these crops in turn gave way to fruit and vegetables for canning in the early part of the twentieth century. However, after 1923 it was discovered that tobacco could be grown on the light soils, and tobacco is now Norfolk County's chief crop. Of the two century farm families in this chapter, one farms tobacco, the other is a descendant of the Culvers.

The Dertinger Family
Windham Township
Norfolk County

Optimists have tried to grow tobacco as far north as Renfrew County, but Ontario's crop — some 175 million pounds of it annually — is produced mainly in the counties that fringe Lake Erie and in Norfolk County in particular. The tobacco-farming areas are easily recognizable by the squat, rectangular drying kilns which line the fields. In summer, the fields are filled with leafy green plants topped by whitish flowers — *Nicotiana tabacum* or tobacco.

Paul Dertinger and his wife, Gabriella, have a century farm in Norfolk County. It is near La Salette, where the flat fields are dominated by a great red-brick Catholic church. In a shimmering miasma of heat, irrigation pumps spray water from Big Creek onto a sea of green tobacco plants, and the brown faces of Caribbean workers in the fields give the illusion of a tropical plantation.

The first Dertinger to settle here was Valentine Dertinger, who came from Bavaria in 1838. He chose the land for its fertility for hay and grain crops, cleared some of it, built a log cabin, and then went back to Germany in 1840 on an important mission — that of finding himself a wife. Not only was he successful in this endeavour — his choice was Josephine Ditter of Hesse — but he also found three other women willing to come to Canada as brides for pioneers. Josephine and Valentine were married when the ship docked in New York. There were eight children of their marriage, of whom Paul Dertinger's grandfather, Benedict, was born in 1843.

Twenty years later, in 1863, the Dertingers replaced their log cabin with the present brick house. Devout Catholics, they gave a portion of their land on Big Creek for a church, a priest's house, a school, and stables. The wooden church burned in the 1890s, and the parish moved to La Salette; all that remains at Big Creek is the graveyard and a wooden cross.

Like most pioneers, the Dertingers started with general farming. They kept cows and sheep and grew peas, which they harvested by hand. By the late 1930s Paul Dertinger's father was growing sweet corn, which he took to the nearby town of Delhi for sale. "But at the peak of the depression, the family was slowly starving to death," Paul Dertinger says, "so my father thought he would go in for tobacco. He built a greenhouse, changed the barn, built four kilns, and had two bachelors who worked with him on a share basis." It was a success: "In 1938 we bought our first car." But for years tobacco remained just a cash crop, part of the general farming operation.

Paul Dertinger did not start out to be a tobacco farmer. He took a degree in economics at the University of Windsor and for a time worked for the Ford Motor Company of Canada in Oakville. What made him return to farming? By 1969 he had six children to support and the farm, he thought, would provide a better living for his family.

Tobacco seed is planted in the Dertingers' greenhouse in the last days of March or in early April. The seed is so fine that it is mixed with water and sprayed onto the seed beds; two ounces of it will provide enough plants for thirty acres.

In the early spring, too, the fields are ploughed, disked, and cultivated. The thirty-seven acres of tobacco that the Dertingers grow is rotated, with wheat or rye grown as a cover crop in alternate years after the tobacco has been cut. The price of wheat, Paul Dertinger says, is lower than it was around 1910, so instead of paying for combining and trucking, the crop is ploughed in to enrich the soil.

By the middle of May, the plants are ready to be lifted and set out in the fields. Lifting the plants is usually done by women seated on rolling carts above the plant beds. It is back-breaking work and back problems are an occupational hazard that Gabriella has not escaped. Once set out in the fields by mechanical planters, the plants must be irrigated, weeded, sprayed, and fertilized, then topped and the suckers removed. The Delhi Experimental Farm provides an excellent service in advising on tobacco-growing, and Canadian tobacco technology is as advanced as any in the world.

Harvesting the matured plants is crucial to the farmer. To get the crop in before the frost comes, the Dertingers employ contract labour from the Caribbean. The expense is high — labour costs amount to twenty-five per cent to thirty per cent of the total cost of production — but "off-shore" labour is preferred by the Dertingers to Canadian or European labourers who cannot or will not work as hard. Nor can Canadian workers be relied on to stay until the crop is in: students, for instance, must return to school or university before the crop is harvested. "If it wasn't for the Caribbeans, we couldn't get in the crop. It takes a number of years to learn the techniques of picking and you have to get the leaves off fast."

Tobacco leaves ripen from the bottom of the plant up and must be picked as they ripen. Pickers sit in bucket seats suspended on an "arm" pulled through the rows of plants by tractor. The process of picking the leaves off singly started about 1931 and is called "priming". It is gruelling work, Paul Dertinger says — unsatisfactory, expensive, and slow — but so far no better method has been found. Whole-plant combine harvesting must come, he thinks, but tobacco plants are brittle and break easily, and tobacco leaves must remain whole throughout the curing process. Once picked, the leaves are sewn onto sticks and suspended in kilns to be cured and dried. Machines that do the sewing have replaced a time-consuming hand-tying operation.

In the early days, kilns were fired by wood and later by coal. They had to be watched day and night to keep the temperature constant, and "curemen" were brought from the southern United States to supervise the stoking. Now the Dertinger kilns are fired on furnace oil and the heat is controlled by thermostat. Even so, Paul Dertinger must check his kilns at eleven at night and again at six in the morning. If the kilns are far away from the house, the farmer may sleep near them. Tired farmers have been known to fall asleep while checking the kilns and to be roasted to death. Paul Dertinger, climbing on the roof one night to check a faulty air vent, fell to the ground and broke a wrist and several ribs.

Once the tobacco has been dried, it is taken to the pack-barn. If all has gone well, the crop will be in by late September. The tobacco, which is still on the sticks on which it was cured, must then be softened by steam, or "cased". The leaves are stripped from the sticks in the strip room and graded by colour. Leaves of uniform colour are tightly packed into bales weighing about sixty pounds each, and are then ready for shipment.

The annual race against frost having been won, the farmer's crop is ready for sale. In the past it was sold to "barn buyers" who went round to each farm, a system vulnerable to abuse. It is now sold through the Ontario Flue-Cured Tobacco Growers' Marketing Board — a name that is admirably explicit. The Board holds auctions in Aylmer, Delhi, and Tillsonburg and these provide the most up-to-date marketing system in the world.

Like any other commodity, tobacco is subject to over-production. Each grower, therefore, is allocated a quota, and since 1976 this quota has been measured in pounds and not in acres. The farmer's quota is divided into four or five shipments and he is allocated dates — now designated by computer — on which his shipments will be sold.

The buyers at the tobacco auctions represent the large exporting and manufacturing firms. For the past seventeen winters, Paul Dertinger has been a buyer for Macdonald Leaf Incorporated, as well as a producer. Initially a Scottish firm with headquarters in Montreal, this company is now owned by R. J. Reynolds Company, the largest buyer of domestic tobacco in the United States. Benefactions by Sir William C. Macdonald, the founder of the firm, led to the establishment of Macdonald Institute at Guelph and Macdonald College at Ste. Anne de Bellevue, Quebec.

What skills does a tobacco buyer need? To begin with, a thorough knowledge of the grades of tobacco — of which, in theory, there are several hundreds — combined with a quick brain and, above all, quick reflexes. Sales are made on an electronically operated Dutch auction clock, a large-faced clock marked in quarter-cent gradations. The clock starts much higher than the anticipated price for a grade of tobacco and the hand drops a quarter of a cent at a time until a buyer makes a bid. A buyer registers his bid by pressing a button that stops the clock, and the clock operates at such speed that it is impossible for two buyers to press the button at exactly the same moment. Six or seven sales can be made in a minute, and a total of two and a half million pounds of tobacco can be sold in a single day at the three tobacco auctions combined.

The tobacco farmer's life, the Dertingers say, is subject to enormous stress. It is said that the per-capita consumption of alcohol is as high in Delhi as it is in Las Vegas. Much of the stress derives from the annual gamble of large sums of money that must be borrowed from the bank in order to get the crop planted and harvested. For thirty acres of tobacco, the cost could amount to more than fifty thousand dollars. With interest at nine per cent, this is a sizeable cause for worry.

To offset this, there is a guaranteed price per pound for tobacco, and there is crop insurance that will protect eighty per cent of the crop; but only from natural disaster — disease, frost, barn fires, tornadoes, and the like.

In addition to the threat of natural hazards, there is the competition of an international market. Production costs in Canada in 1977 were about ninety cents per pound, compared with thirty cents in some other countries. Exports are crucial to the industry, but there are international tariffs, and the United Kingdom, which used to buy a sizeable percentage of the crop, has dropped its imports by a third since joining the European Common Market.

Since 1970, Paul Dertinger says, twelve hundred farmers have left tobacco-farming, and the farm opposite has been sold nine times in ten years. The cost of land has escalated. Agribusiness, he thinks, is not an answer. With larger operations you need more machinery; you need foremen, supervisors, and more labour. "Unless the men are involved financially, they couldn't care less." What has kept the industry going, he thinks, are the "new pioneers" from Europe, the Belgians, Poles, Austrians, Dutch, and Jugoslavs who have worked incredibly hard to establish themselves in a new coun-

try. The 1977-78 list of directors and committeemen of the Marketing Board gives some of their names: Raytrowsky, Homeniuk,
Szucs, DeCloet . . .

All things considered, a small family farm like the Dertingers' is
still the most viable tobacco-farming unit. It demands an unusually
high degree of co-operation from the farmer's wife and family. With
hard work and good management there are profits to be made in
tobacco-farming, and in a good year these may be considerable.
There is time in the winter for holidays, maybe. "There's no way,"
Paul Dertinger says, "that I could be a dairy farmer and milk cows
twice a day!"

The Shaw Family
Woodlawn
Townsend Township
Norfolk County

PROVINCE OF UPPER-CANADA. GEORGE the THIRD by the grace of
GOD of Great Britain, France, and Ireland, King, Defender of
the Faith, and so forth.

Such is the heading on a patent dated "this seventeenth day of
May and forty second of our reign" in "the year one thousand eight
hundred and two" by which Freelove Shaw, who was described as
a "spinster-wife", was given and granted the two hundred acres
comprising Lot 5 in the Thirteenth Concession of Townsend Township in the County of Norfolk.

To have dismissed all of George III's honours and titles other than
"Defender of the Faith" with the words "and so forth" seems almost
flippant. The anonymous official filling in the patent in his neat
copperplate handwriting in the year 1802 may have had second
thoughts, for he has carefully crossed out "and so forth". He has
drawn a line, too, through the word "France". In the middle of the
Napoleonic Wars it was no doubt presumptuous to include that
country among George III's possessions. The word "France" on the
patent is an interesting reminder that English kings did in fact rule
parts of France until the 1400s; while Calais was held until 1558.

It had been the Revolutionary War that had brought Freelove
Shaw to Canada. She was one of the daughters of that former Patriot
chaplain and early Norfolk County settler, the Reverend Jabez
Culver. By 1802, Freelove Culver had married Michael Shoaf, or
Shaw, a descendant of Jacob Schoff, who had come to New Jersey

from Germany in 1752. Michael Shaw was a public-spirited man; his name appears frequently on jury lists of the pioneer courts of the London District.

The present Shaw family still speculate on Freelove Culver's name. Jabez Culver was the founder of Presbyterianism in Norfolk County, so it is hardly likely that he would have given his daughter a name with the connotation it has today, and besides, the spidery writing on the patent could be as easily read as "Truelove". As a family, the Culvers — and there were many of them — delighted in unusual names. Take for example, some of the names chosen for their sons: Ransom, Darius, Ira, Orrin, Mahlon, Leamon; and for their daughters: Calista, Circena, Malissa, Lizanna, Dorcas, and Freelove.

Max Shaw and his wife, Catherine, live on fifty acres of the original two hundred granted to his great-great-grandmother, Freelove Culver. The Shaws grow pears on one of the two remaining pieces of Crown land in Townsend Township that are still being farmed by the original families. The Shaw farm is on the edge of a new development being planned in connection with the Steel Company of Canada Limited's plant at Nanticoke, but "we don't want to sell the farm," Catherine Shaw says. For her sons, Bruce and Frank, it's home.

Great trees dwarf the Shaws' house and barn and their property is appropriately called Woodlawn. The trees include white pine of an unusual size, and the Shaws are justifiably proud of them. They are the last of the trees that are specifically mentioned in the patent, by which George III reserved "to us, our heirs and successors, all white Pine Trees that shall, or may now, or hereafter grow or be growing on any part of the said parcel or tract of land hereby granted as aforesaid."

This was a common stipulation at a time when His Majesty's navy needed the timber for ships' hulls, masts, and spars. Wooden ships have long since disappeared from the Great Lakes and from the oceans of the world, but the Shaw family took the clause seriously, so some of the great white pines — the patriarchs of the forest — are still standing on their property.

CHAPTER NINE

Black Gold and the Domain of Colonel Talbot

*W*est of Norfolk County, the land along the north shore of Lake Erie remained virtually unsettled until the arrival there in 1803 of Colonel Thomas Talbot, a man who was to do more than any other single individual to settle south-western Ontario.

The Talbots were an old and distinguished family who had come to England at the time of William the Conqueror. In 1174 a Richard Talbot was awarded the fief of Malahide in Ireland by King Henry II. A member of the English branch of the family was a champion-at-arms in France during the reign of Henry VI, his most famous opponent being Joan of Arc. He was created Earl of Shrewsbury in 1442 and he and his son appear as characters in Shakespeare's play, *Henry VI*, Part I: "God and St. George, Talbot and England's right".

The Thomas Talbot who settled in what was to become Elgin County was a member of the Irish family from Castle Malahide near Dublin. He began his military career at the age of eleven as an ensign in the 66th Regiment of Foot and was retired on half pay at the age of twelve. Returning to the army when he was older, he sailed in 1790 to join his regiment in Quebec, and in 1791 he became aide to John Graves Simcoe.

At twenty years of age, Talbot was described as handsome, intelligent, and cheerful. He had courtly manners and a cool, confident air. Elizabeth Simcoe's diaries are peppered with references to him: "Mr. Talbot manages all the etiquette of our House, is au fait in all those points which gave weight to matters of no moment." "Mr. Talbot gave a shilling to liberate some wood pidgeons I must otherwise have seen & heard fluttering most disagreeably. I was much obliged to him for his kind attention." " . . . nothing amusing occurred but Mr. Talbot's ineffectual endeavours to paddle a Canoe across the River. The difficulties he met with in his first attempt, & the handkerchief tied round his head a la Canadien diverted me much."[1]

Elizabeth Simcoe was then twenty-six years of age and the mother of six children — a seventh would be born in Canada. She was devoted to her husband, who was considerably older than she; but "the Gov.", as she called him, was occupied with the administration of the fledgling colony. It was Talbot, five years her junior, who organized her balls, walked with her, picked wild grapes in the fall, skated in the winter, and drove her out on hot summer nights. "After the Ladies leave me Mr. Talbot drives me in the Gig towards the landing, the weather being usually too warm to walk, & the Gov. employs two or three hours on writing in the Evening."[2]

The picture of the young Thomas Talbot that emerges from the diary is of an energetic, amiable, reliable young man. What then turned him into the cantankerous despot of his later years?

In 1794 Talbot returned to England and in 1796 bought a lieutenant-colonelcy in the 5th Regiment of Foot. Then, on Christmas Day, 1800, he suddenly sold his commission for 5,000 guineas and returned to Canada. One explanation is that he had been disappointed in love and that this "turned his brain". Another is that in spite of his close connections with two of those "damnedest millstones" — the Dukes of Cumberland and Kent — he was passed over for some high political appointment. Whatever the reason may have been for abandoning his military career, he took up the usual field officer's grant of 5,000 acres in Dunwich Township in 1803 and built himself a log house on a cliff overlooking Lake Erie in what was to become Elgin County. Colonel Mahlon Burwell, his friend and the surveyor of the Talbot lands, was to build himself a house near by.

Colonel Talbot's vision was grandiose. He wished to encourage settlement of the country on the principles of loyalty, obedience, and private industry, but at the same time he was intent on amassing for himself an estate comparable with that of his aristocratic Irish forebears. Thus he arranged with the government that for every settler he placed on fifty acres of land, he was to receive two hundred acres as commission. Although he modified this later by reserving only a hundred and fifty acres for himself, he was nevertheless in a position to assemble a vast acreage, variously described as a palatinate, fiefdom, seigneury, or principality. Aldborough and Dunwich townships were virtually his private domain; by 1850 his personal estate in Aldborough Township alone amounted to 27,650 acres.

The settler, on the other hand, had to complete the normal requirements of clearing ten acres and building a dwelling. He had to stay on his land for five years before he was eligible for a certificate, which could then be exchanged for a patent, and the Colonel decreed that he must clear half the road in front of his lot. If he did not complete these duties he was summarily dispossessed.[3]

At the outset, settlement proceeded slowly. In the fifth year of his residence at what he had named Port Talbot, the Colonel had placed only twenty families on his lands. In 1814 his farm was raided by the Americans; the buildings were burned and his sheep and cattle killed. But from 1819 onwards a horde of immigrants, mainly Scottish and Irish, began pouring into the province and the Colonel was besieged by an army of applicants that he described as a "pest". "Every hour of the days that I have been at home I have been beset by Battalions of applicants . . ." he complained in 1824.[4]

Talbot's irascible temperament and capricious record-keeping soon got him into trouble. The Highlanders who had settled in Aldborough Township claimed that he had "blinded their eyes, lead them astray and endeavoured to swindle them of their rights."[5] In 1837 Sir Francis Bond Head wrote: "If he [the settler] deserts his lot — if he attempts to sell it, assign it, or if he neglects to perform his settlement duties, Colonel Talbot takes up a piece of india-rubber which is attached to his pencil and as he very justly expresses it 'just rubs him out' from which moment the man becomes as much of a nonentity as was the flame of a candle which has been blown out. By the pencil and India rubber Colonel Talbot thus governs in solitude. . . . I need scarcely add that there exists in no country on the surface of the globe an authority more despotic than the power which Colonel Talbot possesses."[6]

One of the prospective settlers, a stalwart Highlander, was so incensed by the Colonel's treatment that he is said to have thrown him to the ground and held him there until he was promised what he wanted. Thereafter, the Colonel forbade settlers to enter his house and he began to do business through "a small compartment of his window" which he opened when he felt disposed to listen and closed and locked the instant he had delivered his reply.

The Colonel was often drunk, "it being his constant practice to take too much brandy," and his language was vulgar and abusive. He was not above setting his dogs on anyone who annoyed him.

A lifelong bachelor, he became increasingly out of tune with the times, as Anna Jameson found when she visited him in the summer of 1837. "The stirring events of the last thirty years" — changes in thought, literature, public opinion — and "the progress of social improvement", all, she thought, had passed him by.[7] His outlook remained rigidly Tory and his uncompromising opposition to the principles of democracy involved him in bitter confrontations with members of Upper Canada's Reform Party.

The Colonel, in fact, behaved as an aristocratic, arrogant

eighteenth-century Irish despot, but under his "vulgar imperti-
nence and tyrranical abuse" there lurked vestiges of a courtly gentleman and of a kindly young man who had given "a shilling to
liberate some wood pidgeons" for Elizabeth Simcoe. His servants
and some settlers to whom he had taken a liking found him kind and
benevolent, and he retained many of his friends throughout his life.

With his lineage and feudal background, the Colonel was anxious
to leave his estates to a member of his family, and at different times
he was visited by his nephews, Julius and Richard Airey. Colonel
Richard Airey and his wife lived for a time at Port Talbot, where they
planted fruit trees and roses and transformed the old house into a
comfortable country seat. Richard Airey was recalled to England in
1851 and to the colours in 1852. It was he who scribbled in a spidery
and almost undecipherable hand the ambiguous dispatch that in
1854 resulted in that heroic and tragic military blunder, the Charge
of the Light Brigade.

Colonel Thomas Talbot died in 1853 at the age of eighty-three and
was buried in the churchyard of St. Peter's Church, Tyrconnel, on a
cliff overlooking Lake Erie about five miles from his old home at Port
Talbot. In Dunwich and Aldborough townships, he and Anna
Jameson — perhaps now joined by John Kenneth Galbraith — are
persons whom some of the local residents most love to hate.

Travelling westwards today from St. Thomas — "named from
Thomas Talbot, with the Saint prefixed for euphony"[8] — along the
old Talbot Road or driving along back roads of Oxford and Elgin
counties, one sees small oil rigs here and there pumping oil from
below the earth's surface. Their yield is part of some 617,000 barrelfuls produced annually in Ontario.

The presence of oil in south-western Ontario was noted by the
earliest white settlers. In March 1793, when her husband returned
from a five-week trip to Detroit, Elizabeth Simcoe wrote in her
diary, "A real spring of Petroleum was discovered on the march by
its offensive smell." It is thought that this was a reference to the
spring on the Thames River north of Chatham at Fairfield. Here the
Indians of Moraviantown had a thriving business, soaking up oil
from the river with blankets and selling it as medicine. Oil was
widely used externally and internally both by Indians and by early
pioneers as a cure for rheumatism and other ills.

In 1858 oil was discovered in commercial quantities at Oil Springs
in Lambton County. Further finds followed at Petrolia in 1861 and
on George Brown's lands in the Township of Zone in 1863. Brown,
the colourful and energetic founder of the *Globe*, forerunner of the
Toronto *Globe and Mail*, had bought four thousand acres of land as a
farming and commercial venture around 1852 and he founded the

village of Bothwell. Here an American prospector, James M. Lick, struck a gusher on the banks of the Thames that is said to have produced oil to the value of ten thousand dollars a day. The village of Bothwell became a boom town overnight. Houses were hastily built; bars, banks, billiard halls, and shops were opened, and huge frame hotels constructed. For a time, Bothwell's future seemed as bright as that of Toronto — some said of New York. But it was not to last. By 1867 only thirty-one of the two hundred and three wells were being pumped and in the same year the town was destroyed by fire. George Brown by this time had sold his lands to a group of Scottish speculators, but many men, James Lick among them, were ruined.[9]

The McKillop Family
Aldborough Township
Elgin County

There is a small park on the cliffs at Port Glasgow in Aldborough Township, Elgin County. From here one can look out over Lake Erie much as Anna Jameson did in 1837 from Colonel Talbot's house. The erosion she described from "the storms and gradual action of the waves" continues to eat away at the cliff face, and along the shoreline there is still a tangle of tree roots and underbrush.

Port Glasgow is sixteen miles west of the Colonel's house and erstwhile "capital", and here the Sixteen Mile Creek runs into the lake. It is a small creek flowing through low, hummocky hills. Only an old fishing boat left high and dry near the lake is a reminder of a once-flourishing fishing industry. But in 1818 the creek was large enough to be used as an anchorage and it was at this inhospitable spot that a party of Scottish settlers from Argyllshire disembarked in 1818. To have landed safely was in itself something of an achievement; some settlers were to drown at Port Talbot while getting their baggage ashore.

Among the settlers were the McGilps or McKillops. They came from Lochgilphead on the North Knapdale shore of Loch Fyne on the west coast of Scotland not far from Inverary, the family seat of the Dukes of Argyll. It was probably the inducement of owning their own land that made them leave Scotland. Before they set sail, spokesmen for the party wrote to the authorities in London "respecting land", and anxiously awaited a reply in Tobermory, before embarking on the *Mars*.

The voyage over was a stormy one lasting sixty-three days. The party landed in Pictou, Nova Scotia, and made their way to Quebec and Queenston, then up the Lake Erie shore by ship to the Sixteen Mile Creek.

Once landed, the McKillops obtained a grant of land from Colonel Talbot and thus became one of the numerous Highland Scots families to settle in Aldborough and Dunwich townships. The land they took up was on Brock Creek, so called because General Brock had camped at its mouth during the War of 1812, while directing the operation that led to the capture of Fort Detroit.

It was late September before the family arrived and it is thought that a hastily built log house was their first shelter. A difficult winter followed soon after:

> One of the settlers of 1818, was . . . Duncan McKillop, whose health soon became so impaired by change of climate and hard toil, that he had great difficulties in procuring the necessaries of life for his family. They had no money to purchase a cow, and Mrs McKillop went to the Thames, 9 miles above where Chatham now is, and earned one by working for Frederick Arnold, who ever after esteemed Mrs. McKillop highly for her heroism and devotion in the cause of her husband and family.[10]

The McKillops, like all the Talbot settlers, had to complete their settlement duties by clearing ten acres of land, building a log cabin sixteen by twenty feet, and clearing half the road in front of their lot — in their case, the Talbot Road. In 1824 they obtained the deed to the land from "the Hon. Thomas Talbot", who received for it a nominal "three barleycorns", an old form of quit rent.

Of Duncan McKillop's four sons, Archibald and Duncan became lumbermen. Their first job was to clear the trees from the highway that runs north from the present town of Leamington, and in time they established a sawmill and a grist-mill in the village of West Lorne. In 1877 the McKillops were listed as the second-oldest family in the township, described as "wealthy farmers and millowners" and among the most substantial residents of Aldborough.

When his brothers turned to lumbering, it was Daniel McKillop, the youngest of Duncan's sons, who took over the home farm. Colonel Talbot did not much care for the Scots and was reputed to settle the English on the best land. The McKillops' land in Aldborough, when stripped of its forest cover, was light and sandy and not particularly promising, given the implements and fertilizers then available. But by amalgamating the family farms and by buying others with heavier soils on which cattle could be pastured during the summer, the family prospered and were well established by the 1850s. Eventually they would own some twelve hundred acres of land.

Two of the next generation of McKillops were listed as fishermen, farmers, and drovers, owning a two-thirds share of the once-flourishing local whitefish-fishing industry on Lake Erie.

There have been four houses on the McKillop farm. The first log house billeted seven army men during the Rebellion of 1837 and served an honourable retirement as a hog-pen. A frame house built in 1845 had a similar fate — it became the top half of a barn. The house that succeeded it in 1895 burned down on Christmas Eve, 1922, and was replaced in 1927 by the present square brick house on the same foundations. Outside in the garden is a great European birch tree, and on the wall facing the old Talbot Road a plaque erected in 1967 commemorating the previous generations of the family.

The present owner, Donald McKillop, is the fifth generation on the farm. He no longer farms intensively — the fields are rented — but there are still sheep here, as there have been for five generations. Even today Donald McKillop's sheep are bothered by wolves. In the early days of the Talbot Settlement, when whisky was eighteen cents a gallon, a local resident who had imbibed too much was left in a fence corner to sleep off the effects of the liquor. The next morning scarcely a shred was found of him or even of his clothing. The author of this story writes that wolves had torn him limb from limb and feasted on the mangled carcase. He adds that after diligent inquiry, conducted around the turn of the century, this was the only case he had heard of in which human life was actually destroyed by wild beasts.

Today there are few farms in Aldborough Township owned by the descendants of the Highlanders who landed in 1818, but in the country as a whole there are many more Argyllshire Scots than are left on the Scottish lands of the Dukes of Argyll, the McKillops among them, who look back on their pioneer heritage and their Scottish ancestry with justifiable pride.

The Burwell Family
Bayham Township
Elgin County

Wilford Burwell and his wife, Madge, live on the 9th Concession of Bayham Township in Elgin County on land surveyed by

Colonel Mahlon Burwell, one of Colonel Talbot's first settlers and the man after whom Port Burwell on Lake Erie was named.

The Burwells were United Empire Loyalists who came to Canada following the War of Independence. Wilford Burwell's farm has been in the family since 1848, when it was deeded to his great-grandfather by a member of the Dobbie family, to whom it had been granted by the Crown.

The Burwells' white house rests at the bottom of a steep, wooded valley on a branch of Otter Creek. In the nineteenth century, the Big Otter and its tributaries were described as "superior mill streams" which in the spring formed "nature's great timber thoroughfare to the lake whereby the wealth of the forest was easily transported to American and other foreign markets".[11] Between 1840 and 1850, hundreds of thousands of oak staves for barrels were exported from Port Burwell, then a shipbuilding town of some importance. But by 1872, the great oaks and pines had been cut from Bayham Township, and by 1877 there was not a single sawmill left in Port Burwell.

In the lumbering period, there was a sawmill on what is now Wilford Burwell's farm, and the house in which the Burwells live was the owner's home. It was built on the east side of the creek and was moved to its present position on the west bank about 1865. It is a house that had two front rooms; it still has two front doors and, according Wilford Burwell, "It was built like a barn, the bedrooms partitioned off like box stalls." The basement timbers and the rafters are held together by cut nails.

Wilford Burwell's mother married twice, both her husbands dying prematurely of pneumonia. In a long life of eighty-one years Mrs. Burwell's two marriages lasted for only ten. Wilford was just eighteen months old when his father, his mother's second husband, died, leaving three daughters and himself, the only son. "My mother had dreams of a boy aged a year and a half growing up to farm for her. I don't know if you'd call it faith, or what, but that's how it worked out."

Life was hard during the Depression years. "To begin with we kept half a dozen cows and chickens. We let the fields out on shares to the neighbours in return for a third of the hay and grain. With what my sisters and mother could make from selling butter to the neighbours, it didn't amount to much."

Then there was the mortgage. "My father had had a large mortgage for those days — eight hundred dollars. We had to save all year to pay the interest and the taxes. As soon as we'd paid one lot of interest, we'd have to start saving again for the next." No bicycle, no toys, no new shoes.

"My one ambition was to grow up fast and work. They say I grew up old. I didn't get much schooling because I went to work at thirteen and I was sixteen when my sisters and I started to farm for ourselves. Our equipment was not the best, but we had a good wheat crop in the first year we started and I paid three hundred dollars off the mortgage. We were away!" After more than forty years, there is relief in Wilford Burwell's voice as he recalls that triumph.

"The year I was twenty-one, I had enough money saved to pay off the mortgage. But this same money was enough to buy a car and I wanted a car so badly. When I left that evening to attend to the mortgage, my mother didn't know if I'd have the mortgage paid or a car in the yard next day. But in the morning there was a receipt on the table, 'Paid in Full', for the mortgage. It was the happiest day I had known."

After the mortgage was paid, there were fences to fix and the barns to be mended. Wilford Burwell gradually built up a herd of pure-bred Holstein cattle. In winter, a hole was cut in the ice for watering the cattle, and pails of water had to be carried up the steep hill for the young stock in a barn at the top. In winter it was slippery. Ashes were put down on the road and a device fixed to the heels of boots to prevent slipping.

In 1955, the Burwells switched to tobacco, which Wilford Burwell now farms with his son, Thomas. The tobacco fields and kilns are on top of the hill behind the house where the cattle barn used to be. Like the Dertingers of Norfolk County, the Burwells know that looking after a tobacco plant is "like looking after a baby". It needs the right heat and humidity and a precise amount of water.

The curing process is a critical part of tobacco-growing: the leaf must be dried and turned yellow without its rotting or going black. During the curing, Wilford Burwell does not sleep at the house. "I have an eight-by-ten room near the kilns with a comfortable bed. I have to get up at night to check the kilns, and I am up for the day by four thirty in the morning. Knowing when to adjust the temperature and humidity is what makes good tobacco. From the start in the greenhouse, until you get it sold, the better you perform each step, the better quality you will get, the better grades and the better price." The Burwells have produced tobacco of the highest grade — a notable achievement.

Everything in Wilford Burwell's later life has been an improvement on the struggles of his youth. And yet he thinks his children may have missed something. "Fifty years ago we would have forty to fifty people here every evening all summer long, swimming in the swimming-hole where the dam was for the sawmill." Then, too, there were horses. A tractor needs no respite, but horses have to rest periodically in the fields and so the farmer has a chance to stop and listen to the birds, a moment to pause and enjoy.

Of his early life he says that everyone likes to do something for themselves and for others. He did something for himself — and for his mother. After that, things got better all the time.

The Kells Family
Enniskillen Township
Lambton County

Lambton County in south-west Ontario faces the state of Michigan across the St. Clair River. Enniskillen, the large township in its centre, was sparsely populated until 1858, when oil was discovered in commercial quantities at Oil Springs. The discovery led to Ontario's oil boom and over the next forty years the population on the township's eighty-two thousand or so acres grew from 238 in 1851 to an all-time high of 5,006 in 1891. By 1977 it was 3,346.

The discovery of oil at Oil Springs was followed by that at Petrolia in 1861. By 1890, Petrolia had become the oil capital of Canada — a boom town and the centre of an intercontinental oil-refining empire that operated the world's first oil exchange.

But it was not oil that drew William Kells to Enniskillen Township. He had purchased one hundred acres north-west of Petrolia from the Crown in 1853, five years before oil was discovered, and settled on the east half of Lot 6, Concession 14. In that year there was only one log school in the township with a teacher whose annual salary was thirty-eight pounds.

William Kells had been born in Kilkenny County, Ireland, in 1821 and came to Canada with his parents in 1824. In 1850 he married Elizabeth Hodgins, a girl of Yorkshire descent. The Kellses were to have eleven children.

William Kells cleared the land and built a log house and barn on the higher, sandy soil near the centre of the farm, leaving fifteen acres of trees that included black walnut, cherry, and black and white ash at the south end. In the 1880s he replaced the log house with a frame house of six bedrooms and built a second large barn.

In 1899 the farm was taken over by his son, William Hodgins Kells, when at the age of thirty-two he married nineteen-year-old Ida Hilda Ellenor. Their eldest son was born in 1902 and was named

Ernest Edward — "Edward" after King Edward VII, who had recently been crowned after waiting impatiently for the throne of England until his sixtieth year.

Meanwhile, test drilling for oil showed that a vein ran north-west from Petrolia, and in 1872 oil was found at Marthaville near the Kells farm. Then it was found on the farm itself. The elder William Kells leased the land to an oil company in the 1890s and at the turn of the century there were seven or eight small wells on the property, bringing up oil from a vein five hundred feet below the surface. In 1902, the year Ernest Kells was born, a particularly good well was drilled at the foot of the orchard, on the east next to the side-road.

When the land was leased, the wells were drilled and operated by an oil company and the farmer's payment was usually in the form of a royalty of every eighth barrel of oil produced. Although "oil was not worth much," Ernest Kells says — eighty-eight cents a barrel in 1884 — it was still found money for the farmer. After her husband took over the farm in 1899, Hilda Kells boarded some of the oil men in the farmhouse and this, in addition to the money from the royalties, was a welcome addition to the family's income.

An ingenious system was devised for operating the pumps that raised the oil from the substratum to the earth's surface. A steam-powered plant or "rig" in a powerhouse worked a system of "jerker" lines that operated pumps for several wells. The largest of these, the Fitzgerald Rig in Petrolia, operated three hundred wells through the jerker line system — all activated from one central powerhouse.

From a spider-wheel in the powerhouse, the jerker lines ran out to wells as far as half a mile away. The jerker lines were made of wooden rods — usually white ash or oak — sixteen feet in length, bolted together and suspended two and a half feet off the ground on wooden posts.

Often the jerker lines ran over land being actively farmed; however, the lines and the wells didn't hamper the farmers in cultivating their crops. They worked round the wells with their implements. The lines were low enough for cattle and horses to step or jump over, and there were places where implements could be taken across them.

Three-poled derricks forty feet high were erected over each well. For a time the three-poled derricks "were as numerous as trees." They were used for raising up the joints of iron casing, joints of iron pump, and the rods to be lowered into the wells. The poles for the derricks were black ash.

As small boys, Ernest Kells and his brothers used to build their own derricks in the orchard and make believe that they were drilling oil wells.

The oil from the wells was stored in underground wooden tanks. The cedar stays for the tanks were grooved and fitted to a circular base and held tightly on the outside by iron hoops. The tanks were almost indestructible — an example of the now-all-but-lost art of making barrels by hand. Much timber went into the making of oil barrels and into firing the steam engines that operated the jerker lines.

The oil was pumped from the underground holding tank into a wooden tank with a capacity of eight or nine barrels lying on its side on a wagon. In early days the wagon was drawn by horses from the farm either to Wyoming (a village north of Petrolia) or to Petrolia itself, where there were refineries. Later, intermediate receiving stations were built and the tank wagon from the farm was pulled by tractor three or four miles to Bunyan, where Imperial Oil had a pumping station to pump the oil to Sarnia twelve miles away.

Where there were oil wells, there was also gas. Some of the wells near Bunyan yielded more gas than oil. The gas came up between the casing and the pump in the oil well and could be used to run the engines for the jerker lines. Such gas was useful on the farms, where it could be burned for lights and stoves, and there were some wells that supplied three or four houses and perhaps a church and school as well. In summer, when it was too hot to burn the gas continuously indoors, gas jets burned outside in gardens and their lights flickered in the country at night. At the Kells farm the excess gas was burned off in the orchard.

At the same time as the wells were operating on the farm, the Kells family were raising cattle for beef, hogs for pork, and keeping dairy cows. The children all helped with milking the cows. Cream was separated to be churned into butter, which was packed into crocks and sold at the Sarnia market some twelve miles away. Vegetables, too, were grown, and apples.

The discovery of oil brought wealth to many residents, but in one way it had an adverse effect on agriculture in Enniskillen Township. It raised the price of land to speculative levels, and speculators who bought it left the land unimproved. And so, as late as 1899, there were still uncleared farms in the township.

William Hodgins Kells died in 1936 and his wife, Hilda, who inherited the farm, outlived him until 1962.

By the 1930s oil levels had dropped and all the wells on the farm were plugged. The machinery, the derricks, and the jerker lines disappeared. All that was left was one holding tank in the orchard and that was filled after a hog fell into it by accident.

Hilda Kells — a bride of nineteen years in 1899 — left the farm to her sons, Ernest and Gordon Kells, when she died in 1962. Gordon Kells bought out his brother's share in 1964. With Gordon's death in 1977, the farm was owned for the second time in this century by a woman — Euphemia Kells, Gordon Kells's widow — who lives in the frame house with the scent of wood smoke in her kitchen and a view from the back windows of the old woodlot.

Ernest Kells, the small boy who played at derricks in the farm orchard, left school to work in the oil industry. He worked on local oil-drilling rigs, then in Oklahoma, New Brunswick, and Quebec. In 1922, he left for Persia and Mesopotamia and remained in the Persian Gulf area, drilling for oil, until 1931. His travels were by no means unique. Men from Petrolia, the oil-boom town, travelled all over the world, and when the climate was suitable they took their wives with them. Ontario's expertise was in demand, and the oil men's children were born in Burma, Borneo, Africa, Europe, Australia, Peru, and Trinidad.

Almost all of this story was told by Ernest Kells and his wife, Hazel. In their house in Petrolia are many mementoes of Ernest's stay in the Persian Gulf area. A knock on their door may herald the casual visitor, or an oil man from Texas in a ten-gallon hat seeking firsthand information on the history of oil.

Beyond the Kellses' back garden is something that is becoming increasingly rare outside the Oil Springs Museum: a complete nineteenth-century oil rig that has been working continuously for a hundred and ten years, and is now owned and operated by Roy Ayrheart. It is exactly as it was except for the engine, which is no longer powered by steam but by an electric motor. Here one can see the jerker lines, the pumps, the three-poled derrick forty feet high made of black ash poles, the wooden underground holding tanks, and a tank wagon. All still working just as they used to on the Kells farm and pumping up a barrel of oil a day — now worth thirteen dollars.

The jerker lines move slowly back and forth in their own timeless rhythm and in one place over the years a forty-foot ash tree has grown round one of the moving rods — a strange compromise between a man-made machine and nature.

CHAPTER TEN

Settlements of the Western Frontier

A severe attack of illness, the combined effect of heat, fatigue, and some deleterious properties in the water at Detroit, against which the traveller should be warned, has confined me to my room for the last three days."[1] Thus incapacitated, Anna Jameson, the nineteenth-century traveller and writer, missed the steamboat that was to take her into Lake Huron and had to wait another six days for her connection.

Thanks to shortcomings in the purity of Detroit's water supply we have been left a pen-picture of Detroit and its environs in the year 1837. It was, Anna Jameson tells us, a "beautiful little city" and of all the places she had seen in the "far western regions" the most interesting. With tongue slightly in cheek she calls it "a most ancient and venerable place, dating back to the dark immemorial ages i.e. almost a century and a quarter ago!"

Five times its flag had changed, Anna Jameson tells her readers. Three different sovereignties had claimed its allegiance, twice it was besieged by Indians, once captured in war and once burned to the ground.

The five changes of flag to which Anna Jameson referred reflect a history which for drama, colour, and human interest would be difficult to equal anywhere in the New World. Located on the narrow channel between Lake Erie and Lakes St. Clair and Huron, the successive forts and settlements where Detroit now stands were the focus of international struggle for over a hundred years.

Across the channel, which we now call the Detroit River, and in places only a few hundred yards away were the low-lying lands that became Essex County. The early history of Detroit is also that of Essex — and of the county immediately to the east, which is Kent. Indeed, it might be said that Detroit was the hinge upon which the history of the whole of south-western Ontario swung.

The story of the struggle for Detroit reminds us that the early history of the province of Ontario, at least as far as Europeans are concerned, belongs to the French, a fact attested to by the origins of two of the century farmers in this chapter: the Bondys, who are one of the earliest families in Ontario with a lineage they can trace back to fifteenth-century France, and the Belangers, who settled in Quebec in 1670 and came to what is still a French enclave in Kent County in 1833.

On August 10, 1535, the French explorer Jacques Cartier named a small bay near Anticosti Island "Baye Sainct Laurens", because the day was, and still is, the name-day of that saint in the church calendar. The name St. Lawrence later came to be applied to the river which Cartier went on to explore. He travelled up it until he reached impassable rapids at a spot which he named *Le Mont Royal* for its imposing hill.

From the Indians Jacques Cartier heard of the Ottawa River and of the Great Lakes beyond, and six years later he returned, this time to establish a colony in the vicinity of Le Mont Royal. The attempt failed, but for two hundred years, until Quebec fell to the British in 1759, it was the French who explored and opened up what is now Ontario.

Ostensibly the spur that drove the French on was the hope of finding a short cut to China and its riches, but the more immediate gains to be had from fur-trading with the Indians soon became the dominant motive for exploration. With the French eager to buy, the Indians were more than happy to trap and sell. As the population of fur-breeding animals declined under relentless trapping, the search for new sources of wealth took the French further and further into hitherto unexplored territory. Some idea of just how massive the onslaught was on fur-bearing animals can be gained from the fact that when Radisson and Groseilliers returned from a trading trip to Lake Superior in 1663, they brought back with them more than three hundred canoes brimful of furs.

Curiously enough, as the French pushed westward they consistently by-passed Lake Ontario, Lake Erie, and what is now southwestern Ontario. The route habitually followed, which had been pioneered by Champlain in 1613 and 1615, took the French up the Ottawa and thence by way of Lake Nipissing to Georgian Bay. Presumably the apparently endless rapids on the St. Lawrence were as daunting to the French as they were to later travellers, but the reason for taking the more northerly route may have been that their guides were Huron Indians whose homelands lay in the Georgian Bay area. Quite understandably, the Hurons wished to keep the fur trade in their own hands; furthermore, they wanted to steer clear of

their traditional enemies, the League of the Iroquois, who dominated the upper St. Lawrence.

At least part of the popularity of the French among the Hurons
rested on the willingness of the former to help them make war on
the Iroquois, who came to detest the French for this reason. In 1648,
and again in 1649, the angry Iroquois swept north to obliterate the
Christianized Huron settlements between Nottawasaga Bay and
Lake Simcoe. They then turned on the Tobacco Indians who lived
west of the Hurons, and on the Atiwandaronks or Neutral Indians, who occupied south-western Ontario, and after decimating
them in battle, laid waste the land that was theirs and emptied it of
its inhabitants.

South-western Ontario remained virtually empty for over a
hundred years. The area was labelled "Nation Détruite" on the
French maps, until the first French settlers around the fort at Detroit
crossed the river and made their homes on the eastern bank at what
came to be called Petite Côte.

It was not until about 1670 that the word spread among the French
that it was possible to get into Lake Michigan via Lakes Ontario and
Erie, though this meant a portage around Niagara Falls. By 1676,
trading posts had been established on the Niagara River, and in the
years to follow, other posts, which doubled as forts, were to appear
on Lake Michigan, on the Illinois and Mississippi rivers, and in 1701
on the future site of Detroit. Called Fort Pontchartrain, it was built
by a man named Antoine Laumet de la Mothe Cadillac — to give
him his resounding name in full.

Yet the name principally associated with the opening up of the
western region is that of Robert Cavelier de la Salle. An unusually
enterprising and independent young man, he pursued both personal riches and the furtherance of French power while still cherishing the increasingly far-fetched dream of a short cut to the Orient. It
was this apparent obsession with China that led to his seigneury on
Montreal Island being dubbed "La Chine". And it was La Salle and
his companions who built the first ship on the Great Lakes, the
Griffon, constructed near Niagara Falls and wrecked in 1679 —
some say at Tobermory near the tip of the Bruce Peninsula. La Salle
was to have led the first expedition down the Mississippi. In the
event, however, it was Louis Jolliet who made the journey, though
he turned back within a few days' travel of the Gulf of Mexico. Six
years later, La Salle led a party that reached the sea, claiming the
entire Mississippi basin for Louis XIV of France and naming it
Louisiana. Later still, a French colony was established on the Gulf,
only to be abandoned. Leading the starving survivors northwards to

the safety of the French posts on the Illinois, La Salle was murdered by his own men.

In 1685 New France had a new governor, the Marquis de Denonville, an experienced soldier and, like other governors before him, determined to put an end to the Iroquois who had gone on the rampage again, this time in the Ohio Valley. He obtained troop reinforcements from France, fortified Montreal, and started to construct a series of new forts, while rebuilding old ones. Fort Pontchartrain became Fort Detroit.

Following the example of his predecessors, Denonville marched into the tribal lands of the Seneca, the most westerly of the Iroquois tribes, burning their villages and destroying their crops. Predictably, the Senecas and other tribes of the Iroquoian League struck back, venting their fury on the settlements around Montreal. In the early morning of a day in August, to the macabre accompaniment of a thunderstorm, the Indians descended in force on Lachine and massacred the inhabitants. The disaster stunned the French and scarcely had they recovered when news reached them from Europe that France was now at war with England.

Breaking out in 1689, "King William's War", as it came to be called in Canada, was the first of a series of conflicts between England and France that culminated in the capture of Quebec by the British in the Seven Years War. That the French preoccupation with the fur trade led to their weakness and final defeat in North America is undeniable. Louis Hébert, an apothecary who settled with his family in 1617 and in whose person European methods of agriculture may be said to have arrived in Canada, was convinced that the strength of New France must be based on the land, as opposed to fur-trading. Hébert set an example with his ordered fields of wheat, oats, and vegetables, and small fruits. But his views were never fully shared by the successive governors of New France.

The first intendant, Talon, also did what he could to promote agricultural settlement in his time, which was the 1660s, and on the seigneurial holdings along the St. Lawrence stable communities were developing. Yet in 1680, of the ten thousand that made up the population of New France, something like one man in five was away in the western forest in search of the easy wealth that the beaver could bring.

Apart from the St. Lawrence settlements, little agriculture was practised by the French in the interior. The two notable exceptions were at Fort Frontenac, later abandoned, and at Detroit. Of these two agricultural settlements, the one at Detroit was the most extensive.

The Detroit settlement had its beginnings very early in the eighteenth century, though it was not until the 1730s that a pattern of holdings began to emerge with long, narrow farms laid out in the seigneurial fashion, one end abutting the Detroit River. Cattle and hogs were raised, corn and wheat grown, while later visitors noted a disproportionate number of horses — the French being communally minded had large numbers of horse-drawn equipages wherein to travel on social occasions.

As time went by, the farms were feeding not just the garrison but the town that was springing up around the fort. At an early date, Detroit had its blacksmiths and metal-workers, its carpenters and masons, and a market where Indian wares could be bought. A report dated 1749 mentions a lumber mill in the locality, besides quarries, one of which was being worked on Stoney Island.

Across the river were the empty lands of the Neutral Indians, that "nation détruite". Excessively low-lying and swampy, what was to become part of Essex County was still thickly wooded with types of trees unknown further north. The woods of south-western Ontario and along Lake Erie were (and what is left of them still are) the northern extension of a deciduous-forest type widespread in the eastern United States, which includes, besides the more commonly known hardwoods such as hard maple, basswood, and walnut, such exotically named trees as tulip-tree, Kentucky coffee-tree, paw-paw, and redbud. Centuries of leaf-fall from this lush forest and the detritus from dead and dying trees had built up on this ill-drained land a rich, fertile loam which those farmers who are lucky enough to be on it praise to this day.

It was onto this land that the Bondy family moved in 1748, crossing over from their older home on the western side of the river. By 1760 some fifty families were living on the stretch of shore between the future site of Windsor and Amherstburg, the Petite Côte. In that year, too, the fleur-de-lis of New France came down over Fort Detroit for the last time.

In the early 1750s, with settlers moving westwards over the Appalachians, Britain claimed that the lands south of the Great Lakes formed a natural extension inland of the colonies along the seaboard. The French reaction was to build more forts south of Lake Erie and they seized a fort from the Virginians which they renamed Fort Duquesne. Later it was recaptured and called Fort Pitt, and later still renamed Pittsburgh. The British government, though France and Britain were not at war, decided to oust the French by force. In May 1755, General Braddock, with 1,500 British regulars supported by 450 militiamen from Virginia under George Washington, toiled westwards over the mountains, dragging cannon behind them. A few miles short of Fort Duquesne, the force was ambushed and routed by a few hundred French supported by Indians. General Braddock died of wounds during the retreat.

The defeat of General Braddock brought it home to the British government, in the person of William Pitt, that the French in North America were to be beaten only through careful planning and the use of massive force. Thus, when Britain and France went to war in 1756, a British and colonial army of some twelve thousand men in over a hundred ships arrived off Louisbourg, the French fortress on what is now Cape Breton Island, to force its surrender after three weeks' siege. Quebec fell to the British under Wolfe in 1759. With the surrender of Montreal a year later, New France ceased to exist. By the Treaty of Paris in 1763, all major French possessions in North America passed into British hands, with the exception of Louisiana.

Scarcely had the war ended and the last of the scattered French forts been handed over by their commanders when the Indians under Pontiac fell upon the scantily held forts and overwhelmed the tiny British detachments that manned them. In the case of one fort, the entire garrison was slaughtered, though exactly when and by whom is a mystery to this day. Six weeks after the rising began there was only one British outpost remaining on the Great Lakes, and that was at Detroit.

Detroit was to hold out until the end of the Indian uprising in 1764. For six months it was under close siege. It survived through the help of some of the French, notably the Bâby family, who at great risk to themselves supplied the beleaguered garrison with food, while half-way through the siege a relief expedition managed to get through, using barges to bring in more men, ammunition, and some cannon.

The Pontiac War may be said to have ended in 1765 when the Indians, realizing that their fight was hopeless, came to a general parley at Detroit. For all its appalling loss of life and destruction of property, the war at least had its beneficial effect on the future policies of the British towards the Indians, policies which kept them for the most part loyal to the Crown in the wars that lay ahead.

A picture of Petite Côte at this time has been left by a soldier, James Smith, who was taken to Detroit as an Indian prisoner in 1757:

Opposite to Detroit and below it, was originally a prairie, and laid off in lots of about sixty rods broad and a great length; each lot is divided into two fields, which they cultivate year about. The principal grain that the French raise in these fields was spring wheat and peas.

They built their houses on the front of these lots on the river side; and as the banks of the river are very low, some of the houses are not above three or four feet above the surface of the water; yet they are in no danger of being disturbed by freshes, as the river seldom rises above eighteen inches. . . .

As dwelling-houses, barns, and stables are all built on the front of these lots; at a distance it appears like a continued row of houses in a town, on each side of the river for a long way. These villages, the town, the river and the plains, being all in view at once, affords a most delightful prospect.[2]

One outstanding feature of French agriculture in the Detroit area was their orchards. Apples, plums, peaches, cherries, and pears were all grown — some, it is said, from trees and seeds brought from Normandy.

The growing Canadian settlements were to experience only ten years of peace between the ending of the Pontiac War and the outbreak of the War of Independence which eventually brought many Loyalists to settle in the area. Some Loyalists came via Niagara to make their way west; and some, like the Dolsens, took up land in what is now Essex and Kent. Others came via Detroit itself to form the nucleus of such settlements as Amherstburg.

As elsewhere in the province, the land belonged to the Indians, and for the first few years the settlers were technically squatters. This problem was not resolved until 1790, when most of the land of what is now Kent, Essex, and Elgin counties, together with part of Middlesex, was bought from the Ottawas, the Chippewas, and other tribes for the sum of twelve hundred pounds; or, very roughly, six thousand dollars.

Actually, no money changed hands. The Indians were paid the equivalent in trade goods. The list makes sorry reading today, including as it does such items as a dozen black silk handkerchiefs valued at thirty shillings, twenty dozen plain hats at fifteen shillings a dozen, thirty ivory combs, and a bullock valued at thirteen pounds sterling.

Towards the end of the Revolutionary War, a census records 321 heads of families in the Detroit area in 1782, with a total population of 2,291. Some 1,100 horses are listed, with about 1,700 cattle, 450 sheep, and 1,400 swine. The bulk of these, both men and animals, will have been on the American side. Essex and Kent remained sparsely populated for years. As late as 1817, some thirty years later, the white population of the whole of Kent was still under the 1,200 mark.

After the Americans won their independence in 1783, there was an uneasy time along the western border, with the British refusing to abandon Detroit and other forts in the western region in order to help pressure the Americans into compensating the Loyalists for their property losses. In 1794, ten years later, the British were still there, as were the English fur-traders, who continued profitable operations in what was technically American territory. With the signing of Jay's Treaty, however, the deepening crisis was averted. The British agreed to evacuate the forts within two years. And so Detroit became American in fact as well as in name, and of those Loyalist families still living on the American side of the Detroit River, some, such as the Botsfords, crossed it in order to remain under the British flag.

Meanwhile, Upper and Lower Canada had come into being, as had Kent and Essex counties, along with seventeen others along Lake Erie and Lake Ontario. Kent was, however, somewhat larger than it is today. Governor Simcoe's Kent had the Thames River as its southern boundary and included, according to a seemingly astonished Surveyor-General who was trying to describe the new county to a friend, all the land "extending northward to the boundary line of Hudson Bay, including all the territory to the westward . . . to the utmost extent of the country called or known by the name of Canada."

The year 1804 saw the beginning of one of the first attempts in Upper Canada at a privately sponsored mass settlement, a scheme developed under the auspices of Lord Selkirk, whose name came to be associated principally with the Scots' settlement on the Red River in Manitoba. Early in 1803 Selkirk brought a party of Scottish emigrants to settle in Prince Edward Island; which done, he came west and was impressed by the possibilities of the land bordering Lake St. Clair. Accordingly, in the following year he assembled 111 emigrants at Tobermory on the Island of Mull. They sailed from Greenock in May, eventually arriving on the site Selkirk had selected in September. His settlement, located near the present town of Wallaceburg, was named Baldoon by Lord Selkirk.

It was intended that the settlement should raise sheep and Selkirk bought a thousand of them in New York State to start the enterprise. These sheep were driven to Baldoon through nearly two hundred miles of bush from Queenston on the Niagara Peninsula — an astonishing feat. Lord Selkirk also brought in a hundred Spanish merinos, a point of some interest to sheep-breeders. It seems that they came from Scotland and Denmark.

The Baldoon settlers ran into trouble from the start. They were totally isolated, with their nearest neighbours, the Dolsens on the

Thames River, nearly twenty miles away and difficult to reach even if they knew the way. As they were reduced to living in tents, sickness spread among them rapidly, with the first deaths occurring within a month of their arrival. At the end of the first year forty-two of them, or nearly half the party, were dead from ague and dysentery.

In the years that followed, a combination of mismanagement and recurring sickness led to the collapse of Lord Selkirk's venture. In 1818 it seems that there were still some twenty families living in the vicinity of the former settlement; but Selkirk, though he attempted to put things right at Baldoon, had long since been absorbed in his Red River project. He sold his holding at Baldoon in 1818, and died in France two years later.

In 1812 the titanic struggle against Napoleon was nearing its zenith. On June 24 of that year, Napoleon marched into Russia at the head of half a million men and such was his hold on Europe that with him were troops from Germany, Poland, Italy, Holland, Denmark, and Switzerland. Meanwhile, the Peninsula army under the Duke of Wellington had begun the 1812 campaign by storming the French-held citadel of Badajoz that lay just across the Portuguese-Spanish border. The fortress, with walls that in places rose a hundred feet above the surrounding ditch, finally fell to direct assault on April 6. The cost was some five thousand dead: and among them was twenty-one-year-old Francis Simcoe, much loved son of Upper Canada's first governor who, as a lively small boy, had delighted Elizabeth Simcoe during her stay in Canada. It was for their son Francis that the Simcoes acquired some land in what is now Toronto and built a house above the Don River that they jocularly called Castle Frank.

Three months after Badajoz and a couple of weeks after Napoleon started his disastrous Russian venture, the United States declared war on Britain and invaded Canada.

It was mainly the long-felt grievances related to the question of impressment and Britain's tight blockade that precluded American trade with the West Indies and Europe, plus a mounting hunger for the empty lands of Canada, that led to the declaration of hostilities. The British navy had become an enormous one, and the crying need was for men to man the ships. The British held that a British subject, wherever he might be found, was liable for impressment in the naval service. What the Americans objected to was the Royal Navy's habit of finding British sailors on American ships, where indeed they were, as the American merchant marine with its higher rates of pay and better working conditions attracted many British seamen to serve in it.

Ironically, the war's immediate cause was removed before it started — the British government unconditionally rescinded their orders relating to the boarding of American vessels at sea even as Congress was deciding to fight. Indeed, towards the end of the war, with American sea-borne trade brought to a standstill by the British blockade, the position was reversed and out-of-work American seamen were signing on in British ships.

For many farmers in Upper Canada, the 1812 war brought welcome prosperity: food became short and prices rose. But for some settlers in Kent and Essex counties, and in other counties of southwestern Ontario, the war meant virtual ruin. It was in Essex County that the Americans first landed and here the first engagements of the war were fought. From the summer of 1813 until the end of the war, with all the defending forces withdrawn, south-western Ontario, while not continuously occupied by the Americans, was open to their raiding and foraging parties, which did not scruple to strip the countryside of food and to burn houses and barns if they felt inclined. One such party drove off nearly a thousand of Selkirk's sheep, taking as well the settlement's large boat and ten smaller ones loaded with food and supplies.

It was a curious conflict in many ways. When food shortages in Upper Canada became critical, it was often Americans who helped out. Many British garrisons were kept going by supplies purchased in the New England states, which from the start had been violently opposed to the war. They had done well supplying the British army in Spain and their sympathies were all with Britain in her long fight against Napoleon. "We will, in no event, assist in uniting the Republic of America with the military despotism of France," declared the citizens of New Hampshire, and similar resolutions were passed in New York and Connecticut. Flags in Massachusetts were halfmasted when war was declared, and a convention in New England debated secession from the Union. By 1814 it was estimated that two-thirds of the British and Canadian forces were being victualled by beef from the New England states.

It was a war that was characterized, at least in the early days, by desperate improvisation on the Canadian side with inadequate forces that had to be hurried, sometimes literally overnight, from one trouble spot to another. Compared with the enormous armies of men being deployed on the battlefields of Europe, the numbers involved in Canada were minuscule. In 1812 there was perhaps a total of about 4,500 British regular troops in British North America, of whom only 1,600 were stationed in Upper Canada. Supporting them were Canadian local units (not to be confused with the short-term militia) such as the Royal Newfoundland Regiment, the Canadian Fencibles, the Canadian Voltigeurs, and the Glengarry Light Infantry, with a total strength of about 4,000 men. Governor-general at the time, and in over-all military command, was Sir George Prevost, who, like Frederick Haldimand before him, was Swiss by birth.

When, in July 1812, General Hull landed at Sandwich opposite Detroit at the head of 2,500 Americans, all that opposed him was a mixed force comprising 100 British regulars, 300 militia, and some 150 Indians led by the chief, Tecumseh. But General Hull was old and sick, with his heart not in it, and instead of marching on Fort Malden in Amherstburg, he procrastinated while his scouting parties fanned out in the countryside. Some of his raiding parties were ambushed, while one party of Ohio militiamen that got near Fort Malden was routed by the Indians under Tecumseh.

General Procter then arrived in the west to take command of the British and Canadian forces, and immediately went on the offensive. Hull retreated, and by August 8 was back across the river at Detroit. On August 13, General Brock, who besides being the senior military commander in Upper Canada was also its acting lieutenant-governor, arrived to direct operations. He led a small force across the river to lay siege to Fort Detroit, and Hull surrendered. A few days later, Brock hurried back to Niagara, leaving Procter in charge of the western frontier. On October 12 the Americans crossed the Niagara River near Queenston. In the battle that followed they suffered some three hundred casualties and left behind nearly one thousand prisoners. However, among the British and Canadian dead was General Brock himself, an experienced soldier with unusual powers of leadership, whom Canada could ill afford to lose.

Back in Detroit, General Procter learned early in the new year that an American force under General Harrison, one of the ablest American generals, was moving north. Taking the offensive, Procter attacked one arm of Harrison's forces with success, but he was unable in the succeeding months to prevent Harrison from establishing himself in a new fort on the Maumee River south of Detroit; nor could he dislodge the Americans from their forts on the south shore of Lake Erie. It was about this time that Captain Laurent Bondy, the ancestor of Ernest Bondy who farms in Petite Côte today, died of wounds returning from a foray on the American side.

From the spring of 1813 onwards, Procter pleaded for more men and supplies. But though promised much by Prevost, by now in Kingston, Procter received little. It was not only Procter who wanted more troops. In February 1813, some prominent citizens, including Matthew Dolsen, had signed a letter to the government which read in part: "At least 1600 men should be stationed at Amherstburg alone. . . . that from want of such a force, and the militia of the District having been kept absent from their agricultural concerns, a very large proportion of last year's crops were destroyed, and that very little wheat was sown last fall. . . ."

Procter soon had further worries. The Americans had started to build more ships, clearly intending to use them on Lake Erie. To help maintain British naval supremacy on the lake, the British laid down a new ship at Amherstburg to be called the *Detroit*, but a report made by Procter as the vessel neared completion was not reassuring: "The *Detroit* will be launched in a fortnight but her anchor is wanted in Kingston. We could lend her guns if she had seamen. . . ." Prevost was asked for additional forces with which to destroy the American vessels on the stocks. He replied: "The ordnance and stores you require must be taken from the enemy whose resources on Lake Erie must become yours."

On September 10, 1813, the naval battle was fought. Fifteen small vessels were involved — nine American and six British — among them the new *Detroit* using guns borrowed from Fort Malden. The Americans won the battle which, lilliputian though it was, laid the whole of the Canadian side of Lake Erie and Procter's flank open to attack.

General Harrison saw his moment and advanced northward. Procter's only alternative was to withdraw and this he did after burning the forts at Detroit and Amherstburg. His line of retreat was up the River Thames, the withdrawal complicated by the fact that he was accompanied by officers' wives and children, among them the Botsford family. At first he determined to make a fight for it at Dolsen's, but his threadbare men, of whom he now had fewer than nine hundred, were discouraged after months of hard service and low rations. Procter was unable to rally them. The retreat continued, with Procter losing barges, boats, and men on the way. Finally, a stand was made near Moraviantown, a mission settlement up-river from the present town of Thamesville. There Procter's small force was overwhelmed by Kentuckian cavalry. Procter escaped, but Tecumseh was killed and his Indians were dispersed.

Further east, the year 1813 saw the Americans in occupation of York, now Toronto, for a week, during which the Parliament Buildings were burned. The halting of an offensive in the Niagara Peninsula was followed by an American retreat in December to their own side of the river after setting fire to Newark, now Niagara-on-the-Lake. Still further east, Americans advancing up the St. Lawrence towards Montreal were defeated in two battles, the last at Crysler's Farm near Morrisburg. In 1814, the Americans again invaded the Niagara peninsula, to be halted in a hard-fought battle at Lundy's Lane near Niagara Falls.

Elsewhere, with the war in Europe nearing its end, the British went on the offensive. The blockade of American ports was intensified, a stretch of the Maine coastline was annexed, and in a fast-moving raid the White House and other public buildings in Washington were burned in retaliation for what the Americans had done at York. However, an attempted invasion of upper New York State was ignominiously abandoned by British and Canadian forces with Prevost scuttling back across the border, his unused and disgusted army behind him. By this time, peace negotiations were already under way in Europe and the Treaty of Ghent was signed on Christmas Eve, 1814. Sadly, the news reached America too late to prevent one further needless, and as far as the British were concerned disastrous, battle, when in January 1815, an invading force was badly cut up near New Orleans.

For the United States, the war they had initiated accomplished nothing; the attempt to add Canada to the Republic had failed, as it had done in 1776. However, the war led to a final ironing out of boundary differences, including the historic decision to place the international boundary between the Great Lakes and the Rockies on the 49th parallel.

In Upper Canada the war had left its legacy of bitterness. Turncoats who had helped the Americans were hanged; others who had fled to the United States had their property confiscated. There was considerable war damage, most of it in what is now south-western Ontario, where from the time of Procter's defeat in the fall of 1813 to the end of the war the Americans had been virtually free to come and go as they pleased. Thus a typical report in January 1814 reads: "The enemy passed Arnold's (near Dolsen's) in number about 130, on their return to Detroit on the 20th ult.; followed by their cavalry, about 60, on the 22nd. They took with them all the flour and grain. . . . They burned Arnold's barn on retiring."

The most devastating raid of all occurred in October 1814. A column of 750 men moved north from Detroit, crossed the St. Clair River, and came into Kent County from the north. Foraging and burning, the American raiders moved up the Thames River as far as Oxford — now called Ingersoll — before turning south and returning to Detroit along the Talbot Road.

One final postcript to the war: in December 1814, a court-martial that was convened in Montreal found General Procter "negligent and deficient" in his handling of the retreat from Amherstburg. It marked the end of his military career. This seemed a shabby way to treat a man who, when all was said and done, had fought bravely and had held the western frontier for over a year with inadequate supplies and forces.

Such were the turbulent beginnings of Essex and Kent counties. Nowhere else in Ontario are there living on the same land descendants of families that helped establish settlements that were growing and prospering at a time when the rest of the province was the domain of the Indians. And nowhere else in Ontario are such vital and living links with the French past.

Today, with their level fields of beans, tomatoes, peas, sweet corn, cucumbers, and other vegetables, it might be said that these two western counties are the market garden of Ontario. But they are much more than that. Kent County grows more grain corn than any other county in Ontario and most of the seed corn, while Kent and Essex together produce two-thirds of Ontario's crop of soya beans. This agricultural wealth is the result of the richness of the soil, the benign climate (Point Pelee in Essex County is the most southerly point in Canada, reaching southwards as far as California does northwards), and the level terrain, which allows for a very high degree of mechanization.

The main problem with this low-lying, if extremely fertile, land is drainage. It was the prevalence of swamps about which the early settlers could do little that held back settlement of the area. Not until an amendment to the Municipal Act was passed in 1866 were municipalities allowed to borrow money for drainage projects and was any real progress made towards reclaiming the wetlands. In the following fifteen years, thousands of acres were drained and brought into production. Today the "government" drains that transect the area with their weirs and pumping stations are prominent features in the flat and ordered landscape of Kent County, while, with some searching, it is still possible to locate the impressive remains of the great wooden and iron "dash wheels" that, in the past, raised the water in the dikes from one level to another.

Of those families that crossed the Detroit River in 1796 to remain under the British flag, some, like the Botsfords, went to Amherstburg; others went north to settle along the Thames River or near Lake St. Clair. Many stayed opposite Detroit, to form the village of Sandwich. Some two miles away, the village of Windsor came into being on land that was part of Colonel François Bâby's farm. It was a stage-coach stop and the place where passengers got down from the coach and into the log canoe that was the ferry over to Detroit. By 1833, Windsor boasted nearly twenty houses and was likely, one traveller said, "soon to eclipse Sandwich and . . . rival Chatham". Later, another traveller commented that "the village of Windsor is a new place, formed in consequence of the American tariff, to enable the inhabitants to smuggle British goods across the river. . . . a man coming over from Detroit buys cloth for a suit of clothes, gets them made, and then marches to Detroit with the new clothes on his back and the old ones in a bundle, under the very nose of the Collector of Customs." That was in the 1840s. *Plus ça change, plus c'est la même chose.*

Today the city of Windsor looms over the fertile fields of Essex County, while from miles away across the flat landscape, one can see the traffic thundering ceaselessly along the Macdonald-Cartier Freeway.

The Dolson Family
Raleigh Township
Kent County

The Indians called the river Eskunissippi; early French voyageurs called it Rivière la Tranche, winding as it did then between high banks topped by tall trees. Governor Simcoe travelled along it on his way to Detroit with Joseph Brant and twenty Indians — "no European having gone that track,"[3] his wife wrote — and renamed the river Thames. For years it provided the only highway into the heart of the prairie, swamp, and forest that is now Kent County.

Roger and Winifred Dolson live on the banks of the Thames River on a farm long known as the oldest in Kent County. Their first Canadian ancestor was named Van Dolzen, a man of property who fled from Northumberland County, Pennsylvania, to Niagara with other Loyalist families during the American Revolution. Their family name has evolved since to Dolsen and then Dolson.

The first Van Dolzen eventually left Niagara, preferring to settle at Petite Côte, across the river from Detroit. When Patrick McNiff surveyed the course of the River Thames in the fall of 1790, two of Van Dolzen's seven sons were established on its banks: Isaac on the south or what would become the Raleigh Township side, where the present Dolsons still live, and Matthew across the river in the future Dover Township.

During the Revolutionary War, Matthew Dolsen, according to his own statement, "was harassed and imprisoned in Northumberland

Jail on account of his loyalty to the British Government, and was obliged to leave his farm, and lost his crop and all his cattle and stock as the rebels threatened his life. He fled to [New] York to join General Clinton [but] was taken and imprisoned and one of his brothers killed by his side. . . . He made his escape after being long confined, and came to Niagara. . . ."[4]

At Niagara, Matthew Dolsen joined Butler's Rangers. Later he made his way to Detroit, where he bought a lot; he also purchased a farm in Petite Côte near that of his father. When he moved to the banks of the Thames in Dover Township, he established a grist-mill, a distillery, a tavern, and a blacksmith shop. Matthew is believed to have built one of the first ships on the Thames River, in which he ferried goods back and forth to Detroit. So prosperous did his settlement become that it was referred to simply as Dolsen's, and it was the most important centre in what is now Kent County until about 1818, when it was superseded by Chatham.

Between the years 1798 and 1810, the Dolsen family received large land grants in Raleigh and Dover townships, including a grant of two hundred acres to Hannah Field, wife of Matthew Dolsen. Hannah was no less a character than her husband, and with the nearest doctor some fifty miles away in Sandwich she acted as unofficial physician to the settlements. An oft-repeated family anecdote concerns two young daughters of Thomas and Martha Smith who in the winter of 1798 became lost in a blizzard. They were not found for twenty-four hours and by that time, Mary, aged eleven, was dead. Ann, aged thirteen, was still alive but her legs were frozen. Hannah Dolsen, aware of the danger of gangrene, amputated both her legs, operating on the kitchen table without antiseptics or anaesthetic except, perhaps, some of Matthew's whisky and a bullet to chew on.

Martha Smith, the mother of Mary and Ann, survived these tragic events by less than two months; Ann Smith lived for another seventy-two years. When she died she left a grant of land for the erection of the church of St. Thomas, Dover, over the graves of her parents and her sister.

The location of their lots on either side of the river embroiled the Dolsens in the events of the War of 1812. Members of an American raiding party seized flour, whisky, and salt from the home of Isaac Dolsen, then camped for the night at Matthew Dolsen's, making off with bales containing four hundred Hudson's Bay Company blankets and a roll of cloth. Then, in the fall of 1813, General Procter's retreating army stopped at Matthew Dolsen's on the night of October 1. In addition to baggage, supplies, and women and children, Procter had with him Chief Tecumseh and some eight hundred Indians.

Fast on Procter's heels came General Harrison's American force including the mounted but undisciplined Kentuckians. Like Procter, Harrison sent his heavy baggage and stores up the river in boats — fifty of them protected by three gun-boats. On the night of October 3 the Americans were camped four miles below Matthew Dolsen's, but they caught up with Procter on October 5 and defeated him at Moraviantown, where Tecumseh was killed. On their return down-river, the American infantry again camped at Dolsen's. Their depredations and those of the Indians, plundering and pillaging as they went, almost ruined the settlers. But the Dolsens and others like them were spared an even worse fate: General Harrison's orders to wipe out all settlements on the Thames River were countermanded by the American president, James Madison, and never put into effect.

Among Roger and Winifred Dolson's old family documents is the will of Daniel Dolsen, who died in 1853. Its legal description of the land holding reads: "commencing near the centre of the said lot fourteen at the centre of a large walnut tree now standing near the River Thames, then south forty-five degrees east seventy-five chains, then north forty-five degrees east sixteen chains, then north forty-five degrees west to the River Thames aforesaid, and then westerly along the water's edge with the stream to a point at north forty-five degrees west from the centre of the said walnut tree, thence south forty-five degrees east to the centre of the said tree."

Trees were perhaps more reliable markers than survey stakes, which, if they did not suit the settlers, were often removed, but one of Roger Dolson's three sons who tried to follow these directions found himself in a hopeless muddle, the "said walnut tree" having long since disappeared.

Victorian piety is mixed with practical details in the old Dolsen wills: "My son Daniel is to reserve my watch. My wife Elizabeth is to live on the said farm and to receive thirty dollars a year while she shall live."

"There were those who were favourites and those who weren't," Roger Dolson adds. "There was one heir who was left a single dollar."

The Dolsons live in a brick house that was built about ninety years ago for Roger Dolson's uncle, who was planning to be married when he died suddenly of appendicitis. Across the road on the river bank is the old Dolsen cemetery, including the graves of a Gilbert Dolsen and three of his four wives. Erosion from the river has eaten into the bank and the headstones have been moved. The average age of the dead is fourteen years and there are many infants.

"My grandfather had six hundred and forty acres here," Roger

Dolson says. "Now all that's left is one hundred. . . . I turned over to cash crops about twenty-five years ago. Now I rent the land out. None of my sons will take over the farm; I expect when I'm gone it will be sold. Chatham keeps gobbling up the land. It's only two miles away.

"Buy a farm? You'd never pay for it. Land along the road here, you could get three thousand an acre for it. How in the world could you pay that and farm? You just couldn't do it."

The Botsford Family
Maple Hill Farm
Malden Township
Essex County

By 1635 King Charles I of England had manoeuvred himself into a disastrous position. He desperately needed money to pay for ships to protect England in the French and Dutch wars, but there was no Parliament to vote him any. He had dissolved it himself six years earlier. Pawning the Crown jewels was one expedient to raise funds. Another was the imposition of a tax known as "Ship Money", a method by which funds were raised to provide new vessels for the navy.

The "Ship Money" tax caused widespread consternation. John Hampden, a Buckinghamshire squire, contested its legality in one of the great cases in English judicial history, a case he ultimately lost. So great was the antagonism aroused by the tax that many people left England for the American colonies, among them the Botsford family.

The Botsfords were Congregationalists. "Old traditional hard-shells" their descendant, David Botsford of Amherstburg, calls them, and their family history reflects the uncompromising independence of this nonconformist faith. They left the little town of Shalgrove in Hertfordshire for Milford, Connecticut, in 1637, along with thirty or forty other families under the Reverend Peter Prudden, and in Connecticut they established a short-lived form of communal government based upon the Bible.

David Botsford's great-great-grandfather, Henry Botsford, went from Connecticut to Detroit and there became a captain in the Provincial Marine of Upper Canada. He married a girl of French and Indian descent, and after Detroit was ceded to the Americans following the War of Independence, this Loyalist family moved across the Detroit River to Essex County, where, on June 8, 1790, Henry

Botsford had bought a lot in Petite Côte facing the Detroit River from Matthew Dolsen. The Botsfords were, in David Botsford's words, "professional and professed patriots".

Continuing the story of his family, David Botsford says that his great-great-grandfather was later in charge of the small boats on the River Thames during General Procter's retreat in the 1812 war, when officers' wives and children were trying to keep up with the army. "My great-grandmother was a baby at the time, and her mother had brought along a pillow to lay her on. When the Americans caught up with them, a soldier, looking for gold, ripped open the pillow, scattering the feathers. My great-grandmother was very indignant and protested to the American general. 'Ma'am,' he said, 'you must excuse them. They are wild men from Kentucky and I can't do anything with them.'"

After the War of 1812, the Botsfords bought the land near Amherstburg on which they still live. It had been first owned by a Commodore Grant, whose daughter was shot through the cheeks in the retreat up the Thames River, and her executors sold it to David Botsford's great-grandfather. Today, David Botsford, his wife, Effie Loretta, his brother, Andrew, and a son and grandchildren, live in a family complex of three houses and grow cash crops as the family has always done — now corn and soya beans.

Before his retirement, David Botsford was curator of the Fort Malden Museum and his knowledge of local genealogy and history is prodigious. Life for the first two generations on the Botsford farm was hard, he says. They relied for food principally on hogs and corn. There were few schools, and consequently grandparents were better educated than their grandchildren, rather than the reverse. Two of the second generation on the land, David's great-uncles, went off to fight in the American Civil War and one was a prisoner of war in the south. There was intense Canadian interest in this struggle. When news of Lincoln's assassination reached the area, there was a spontaneous observation of a day of mourning. The Botsfords remember this because "our old barn on the farm was being built at the time, but work was knocked off as soon as the news was heard."

David Botsford's grandfather raised general-purpose horses on the farm, "good enough for the road, but heavy enough for the plough". The family grew tobacco, and then David's father became interested in cattle — first in Jerseys, then in Holsteins.

"In the 1890s my family started a retail dairy in Amherstburg and it ran until 1932, when the extra cost of pasteurization put it out of business. It was hard to make a living from the dairy because there were five or six in the town where two would have done. We managed for a time because we had the contract to supply milk to the men on the American tugs and dredgers that worked on the channel in the Detroit River. But the hours were terrible. We had to meet the schedule of the tugs and this meant sometimes supplying milk at midnight or at two o'clock in the morning. And we had other troubles . . . our customers became our friends and when hard times hit, we had to carry them. After a while we had more debts on the books than we could sustain. . . ."

The earliest European history of this part of Essex County belongs to the French Canadians. By 1776, there were more than two thousand settlers on both sides of the Detroit River, keeping cattle, sheep, horses, and hogs. While not noted for the excellence of their farming, the French left one notable legacy. This was their cultivation of fruit trees and especially of pears, the seeds of which were said to have been imported from Normandy by French missionaries. Later, David Botsford's great-uncle had an orchard with many named varieties of fruit, including the Botsford pear, named after him. One russet pear tree in the Botsfords' garden is now over a century old.

In spite of an attempt to promote dairy products in Ontario between 1880 and 1890, Essex was never much of a dairy county, "because Essex farmers didn't like to be tied down." "As far as I know," David Botsford continues, "there was only one cheese factory in the area on the Anderdon-Malden town line. It was sold and the building became the Cheese Factory School with the cooling-room used as a church." Around 1910, fluid milk was sold in Detroit, transported by the electric-car service that ran between Amherstburg and Windsor at the time, then across the river to Detroit in cans, "but a tariff imposed by the States put an end to that.

"Amherstburg was once a British naval shipyard and the farmers in the area were offered a bonus for growing hemp for cordage. After the War of 1812 there was no market for hemp, but it had run wild by this time and can still be found wherever the ground is extra rich. . . ." Like flax, David Botsford says, it had to be retted down, a process by which the fibres were softened by soaking. "There was a certain sickness associated with the retting. The active ingredient in the hemp was absorbed through the skin and this gave the people who worked with it hives." Today, hemp is more commonly known as marijuana, and considerable surprise was caused locally in 1977 when an acre of it was found growing inside a cornfield in Kent County.

David Botsford also has something to say about growing tobacco.

"The Jesuits found tobacco growing in the Indian settlements on the south side of Georgian Bay in the early 1600s, and around Amherstburg it was grown by fugitive slaves in the 1820s. These former slaves had small holdings and seven or eight acres of tobacco would support one family. But it was hard work. All the hoeing and planting and picking off the bugs had to be done by hand. The method of curing was air drying and our old barn had rows and rows of nails in it on which the individual 'hands' of tobacco were hung to dry. The market for tobacco from this area was Cork, Ireland. The next upsurge in tobacco was around 1900 when it was flue-cured in kilns in the Colchester area, but gradually the land around here became too expensive to grow tobacco and the tobacco-growing area moved to Delhi."

The three houses on the Botsford farm replaced log dwellings built when three Botsford brothers married three sisters. The house in which we sit was built in 1870 from bricks made on the farm. The living-room is lined with books, and long rows of files contain David Botsford's work of genealogical research. He concludes our visit by telling the story of how his parents met. His mother, Captain Agnes Patterson, was a Scottish girl from Nova Scotia and, at the age of eighteen, an officer in the Salvation Army. She was sent to work in Ontario, but the Army was so poor at the time that there was often no money to pay for her transportation. Once relays of sleighs were organized to take her across Ontario. In 1897 "she rode into Amherstburg in the Windsor coach and met my father. . . ."

Although this Loyalist branch of the Botsford family has lived in Canada since the end of the eighteenth century, its American connections are maintained. Each year a family reunion is held on the original lot in Milford, Connecticut, which the Botsfords have owned since their resentment at the imposition of the "Ship Money" tax drove them out of England in 1637.

The Belanger Family
Dover Township
Kent County

Roland Belanger is a French-speaking Canadian whose family has lived in English Ontario since 1833. Before that they had lived since 1670 in Quebec, where some members had married into Scottish families. Intermarriage with other nationalities continued when they settled in Paincourt (or Pain Court, as the early settlers called it), some seven miles from Chatham.

"My grandmother on the Stirling side, her father was a Scottish military man," Roland Belanger says. "He could speak no French and his wife could speak no English and together they raised a family. My grandmother on the Belanger side was Pennsylvania Dutch. She died one winter and they took her body across frozen Lake St. Clair in a sleigh so that she could be buried with her own people in Michigan. Some of my relatives were named David, which is not a French name; they were Lebanese and farmed on the River Road. I am proud of all my ancestry and just thankful I'm here, that's all."

Roger Belanger farms near Paincourt on what he thinks is some of the best land in Canada. On his travels — to Brazil, the Far East, and Europe — he says he has seen none better. But until Kent County was drained, the richness of the soil was not apparent. It was a wild, swampy, and desolate land, the home of muskrat and waterfowl, bordered on the north by Lake St. Clair and intersected by the Thames River and by the Paincourt Creek.

In 1815 seven French families moved into this inhospitable landscape and settled on the creek bank a mile or so north of the river. Then in 1829 the Pain Court Block, as it came to be called, was surveyed by Charles Rankin and French families started moving in from Quebec. Until the land was cleared and drained, the settlement was desperately poor and often near starvation. Missionaries from Sandwich who came to minister to "les fidèles de la paroisse La Tranche" called the settlement "Pain Court" — the bread was short and food scarce.

Paincourt is now a village in a flat rural landscape, a French enclave within a predominantly English area. Its buildings are dominated by the Church of the Immaculate Conception, and near by are the French-language elementary and junior high schools. These three buildings are the nucleus of the French community. Roland Belanger derives a quiet satisfaction from the French culture that has survived here, one that possesses its own traditions and elements of its own language.

"My family left Normandy in 1670. When I went back to France on a visit, people could not believe that someone from Ontario would speak a French so close to Norman French." The purity of Paincourt French has always been a source of pride. An anonymous resident wrote in 1921 of a number of distinctly local words: *brunante* for twilight, *poudrerie* for blizzard, and *fret* for cold. He listed, too, the fifty-two founding families in the area, most of whom first settled in Quebec well before the end of the seventeenth century.[5]

Like many other French boys raised in Kent and Essex counties before the Second World War, Roland Belanger was educated at

Ottawa University High School, learning Latin and Greek along with thirteen other subjects. It cost about $320 a year to send a boy to school in Ottawa, a substantial outlay for some families during the Depression. During the Second World War he served in the Military Police, and he has been the French-speaking representative on the Kent County Board of Education for thirty years. In 1960 he was left a widower to bring up a family of one son and six daughters, the youngest a year old. He has encouraged all his girls to have professions "because you never know what may happen". His son is sales manager for King Grain Limited, the internationally known company founded by Albert Roy of Paincourt. "Maybe it will be the husband of one of my daughters who will take over the farm."

The original Belanger land grant of fifty acres has been expanded to five hundred. Roland Belanger and two of his brothers have incorporated themselves as a limited company, Belanger Farms Limited, operating under a charter from the province of Ontario "for farming purposes, for the protection of our children, and to retain the family farms".

On this rich land, Roland grows seed corn, peas for canning, seed wheat, seed soya bean, and Burley tobacco, having given up the mixed farming of his earlier years. The Belanger farm buildings are immaculate, so neat and well painted that they look almost like a set of a child's bright toys in the flat Paincourt landscape.

The Belanger family has come a long way since Roland Belanger's Pennsylvania-German grandmother made wheat-straw hats to send down the Thames River by chaloupe for sale in Detroit. Her grandson has travelled the world, but for him it's Canada that counts. "The survival of Canada," he says, "that's what matters to me."

The Bondy Family
Sandwich West Township
Essex County

*I*n 1733 a baby named Joseph Bondy was born at Detroit. He was the son of another Joseph Bondy, born in Montreal in 1700, the grandson of Jacques Bondy, born in Quebec in 1660, and the great-grandson of Thomas Douaire de Bondy, born in France in 1626 and drowned near his home on the St. Lawrence River, leaving a rich young widow and four small children. Thus, by 1733 the Bondy family could already claim that four generations of their family had lived in Canada, while in France their family history went back to 1486.

The Bondys followed the pattern of settlement in the Detroit River area, crossing to the Canadian side around 1748 and settling in the fertile plain of the Petite Côte district. Laurent Bondy, the son of the second Joseph, was born in 1771 and lived in Petite Côte near the Detroit River on land which the Bondys still own. Near by was the Petrimoulx grist-mill — the first mill in Sandwich West — which he operated.

Laurent Bondy was an industrious and prosperous man. During the War of 1812 he became a captain in the Militia and organized a group of Canadian volunteers, leading them across to the American side, where they met the enemy at Pointe-aux-Raisins. During the battle, Captain Bondy was mortally wounded. He lay helplessly on the beach at the foot of the rapids until his son Laurent, who had been fighting in the same battalion, laid him in a canoe and set out on the river to take him back to Petite Côte.

It was a sad crossing in the dead of night. The dying father told his son where to find his money, hidden in the stone mill. He bequeathed to Laurent his sword and his beautiful cream-coloured war-horse. Before they reached the far bank, Captain Bondy was dead.

The cache of which he had spoken was later found in the walls of the mill, paper currency that had been packed in bottles and sealed with wax. The bottles had been placed in holes and these had been carefully filled and plastered over to avoid detection. The young Laurent divided the money equally among his brothers and himself, and the war-horse was sold. But Laurent kept the sword, and it is still a treasured possession in the Bondy family.

Ernest Bondy, one of the great-grandsons of Captain Laurent Bondy, settled on a farm previously owned by his father on the Malden Road. He was Clerk of Sandwich West for over thirty years and a Justice of the Peace. His grandson, another Ernest, now lives on the same farm with his wife, the former Aline Caron of Paincourt, six sons, and one daughter. Ernest Bondy talks easily about his farm and his family. "In 1960 I bought the farm from my father. He farmed it all his life and I have farmed it all of mine, but now I do it on a part-time basis. I run an insurance business as well. I couldn't support seven children on this small farm. The original holding was bigger but it was divided about five generations ago. I have thirty-six French acres, which are not quite as large as English acres." The farm is the characteristic French shape, long and narrow.

"When I was a young man we were in pure-bred Holstein cattle. Cattle were our main business until 1961, when we sold out because bulk tanks came in. This farm was too small and we could not expand because of the price of land in this area.

"The Bondys have been in Canada for at least eleven generations. Many of them have been farmers and gardeners — perhaps gardeners more than farmers — growing vegetables for the Detroit market. At one time this area was all market garden, although I can remember some of the original bush which was not broken up until 1940. Now I grow sweet corn and peas for Green Giant of Canada. We have been growing for them ever since the company was established in Canada in 1927 and we have never missed a year. Mind you, it is much easier now because of the machinery. Some years ago we had only seven acres of sweet corn because we had to pick it all by hand. This year we had seventy at this farm and another, and the picking was all done by machine.

"My dad bought his first tractor in 1935. This year I insured a tractor in June for sixty thousand dollars and the same farmer had bought a combine in March for fifty-seven thousand dollars. One hundred and seventeen thousand dollars for two pieces of equipment! And this when farm prices have dropped. Corn is one dollar and sixty-one cents a bushel and you need at least two dollars and fifteen cents to break even."

This branch of the Bondy family has retained the French language and identity during the two hundred and more years of settlement in Petite Côte. The congregation of beautiful St. Joseph's Church, with which the Bondys have been connected for generations, has remained French-speaking and now has about six hundred French families as parishioners. But, says Ernest Bondy rather sadly, this may change as English-speaking Catholics move into the new subdivisions in River Canard. "If one family cannot speak French, then it is only polite to speak English."

Like many farmhouses, the Bondy house has been much altered in the hundred or so years of its existence, but the original stonework and beams are still in the basement. Under the carpet in the living-room is a trapdoor leading to a storage space where cases of liquor were hidden during the years of prohibition.

Outside, the barns and drive sheds form three sides of a rectangle and the impression they give is of a farm in Normandy rather than Canada. Behind them are the flat, fertile fields of the Petite Côte.

"After I left school," Ernest Bondy concludes, "I went to the Ontario Agricultural College in Guelph, but my father became ill and I quit. I was the only son to take over the farm and I've never regretted it. Farming is hard to compare with anything else; it's a way of life more than a job. If you're a real farmer, you can't be happy at anything else."

CHAPTER ELEVEN

The Huron Tract

*F*rom the earliest days in Upper Canada land had been used as a reward for services rendered. It had gone not only to Loyalist settlers, but to senior military and naval men, worthy civil servants, and members of the judiciary. One chief justice was awarded no less than 12,800 acres by a grateful administration. Even government surveyors were paid in kind, as it were.

In the 1820s it was found that a staggering eight million acres had been given away — about one-quarter of all the land that is now southern Ontario. Of these eight million acres, only three million were occupied. The rest was "wild land", much of it in the hands of speculators.

Another three million acres were locked up in what were known as the Clergy and Crown Reserves. The Clergy Reserves had been set aside to provide the established or Anglican Church with a future source of funds. In the case of the Crown Reserves, the proceeds of sales went to the administration itself, giving it, at least in theory, a degree of independence from a possibly parsimonious legislature. Some of these reserves, both Clergy and Crown, were in sizeable blocks, others were scattered throughout the townships; and these the settlers detested.

If it abutted on navigable waters, the standard township as defined in Simcoe's time consisted of a tract twelve miles deep and nine miles wide, divided on its longest axis into fourteen strips or concessions, each of which was subdivided into twenty-four lots. Inland the townships were ten miles square. But wherever they were, two out of every seven lots were withheld from settlement, one assigned to the Clergy, the other to the Crown. Thus, in a township with, say, 336 lots, there might be 96 reserved lots, scattered more or less at random, leaving some settlers boxed in by land they could never acquire, however desirable. Furthermore, uncleared land was an open invitation to squatters or illegal lumbering operations, besides providing, in early days at any rate, cover for bears and wolves.

The picture that emerges of Upper Canada in the early 1820s is of 100,000 or so people scattered for the most part in archipelagoes (or collections of islands) — as represented by the townships — with the townships themselves perhaps widely separated by undeveloped tracts owned by absentee landlords. Clearly, something had to be done to tie the whole thing together.

While pondering this problem, the Lieutenant-Governor, Sir Peregrine Maitland, was being made acutely aware by the home government of the need to economize. Indeed, his tightened budget was placing him and his administration increasingly at the mercy of the Legislative Assembly, which with its growing political maturity was showing a distressing tendency to appropriate any funds that might be available. It was time, perhaps, to cash in on the Crown Reserves; but how, with so much other land for sale, could this be done?

The answer was to come from John Galt, though he provided it in the course of addressing himself to a quite different problem — namely, how to obtain compensation for those who had lost property in the War of 1812, already some years in the past and conveniently fading from the memories of the civil servants in Whitehall.

At the time the total amount claimed in war damages was in the order of £400,000, some of it by farmers in the western counties over which the Americans had ridden rough-shod for so many months. The figure was subsequently reduced, but, even so, the British government with its many preoccupations was in no state to give its full attention to claims by settlers in what was after all only an imperial backwater. The claimants decided that Whitehall needed prodding by someone on the spot, and Galt was the man they selected to do this.

John Galt is often referred to as "John Galt the novelist", though most people would be hard put to it today to name anything he wrote. In his day, however, he had a large following. Poet and playwright, as well as novelist and biographer, Galt was a product of Scotland's "Golden Age" and ranked with Sir Walter Scott as one of Britain's leading literary figures.

But John Galt was by no means a sedentary man of letters. Son of a sea-captain turned merchant, he spent his youth in Greenock, a port redolent of history and of maritime enterprise. At the age of sixteen Galt worked in a customs house for a while to improve his penmanship and then, after a spell with a firm involved in the Canadian trade, he went into business for himself. In 1804 when he was twenty-five he took himself south to London, where he became involved in several business enterprises, all of which proved unsuccessful.

Then he was off again, this time to the Mediterranean, where he had an exciting time promoting a scheme for running cargoes of forbidden British goods into Napoleon's Europe. In 1812 he was back in Gibraltar in connection with a similar clandestine enterprise, but that too proved abortive. With his armies chased out of Spain by the Duke of Wellington, Napoleon's grip on Europe had started to loosen. It was while he was in Gibraltar that Galt first pondered what the future might hold for thousands of demobilized soldiers. Somewhere, perhaps, a place could be set aside for these men to whom Britain owed so much.

Thus, a letter that arrived in 1820 asking Galt to undertake the Canadian claimants' case struck several sympathetic chords: his curiosity about Canada, his love of far-off ventures, and his concern for the plight of the discharged soldier. The letter was of interest for another reason. Galt was hard-up at the time and the claimants were offering a commission: three per cent of whatever could be wheedled out of the government.

John Galt took up the case with enthusiasm, laid siege to Whitehall, and finally obtained an assurance that part of the claims would be met, provided the province matched the British contribution pound for pound.

Upper Canada had no money to spare and matters reached an impasse. However, after discussing the problem with Alexander MacDonell, Upper Canada's first Roman Catholic bishop, Galt came up with a solution. Why not, he suggested, form a company that would buy up the Clergy and Crown Reserves? The provincial government would be able to use the proceeds to pay off the war claims and part of the administrative expenses of the province — just what the British government wanted; while the company would make its money by developing and selling the land. Galt's idea caught on. After all, the company approach to land settlement had often met with sucess in the United States, and indeed was already being used by the British in Australia. And so, Whitehall agreeing, the Canada Company was formed, in London, with a million pounds in capital subscribed by British merchants. The Crown was to convey to the company, with some exceptions, all Crown Reserves in Upper Canada and half of the Clergy Reserves.

However, these arrangements, made as they were without so much as a nod in the direction of Upper Canada, were being viewed rather coldly by Sir Peregrine Maitland, not to mention members of the Family Compact, who were always sensitive to outside interference in the affairs of what they were coming to regard as their exclusive bailiwick. In the early 1820s this self-perpetuating oligarchy of highly placed officials and churchmen was reaching the zenith of its power, and it was one of its leading members, the Reverend John Strachan, who now raised a difficulty. He complained that the Clergy Reserves were worth far more than the Canada Company was planning to pay for them.

Rather than take on Strachan and possibly the whole of the Church of England as well, it was decided that the Clergy Reserves would be left out of the deal. The company would receive instead a tract of land in the west that had recently been acquired from the Chippewa Indians.

And so what became known as the Huron Tract came into the possession of the Canada Company. Roughly triangular in shape, with its base on the Lake Huron shore and its truncated tip nudging what had been the Indian lands in the vicinity of Waterloo, the Tract comprised most of what are now Huron and Perth counties. For just over 1,384,000 acres of Crown Reserves and 1,100,000 acres in the Huron Tract, the company paid £344,375.7.2d., roughly ninety cents an acre at the rate of exchange then prevailing.

The company was allowed to withhold part of the purchase price to pay for capital improvements in the Tract. The rest was to be paid in the form of annual instalments, out of which were to come monies to run the provincial civil service, thus allowing the home government to withdraw its annual grants. Other sums were to go to the support of the Roman Catholic and Presbyterian churches and towards the construction of a college. Out of the same money Colonel Talbot was to be paid a pension of four hundred pounds a year, while officers of the land department, who were being done out of their fees in connection with Crown Lands they no longer had to administer, were to be suitably compensated. Finally, whatever was left over was the provincial government's to use as it wished.

The only people, it seems, who got nothing whatsoever out of the deal were those who, in a sense, had started it all — the claimants for war damage. In fact, though Galt did not know it, they had been left out of the negotiations right from the start. In the course of time, however, they were to be partially compensated.

As for John Galt, he was now the excited Superintendent of the Canada Company. Reaching Upper Canada in December of 1826, Galt was soon bustling about the provincial capital at York promoting the company's affairs, and in his obstinate and impulsive way he succeeded in offending the Lieutenant-Governor within two days of his arrival. However, he had no time for the niceties of protocol as he busied himself with his plans and maps, and issued instructions to his fellow Scot and right-hand man, "Tiger" Dunlop.

Dr. Dunlop had seen active service in Upper Canada during the 1812 war when as an army surgeon with the 89th Foot he ran emergency field hospitals at the battles of Crysler's Farm and Lundy's Lane. With the war at an end, he became bored with barrack life at York, a "dirty straggling village" in his words, and volunteered to help build a military road from Lake Simcoe to Penetanguishene on Georgian Bay. It was then that he fell in love with the frontiersman's life, a love that was never to leave him.

In 1815 the 89th was ordered back to England — Napoleon had returned from Elba to enjoy his last short-lived return to power — but the regiment was still on the sea the day that Waterloo was fought, and by the time it landed the war was over. Dunlop, now on half-pay and at a loose end, shipped out to India, there to become involved, curiously enough, in another land development scheme on the Hoogli River, where an over-abundance of tigers was apparently standing in the way of orderly settlement. It was his alleged prowess in eliminating this unusual environmental hazard that earned him his nickname.

Back in Britain after a bout of fever, "Tiger" Dunlop eventually gravitated to London, where he worked as a journalist, and it was there that he met John Galt, who offered him a job with the Canada Company. He was to become Warden of Woods and Forests, an appealing if somewhat romantic title, exactly the sort of job he was looking for.

Capable and energetic, this massive red-headed man was to become something of a living legend in Upper Canada, going about his business in bush-clothes and trailing clouds of snuff. Fond of practical jokes and a perennial bachelor who liked to know where his next drink was coming from, "Tiger" Dunlop made a host of friends, from the highly placed to the newly arrived settler.

In the spring following their arrival in Canada, John Galt and the "Tiger" were to found the city of Guelph. Galt had decided that the start of the company's operations in the Huron Tract should be marked by an occasion of suitable solemnity and he had stage-managed a small ceremony centring upon the felling of a symbolic tree. As it happened, he and Dunlop managed to lose themselves in the woods on their way to the selected spot where others awaited them, while to make matters worse they got soaked in a torrential downpour. However, they arrived at the rendezvous by nightfall and Galt held his little ceremony, though he found Dunlop's efforts to turn the whole thing into a party a little jarring. A tree was duly felled and as of April 23, 1827, there was a Guelph in Upper Canada.

John Galt had chosen the name in honour of the Royal Family — whose family name it was — and in doing so he put his foot in it again. The directors of the company in London had thought it would be politic to name the new town after Viscount Goderich, who happened to be Chancellor of the Exchequer. They insisted that Guelph was not Guelph but Goderich, and went on so insisting for several months. But Galt was adamant, though he made amends by giving the name of Goderich to another townsite on the shores of Lake Huron, selected by "Tiger" Dunlop in the course of a strenuous summer-long survey of the Tract that he embarked on within a few days of the famous tree-felling ceremony.

For all his snuff, whisky, and boisterous approach to life, Dunlop was an erudite man, his reports to the Canada Company ranging knowledgeably over a wide variety of subjects and not without touches of humour. Thus, in an account of the Huron Tract that deals with its geology, waterways, forest cover, and soil fertility, he gets on to the subject of swamps, of which the Tract contained not a few. "It may be proper to mention the dry swamp *lux a non lucendo* for it is no swamp at all, but cedar and swamp being so indissolubly associated in the brain of a Canadian that he is puzzled to account for the former without the presence of the latter, so when he finds cedar growing on dry land he immediately pronounces it to be a dry swamp, which incongruous appellation I doubt not he would apply to Mount Lebanon itself."[1]

On his return from his survey of the Tract, Dunlop threw himself into the task of preparing Guelph for settlers. The next summer, that of 1828, he was back in the bush again cutting an eighty-mile trail from Waterloo to Goderich, via what is now Stratford. It was an appalling summer — "unprecedently unfavourable for outdoor occupations" in Dunlop's view; "the rains fell so incessantly . . . that on an average, taking advantage of every fair moment there was not three days work obtained in each week. . . ."[2]

Bad weather was not Dunlop's only problem. Commenting that he and his work-crews were lucky to escape the "malignant remitting fever" that gripped the province that summer, he goes on to say that "agues and milder fevers frequently terminating in dysenteric complaints were exceedingly common. . . ."[3]

Bad weather and disease notwithstanding, Dunlop got his men through to Goderich, and what's more, turned them right round again and set them widening and improving the trail to make it passable for wagons, laying the road that one day would become

Highway 8. By the end of that summer the job was done and the interior of the Tract and what are now Perth and Huron counties were accessible from both east and west.

In concluding his report on those months of ferociously hard work, Dunlop made a recommendation that throws an interesting light on the range of abilities expected in those days from an educated man. Such medical men as the company chose to send to Upper Canada should also, he suggested, be mineralogists as well as good naturalists.

"Tiger" Dunlop was to stay with the Canada Company for a number of years. Later he went into politics, to become, rather sadly, something of an anachronism, a relic of frontier life in a world increasingly dominated by the businessman. He ended his days as Superintendent of the Lachine Canal, dying in a shabby house on the canal's edge in 1848. However, the sordidness of his surroundings on the day of his death was more than made up for by the dignity of the place where he was buried — a site he shares with his brother high on a bluff overlooking the Maitland River and the town of Goderich which he founded.

John Galt, for all his dedication, enthusiasm, and hard work as Superintendent, was soon superseded. The company directors in London thought he was spending too much with too little result. He was recalled in the spring of 1829 after being on the job for just over two years. He arrived in England totally destitute.

All those in the provincial hierarchy on whose toes he had trodden so firmly were glad to see the last of him no doubt. From the directors and shareholders of the company that he had so successfully launched he received not so much as a vote of thanks. Only the settlers themselves were sorry to see him go. For whatever bad name the Canada Company was to acquire in later years, under John Galt it had been honest and humane in its dealings.

Back in England and unable to disentangle his financial affairs from those of the Canada Company, he declared himself bankrupt at one point, to find himself consigned to a debtors' prison. Meanwhile, he took to his writing again and became involved in other settlement schemes, this time in Lower Canada. Five years before his death in 1839, he was still being dunned by the Canada Company for an alleged debt.

In the eleven years between 1829 and 1840 the Canada Company settled over six thousand people in the Huron Tract, and among them were the forebears of the century farms whose family history is told in the pages that follow. As for the Canada Company itself, it was also long-lived. In fact it was not finally wound up until 1953, though by then its activities were confined to the administration of farm mortgages — and some of those too were over a century old.

The Whyte Family
Holm Farm
Hullett Township
Huron County

On June 7, 1932, Margaret McMillan Whyte's father, Thomas McMillan, died after being crushed by a horse. It was one of a series of family tragedies that left Margaret, then unmarried, in charge of a large farm at the age of twenty-one. In the space of a few years she had lost her mother, both her brothers, and her father.

Margaret Whyte's grandfather, John McMillan, left Scotland in 1843. His was a background of poverty and he never had more than a year of schooling in his life. He broke a seven-year apprenticeship to a shoemaker by running away after four years to work for eighteen hours a day in an ironworks in Lanarkshire, earning by this means enough money for a steerage passage to Canada.

John McMillan took up land from the Canada Company in Hullett Township, Huron County, in 1844. He built a log cabin at the back of the property near a spring-fed creek, and over the next seven years chopped, cleared, and fenced ten acres of hardwood bush. So discouraging was this period that he would gladly have returned to the hardships of Scotland; nevertheless, he possessed some notable qualities: great physical strength, an ability to learn and to apply what he had learned, wit, force, and a ready command of language. It was only a matter of time before he became one of the most successful and innovative farmers in the county. In 1880 he was selected as a member of the Agricultural Commission appointed to report on farming conditions in Ontario. He lectured at the Ontario Agricultural College, Guelph, and in 1882 was elected to the House of Commons as Liberal member for South Huron. Before his death in 1901 he would be re-elected three times.

For many years John McMillan and his youngest son, Thomas, were the largest patrons of the local cheese factory, milking from twenty to twenty-five cows. The McMillans were among the first in Ontario to use silos. They built one of octagonal shape in the corner of the barn about 1889 and erected "a huge cement structure" about 1897.[4] Forty acres of corn were needed to fill the silos, all cut by men with short-handled hoes. In later years, Tom McMillan grew sweet clover for silage.

In 1879, the McMillans built a large barn to house a beef operation that would thrive for forty-eight consecutive years. Tom McMillan crossed the Atlantic many times taking cattle to sell in Glasgow, and for five years between 1893 and 1898, the McMillan cattle fetched the highest price for imported cattle on the Glasgow market. By bringing back Clydesdale horses, Tom McMillan also made a profit on his return voyage, on one occasion as much as a thousand dollars for a carload, a tidy sum for the day.

Cattle were also exported to the United States. The Buffalo *Daily Record* had this to say of the McMillan cattle in 1913: "The two highest priced loads of Canadian steers that were ever marketed here were sold today, the price being $13.50. Opinion among order buyers . . . was generally that they were beyond doubt the best finished cattle that were ever offered for sale at Buffalo out of the Dominion. . . ."[5]

In 1890 Tom McMillan built a large brick house on the farm and the following year he married Mary McLean, a local girl and an admirable helpmate. "They had four children," Margaret Whyte says. "John, born in 1892; William, born in 1895; a daughter who died at birth; and myself, born in 1911. It seemed in some ways that I was an only child, my brothers were so much older — sixteen and nineteen years older — but I grew up in a very happy family. I can't remember anything unpleasant about my childhood at all."

Like his father, Tom McMillan was elected Liberal member for South Huron in 1925. Then, when Margaret was fifteen, her mother became seriously ill. "My father was on his way to Ottawa for a crucial vote, but they wired him at Kingston to get off the train and come home. Mother was dying."

The year after, Tom McMillan took Margaret with him to Ottawa. She accompanied him to many events, including the opening of Parliament, and, although she was a girl of only sixteen, to a ball at Government House. She recalls how proud she was of her father and remembers, too, that she heard the carillon in the tower of the Houses of Parliament ring for the first time in 1927 to commemorate the Diamond Jubilee of Confederation.

Margaret's older brother, John, had died in 1921. "He was corn-harvesting for a neighbour and a boil behind his ear became infected. He came home sick on Tuesday night and he was dead on Saturday." Her brother William died suddenly of a heart attack in 1931 at the age of thirty-six.

"I said I'd stay at home," Margaret Whyte says. "My father was still a member of Parliament, but we had a housekeeper and we had hired men. In June of the following year, my father was home and he and a hired man were cutting the hoof of a young horse. It lunged and pinned him against a stall, rupturing his pancreas. He died the next day. . . . So there I was, twenty-one years old and left with a big farm.

"Dignitaries from Ottawa came to the funeral, including Prime Minister Mackenzie King. Later, I was approached by both the Minister of Justice and the Postmaster General, who asked if I would stand for Parliament instead of my father. They thought that if I did, a by-election might be avoided. But I felt inadequate and I refused."

While a student at Macdonald Institute in Guelph, Margaret McMillan had met a young man named Wilfred Whyte. She married "Nick" Whyte and they had a family of six children. For a time the Whytes carried on feeding steers, just as Tom McMillan had done, but Nick's main interest was in poultry. In the 1940s he built one of the first large broiler barns in Ontario. In January 1963, just after sixteen hundred broilers had been loaded out for market, the barn burned. There was a blizzard at the time and the snow was so deep that fire engines could not reach it. The Whytes replaced the building with their present far larger and fully automated barn holding up to ten thousand broilers.

Over the years the Whyte farm has grown and is now fourteen hundred acres in extent. Margaret Whyte's four sons handle its management and operation. The old cattle barn still stands, and near it is the silo described as a "huge cement structure" in 1897 but small to modern eyes. The outlines of the old brick house are solidly late-Victorian; inside are many mementoes of the family's past. An imposing front staircase leads upwards to bedrooms furnished with beautiful old wooden high-backed beds made locally in Seaforth. Behind the kitchen is a portion of an earlier building, a frame house built by John McMillan.

Like many century farmers, Margaret Whyte fully appreciates her farm, and her family history. "We all have so very much to be grateful for . . . a priceless heritage from our forebears."

The Hodgins Family
Biddulph Township
Middlesex County

"You have to realize that I'm a farmer. I like to have a field in hay for a year or two, then pasture it for a year or two. After that I plough it up and sow wheat on it. Then I sow corn on the wheat stubble, then grain on the corn ground and seed it down again.

Then it's a couple of years in hay or pasture. I've always firmly believed that your land will stay good forever if you follow a rotation like that. Some modern farmers seem to think that you can grow corn for fifty years in a row. There may be money in it, but there's also trouble."

The speaker is Austin Hodgins of the Coursey Line, near Lucan in Biddulph Township, about nineteen miles north of London. In discussing crop rotation, he is touching on a subject about which at least something has been known since the time of the Romans. It was practised in medieval Britain, and, later, such English agricultural innovators as "Turnip" Townshend and Coke of Norfolk focussed the attention of English and Scots farmers on the significance of rotation if land is to be kept alive and fertile. The Roman poet Virgil, himself a farmer, advocated crop rotation in 29 B.C. when he published *The Georgics*, a handbook for Roman farmers, written in verse, that is also a plea, familiar enough, for greater government recognition of the importance of agriculture. Thus we find Virgil telling us, for example, that barley exhausts the soil and must be rotated with leguminous crops such as beans if the land is to retain its health. Austin Hodgins makes much the same point with his reference to corn.

Lieutenant-Colonel James Hodgins — "Big Jim" Hodgins — was the first white settler in Biddulph Township. He was born in 1785 in Ireland, near Nenagh, Tipperary County, and was a descendant, it is said, of an officer in Cromwell's Irish army. In 1832 he and a few close relatives decided to emigrate to Canada, where James's three brothers, John, Adam, and Thomas, were already working on the Rideau Canal. Adam Hodgins had helped with the survey of the Huron Tract the previous year and this is assumed to be the reason why James Hodgins made his way westwards and took up a lot on Concession 3 of Biddulph Township, a lot that is still in the possession of the Hodgins family.

James Hodgins' sons and some of the relatives who had come with him settled on the same line, at first known as "Big Jim's Line" but later as the "Coursey Line" with the arrival of several families of that name.

In 1835 James Hodgins became an agent for the Canada Company, selling farms in Biddulph Township. "It was rather like a modern lottery," his great-great-grandson, Austin Hodgins, says. "It seemed that if he sold so many farms he got one free. He ended up with fourteen farms, and as he had five sons, the farms were distributed among them and among the relatives who came from Ireland."

James Hodgins also secured a grant of several acres of land for the erection of St. James Church, Clandeboye, where a cairn and a tablet were erected to his memory in 1932, a century after his arrival.

In Ireland, James Hodgins had been chief of the Royal Irish Constabulary at Borrisokane, Tipperary. When the Mackenzie Rebellion broke out in 1837, he drilled recruits for protection against the rebels and was appointed lieutenant-colonel of the 6th Battalion of the Huron Militia.

In 1844, Colonel Hodgins returned to Ireland to encourage other families to emigrate to Canada. Owing partially to his efforts, Biddulph Township became largely an Irish settlement, part Protestant and part Catholic. The Irish emigrants, some of whose families had suffered poverty and degradation in Ireland for centuries, brought with them to Biddulph the hatreds of the past and the secret societies — the Oak Boys, the Whiteboys, the Ribbon Men — that in the bogs and lonely glens of Ireland had dispensed their own kind of hedgerow justice.

Among the families whom the Colonel induced to come to Canada were the Donnellys. The story of the Donnelly feud and of the brutal murder of James Donnelly and his family near Lucan in 1880 has been told many times. It is possible, Austin Hodgins says, that the Colonel may have given Jim Donnelly permission to squat on a farm on the Roman Line — the cause of all the trouble. When Jim Donnelly was sentenced to be hanged for the murder of Patrick Farrell in a drunken brawl, it was Colonel Hodgins who drew up and signed the petition for leniency that resulted in the sentence's being commuted to seven years' imprisonment. Until his death, Colonel Hodgins remained the Donnellys' friend. "There's just one God, and that's 'Big Jim' Hodgins," Jim Donnelly is reported to have said. "He took the rope from around my neck. . . ."

Colonel Hodgins represented Biddulph in the Huron District Council in 1842. He was the first elected Reeve of Biddulph and a Justice of the Peace, setting an example of public service that many of his descendants have followed.

"Deputy" John Hodgins, a son of the Colonel, was Deputy Reeve of Biddulph Township from 1868 to 1872 and Reeve from 1872 to 1876. His son, Charles Constantine, was successively Deputy Reeve, Reeve, Warden of Middlesex County, and a member of the legislature of Ontario. In 1894, Adam Hodgins was a member of Parliament in Ottawa. In 1964, Wilson Hodgins was elected Reeve of Biddulph Township — the fifth generation, including the Colonel, to fill the Reeve's chair.

Austin Hodgins has been no exception to this family tradition. He has served the township for thirty years as councillor, reeve, and township clerk. "I only missed one council meeting and that was when I was on my honeymoon." He has been elected by acclamation in twelve consecutive elections. As reeve, he had to attend County Council meetings in London, some nineteen miles away. At the time he was milking sixteen cows. During the evening break between five and eight o'clock ("I was never much of a man for a drink"), he would drive home, milk the cows, have his dinner, and be back in his chair on time.

Austin Hodgins served in the 23rd Field Artillery, 4th Canadian Armoured Division, during the Second World War. He met his wife, Dolly, in Holland in 1945 after the fighting was over. She came to Canada in May 1951 and they were married in September of that year.

"When I got home from the war in 1946 my father had been farming for thirty years. He was worse off than he had been when he started. I took over the farm and the debts. We had good times after the war. Everything you touched made money. We were young, strong, and ambitious, and we just went as hard as we could go.

"For the first few years I had sixteen Ayrshire/Shorthorn cows that I milked by hand, two hours in the morning and two hours in the evening. After about five years I bought a milking-machine and increased the herd to twenty, which I could then milk in half the time. I bred these cows to a Hereford bull and would buy about ten-or twelve-day-old Hereford calves, so that I raised about thirty each year. In the fall I would buy a carload of western Hereford calves, making a total of ninety; I would feed them in the barn for the winter, grass them on the River Farm in the summer, then sell them in the fall."

With the proceeds from selling hogs and cattle, Austin Hodgins soon had the land paid for. Then, in 1971 the barn blew down, so he cut back on the stock. "The Clerk's job takes up more and more of my time, so now I keep twenty-six cows and four sows, and whatever they raise I keep until they are finished."

There are still eight Hodgins families, including Austin Hodgins', on the Coursey Line. Vincent Hodgins lives on the Colonel's old lot; down the road, Rosco Hodgins operates a farm airstrip with five aircraft used mainly for crop- and forest-spraying.

Then there's Clint. A story goes that Clinton Hodgins, who lives near by, had to be tied into the seat of a sulky by his father, "Racehorse" Sid, so that he could exercise horses at the age of four. Clint devoted his life to harness-racing and in 1973 became a member of the United States Harness Writers' Living Hall of Fame.

A colourful character on or off the racetrack, he owns a stock farm in Orlando, Florida, and one adjoining his home in Biddulph. Clint was born in 1906, and if it were not for ill-health, Austin Hodgins says, he would be driving horses still.

By contrast, Austin Hodgins has devoted his life to his farm and to the township. The interior of his house reflects a mixture of two cultures — Canadian and Dutch. In his study, with a view across the fields from the window, Biddulph Township papers are neatly stacked. A portrait of the Colonel, whose years of service to the township have been matched by succeeding generations, hangs on the wall, an expression of approval in his gaze.

The Stevens Family
Stonetown Farms
Blanshard Township
Perth County

Since May 2, 1670, when King Charles II granted a charter to the Hudson's Bay Company, the fur trade has been big business. In 1978 finished furs to the value of over two hundred million dollars were sold in Canada, with exports amounting to more than seventy million dollars.

David R. Stevens of St. Marys, south of Stratford, Ontario, is a century farmer who is a breeder of the mink and fox that go into the making of Canadian fur coats. He is also a Master Breeder of Holstein cattle and a breeder of pure-bred Yorkshire hogs.

David was born on Lot 5, Concession 15, in Blanshard Township, where his great-grandfather, Faithful Stevens, settled on land obtained from the Canada Company in 1853. Faithful Stevens came from Cornwall, England. The names of his two brothers — Peaceful and Thankful — suggest that the family were perhaps Puritans or Quakers.

The lot that Faithful Stevens chose is on low hills where the Avon and Thames rivers meet, about four miles north of St. Marys. Faithful chose well. At the back of the farm where David Stevens has dug out a trout pond, there are springs producing two thousand gallons of sweet water an hour.

David Stevens was born in a frame house on the farm and has worked on it from the time he was a small boy. "I can remember my father drawing grain. I was too small to pitch sheaves but I could put them in place and tramp them. While we worked my father would tell me about the area and the settlement of the property. He told me that the centre of the farm was cleared in his time. One man was hired to cut the trees . . . it was all done by axe."

David left school at the age of twelve to help his father with a herd of Shorthorn cows, Yorkshire hogs,and a flock of Plymouth Rock hens. Times were hard in 1921 and there were four older sisters to be educated and two younger children.

It was the location of the farm that fostered young David's interest in trapping, for from the farm the road to St. Marys winds along the Thames River, and there he trapped his first muskrats, skunks, and "coons". "I don't know where else I would have got my spending money." On Sundays he drove the buggy into St. Marys, taking his younger brother and sister to Sunday School. While waiting for them, he used to visit a retired undertaker, J. O. Mitchell, who kept a small fox ranch in the yard of his town home.

In 1921 David Stevens trapped his first mink, "way back from the river where I had set a trap for a skunk. I got $4.25 for the pelt." By 1924 — when he was fifteen years old — he was already exploring the possibility of setting up a mink farm. "I had spent many Sundays with Mr. Mitchell and I saw that his net income from the foxes in his yard was greater than that from our 150-acre farm. . . . I went on trapping and caught more each year. In 1926 I caught eighteen wild mink — a record for any trapper." In that year, at the age of seventeen, he was ready to start his mink ranch.

"I wanted to get breeding stock from an area where there were wild pelts. The Labrador mink sold for twice the price of native Ontario mink because of its much denser fur. In 1924 or 1925 they were fetching up to thirty dollars a pelt, but it was impossible to get live mink out of Labrador.

"The mink from the Lac St. Jean area near Chicoutimi in Quebec were second best. So I bought a pair of mink in 1926 from a French rancher at Deschambault, bought them by mail order for a hundred and fifty dollars. The mother mink raised four kittens that year — two of them female. I'd had a good trapping season and saved seventy dollars, so I bought another female mink from a man in Saskatchewan. I should never have done it; its fur was much coarser and it didn't do the herd any good."

By 1938, twelve years later, David Stevens had built up a herd of 300 females and 150 males. He and his son John, who manages the present mink and fox ranch, now have 2,500 females and 650 males.

On a large mink ranch, David says, "you'd be lucky to get 8,500 kits from 2,500 females." Only so many of the mink will produce, some never conceive, and some kits die. Mink breed only once a year. "That's why it's so doggone important to get every female pregnant between late February and the end of March." But for these six weeks, the male mink has no interest in sex. In fact, the male reproductive organs dry up and sometimes the males become sterile. For this reason, sperm tests have to be done on each male. "One year I had thirty-six females bred by a male and I had thirty-six females without a kit.

"There's a better net profit in the fur business than in most livestock operations, but it's still terrifically risky. In 1938 I had 950 young mink and that fall lost 600 from distemper, which we didn't have a vaccine for at the time."

There is no way of marking or tattooing a mink for identification, so every animal's pedigree is written on a card that must stay with it. When the female is taken to the male for breeding, the card goes with her. When she comes back, the card comes back. With 2,500 females this alone is a sizeable amount of record-keeping.

To be successful with a breeding herd, fifty per cent of the animals must be renewed each year; that is, fifty per cent are new kits and fifty per cent are two-, three-, and four-year-olds. Almost every year, too, small quantities of new blood are introduced. Line-bred males and females are bought from other ranches and their breeding results observed to see if they produce as good or better mink.

The mink are housed in cages in long, low sheds. They are fed twice a day and each animal has its own water supply. In the whelping season, females are provided with nesting boxes packed with shavings. A mink pelt reaches maximum quality at eight months of age. The mink are killed by injection, the most humane method available, and the pelts stripped of their layers of fat. The fat is then sold for the manufacture of perfume.

There are thirteen different colours in mink, including "jet", "demi-buff", "pastel", "sapphire", "violet", and "pink". Buyers from all over the world come to the Hudson's Bay Company auctions in Montreal, where prices have ranged as high as $114 for a single demi-buff pelt.

In addition to mink, the Stevenses have 350 breeding foxes — red, silver, and cross-fox. "You'd be amazed at the difference in the shades of red," David Stevens says. "We have a pen of twenty-two red-fox pups. . . . If you have any eye at all you can tell that there are two pups there that have twice the value of any of the rest — and they're all red foxes."

As well as having the mink and fox ranch, David Stevens has a Holstein herd of distinction for which he was awarded his Master Breeder's Shield in 1964. The Holstein herd and the field crops are managed by his son Donald, while Jacob Crowder, who has been with the Stevens family since 1940, manages a herd of thirty to forty pure-bred English Yorkshire sows on Faithful Stevens' old farm.

How is it possible to run three such diverse operations? Well, they all started small, David Stevens says, and developed slowly. Each is kept entirely separate from the others, and except for rush periods in the year, the six to eight men who work on them full time do not switch from one operation to another.

What now gives David Stevens greatest pleasure is the trout pond on Faithful's old farm. His grandchildren, the sixth generation of the Stevens family, can swim in the pond and it is here that he finds a peaceful haven on the farm where he was born.

CHAPTER TWELVE

The Heartlands and North to Georgian Bay

*B*y 1841, when Upper and Lower Canada were united and the former was renamed Canada West, most of what is now southern Ontario was settled, if sparsely so in some areas. But north of a line drawn diagonally between Goderich on Lake Huron and Lake Simcoe, the land was still all but empty, the only settlements being those on Georgian Bay.

From the late 1830s onwards, however, roads had been pushed steadily northwards, and the last of the unoccupied territory north of the Huron Tract was being opened up for settlement. A number of Irish came to take up land in what was known as the Queen's Bush, many of them from Ulster. Highlanders came to the area in the 1840s, to be joined later by their Lowland compatriots. And among the first settlers were escaped slaves from the United States.

Meanwhile, to the south and to the east of the Huron Tract the towns were growing. The site of Simcoe's London remained empty until 1827, when six commissioners (one of them Colonel Talbot), entrusted with building a new gaol and courthouse in its vicinity, went on to draw up plans for the town. There was some question whether lots within the proposed town should be disposed of through Talbot or by the government, an issue which prompted an impatient letter from the Colonel asking the authorities to make up their minds. "I am astonished," he wrote, "that you folks at York are not quicker."[1] Talbot was to be connected with the development of London until the 1840s, by which time the town could boast of some three or four thousand people as well as its handsome gaol and courthouse.

In the mid-1840s, John Galt's Guelph was also thriving, with a population of over twelve hundred. It, too, possessed what was considered to be an eye-catching gaol and courthouse; so much so that one contemporary writer complained that the buildings were placed "in a bad situation, being almost out of sight".[2] Woodstock was then almost as large as Guelph, but Waterloo and Berlin — the future Kitchener — were still villages of only a few hundred people.

These growing villages and towns were to impinge little, in the physical sense, on the farmlands to their north and east, which today constitute the agricultural heart of Ontario. Though the combined area of Huron, Perth, Middlesex, Oxford, Wellington, and Waterloo counties adds up to less than thirteen per cent of the area of southern Ontario, within these counties there were, in a recent year, over a quarter of the more productive farms in the province. In that same year, these six counties produced a fifth of all the oats and hay grown in southern Ontario, together with nearly a quarter of all the winter wheat and well over a third of the barley and corn.

At the same time, the farmers in these counties were raising nearly a fifth of the sheep in southern Ontario, nearly a third of all the cattle, and almost half of all the pigs. Roughly a third of all the milk produced in southern Ontario originated here, and of that third, half came from Perth and Oxford counties alone.

This astonishing performance is made possible by generally fertile soils combined with a relatively benign climate that sees moisture-laden winds blowing in from both Lake Huron and Georgian Bay. These same bodies of water ameliorate temperatures, giving a greater number of growing days than one might expect from the latitude.

However, there is more to the high productivity of the area than that. A farmer is nothing without his market, and ready access to this is provided by Highway 401, which runs through the lower part of Waterloo, through the middle of Oxford, and across the corner of Middlesex County. Of more basic importance, though, is the stability that still prevails throughout much of the region, which is, as yet, relatively untroubled by urbanization. Without that stability an efficient agricultural industry such as there is there today would never have emerged.

In the 1840s, when settlement of the Queen's Bush began, the villages on Georgian Bay were developing, if slowly. The first of these had sprung up in the vicinity of Penetanguishene, where a naval base had been started during the War of 1812, during which Georgian Bay and Lake Huron had been the scene of a naval conflict even tinier in scale than that on Lake Erie in 1813.

In the opening days of the war, the British had captured the American fort at Mackinac which guarded the strategic strait between Lakes Michigan and Huron and had so gained control of the upper lakes. To contest this, the Americans, in the summer of 1814, sent a fleet of five ships laden with troops to retake Fort Mackinac.

They failed, but having destroyed the only British ship of any size left on the upper lakes — the schooner *Nancy*, which had been sheltering in the Nottawasaga River near its mouth — the Americans withdrew, leaving only two of their ships behind to blockade Fort Mackinac. En route for Mackinac, Lieutenant Worsley, R.N., commander of the late *Nancy*, and his men came across one of the American schooners; they boarded and captured it, assisted by men from Fort Mackinac. When the second American ship sailed up to rejoin her consort, the performance was repeated, and the British were once more in command of the upper lakes.

In order to secure the back door to Upper Canada, it was decided in 1815 to build a major naval installation at Penetanguishene. It was this project that brought Dr. Dunlop north from the detested York to supervise the construction of a military road from Lake Simcoe to the site of the proposed base; and it was while he was thus engaged that the "appalling intelligence" reached him that the war was over, leaving him and his brother officers with, as he put it, "half-pay staring us in the face".[3]

After a brief pause, however, the work on the new installation went forward, with Penetanguishene eventually becoming a naval base and garrison town of repute. The base was not finally closed down until 1852, by which time there were small settlements at what are now Collingwood, Thornbury, Meaford, Owen Sound, and Wiarton.

It was the coming of the railways that accelerated the development of the region. In 1855 the first wood-burning locomotive puffed into a station known as Hen and Chickens Harbour. Renamed Collingwood, the settlement benefited enormously from the railway, particularly as it remained the only rail-head for some years. The railway was not extended to Meaford until 1872, while a year later Owen Sound, known as Sydenham in its earlier days, was directly connected with Toronto by a narrow-gauge line. In 1882, the railway finally reached Wiarton.

Many of those who stepped off those first trains at Collingwood were loggers, drawn to the region by the lumbering operations which dominated the economy of Georgian Bay during the last half of the nineteenth century, and which by the early years of the twentieth had put paid to the magnificent pineries that once fringed it. However, the lumbering industry in its heyday helped bring prosperity to the region and to those who settled in it — though not to many who had taken up land in the Bruce Peninsula. The Peninsula had been opened to settlement in the early 1850s, and there for a number of years timber rights belonged to those who had bought them and not to the settlers, who were allowed to cut timber only for their own immediate use. In debt, and with no source of income, many settlers on the Bruce left their holdings when the loggers finally came to clear their land, only to reveal barren and infertile soil beneath.

As the last empty lands to the south of the Bruce started to fill with people, the two Canadas federated with Nova Scotia and New Brunswick in 1867 to form the Dominion of Canada. Canada West became the province of Ontario.

The MacKay Family
Faralary Farm
East Zorra Township
Oxford County

The Max MacKays live north of Woodstock in Oxford County — surely one of the more beautiful in south-western Ontario, with its rolling hills, its many trees, and its farmhouses framed by avenues of maples.

The MacKays' grey stone house, sporting gables and decorative white trim, is set among well-kept lawns that slope down to the road. Walnut and catalpa trees, a pond, and the long, white rail fences combine to give an impression of a carefully tended country estate.

Oxford County is the "dairy pasture" of south-western Ontario. Its capital, Woodstock, proclaims proudly that it is the dairy capital of Canada, and the town boasts a full-sized black and white statue of a famous Holstein cow, Springbank Snow Countess, "World Champion Lifetime Butterfat Producer between 1919 and 1936". It is not surprising, then, that the MacKays are dairy farmers. They milk about sixty Holstein cows, and Max MacKay is a director of the Oxford County Holstein Club as well as being a member of the County Milk Committee of the Ontario Milk Marketing Board.

The farm is named after the place in Scotland where the MacKays originated — Faralary or Farlary, near Golspie on the east coast. Here the North Sea beats on a desolate coastline. Inland is a country of rocks and gorse, moors and moss, and a few fertile glens and straths. Most of these wild and lonely lands belonged at the turn of the nineteenth century to the hereditary MacKay chief, Lord Reay, and to the wealthy Countess of Stafford, afterwards Duchess of Sutherland, whose vast estates stretched from coast to coast across the north of Scotland.

The Countess of Stafford was not an unkind woman, but she lived far away in London and she brought, perhaps unwittingly, disaster on her people. As mentioned earlier, in 1813 under her direction or that of her factors, the homes of her tenants were pulled down and burned and her clansmen evicted, among them the MacKays. This to make way for sheep-walks.

The Countess also raised men from her estates for service in the armies of George III. The 93rd Regiment — the Argyll and Sutherland Highlanders — noted for its bravery and steadfastness, saw much service under Wellington in the Napoleonic Wars. After the wars a captain in the regiment, William MacKay, took his discharge and, leaving Sutherlandshire with his brother, Angus, emigrated to North America in 1819.

After landing in New York, these two brothers found work for a time on the Erie Canal. William came on to the Township of Zorra the following summer, and settled on a farm on the 9th Line. He built a shanty, using a blanket for a door, and "night after night Captain MacKay would be wakened by wolves pawing at the blankets."[4]

After some years, hearing that his relatives were among the crofters being evicted from the Sutherland estates, Angus MacKay went back home to Scotland and persuaded a shipload of them to return with him to Canada. They arrived in the autumn of 1829 to make their way to their future home east of Embro, a village that had its namesake on the east coast of Scotland.

Twenty-seven years later, in 1856, a certain John Sutherland and his wife, Elizabeth, bought a farm on the 9th Concession of the Township of East Zorra. They were a childless couple and they adopted a nephew, John Sutherland MacKay. In a will dated November 25, 1867, John Sutherland bequeathed to his "beloved wife, Elizabeth Sutherland, the sum of sixty dollars annually of lawful money of Canada in lieu of dower to be paid in half-yearly instalments" and to his nephew, John Sutherland MacKay, "his heirs and assigns for ever, the west half of lot No. 14 on the 9th Concession of the Township of East Zorra. . . ."

It was John Sutherland MacKay who built the big stone house, starting it in 1872 and finishing in 1876. The stone walls are twenty-two inches thick and the woodwork in the interior has been artificially "grained". A workman spent a winter painting a pattern of complicated lines and swirls in imitation of a natural wood finish.

Max MacKay, the present owner of the farm, is John Sutherland MacKay's grandson. He is married to the former Arlene Boyce. Of their family of seven children — three sons and four daughters —

all three sons intend to farm and his two eldest daughters are married to farmers. "I don't think any of our family has any desire to live in the city," Arlene MacKay says. "We have never talked against it but they seem to enjoy the freedom and privacy of rural life. We are firm believers that the family farm is an important institution."

Over the years the MacKay farm has grown from one hundred to almost three hundred acres. The eldest son, Gordon, has bought a farm on the Embro Road that is worked with the home farm. The MacKays' was a mixed farm for many years: pigs, cows, and chickens. "In 1960 we had to get rid of the pigs and put in extra cow stalls. In 1972 we got rid of the hens. Now we dairy. Corn is our main cash crop. We combine corn in the fields, dry it, put it in bins, and sell it out during the winter."

The MacKays are a well-travelled family. "Last year Gord won a trip to the British Isles for five weeks as a provincial representative of the Junior Farmers' Association. He stayed with young farmers in England, Scotland, and Ireland." Max and Arlene MacKay have been to Scotland, New Zealand, and Australia on farm tours, and to Jamaica and the Dominican Republic. They found that the contrast between dairy-farming in New Zealand and in Ontario was startling. "In New Zealand, farmers can keep a hundred and fifty cows on fifty acres and just pasture them out. They don't have to feed any chop in the barn. To bring up their production, they just add another cow. One farm where we were billeted for a night had no implements but a tractor, a two-wheeled trailer, and a mower. They'd cut the hay, take it and dry it, and when there wasn't enough feed, throw some out to the cows. They bought no feed supplements . . . they didn't buy a thing . . . and they had no big machinery. There, five thousand dollars would buy all the machinery you'd need. But here the climate is harder and animals can't be pastured in our Ontario winters."

In Scotland, the MacKays were struck by similarities in the landscape. The rolling hills of Ayrshire were reminiscent of those of Oxford County, although perhaps this coincidence was only a matter of luck. Before his land was cleared, the early settler contemplated a scene dominated by the dense forest that once stretched across south-western Ontario.

Not so long ago in the kitchen of the MacKay home there were hooks to support drying-racks for apples. Now there is a closed-circuit TV screen to show what is going on in the dairy barn. Max MacKay is an inventive person who takes advantage of technological advances. He built his own milk cooler before one was available commercially, installed coolers in the pipelines so the milk is cooled immediately, and built a cylinder to open and close the milking-parlour door. He is now interested in solar heat. In the MacKay family, past and present come together in a very practical way.

The Bothwell Family
Bothwell Manor Farm
Sydenham Township
Grey County

*T*he house on the Bothwell Manor Farm is unusually impressive from first glimpse. Set back from the Owen Sound–Meaford road in stately isolation, it is a house in the architectural style of the French Renaissance period at its most imposing. This was a style that spread through Europe and America in the Romantic period of the 1870s and 1880s, and it was the style in which John Bothwell chose to build his fine new three-storey home in 1886.

The mansard roof in which are set bull's-eye dormer windows is typical of the Second Empire period. The walls of the two lower storeys are of solid brick, fourteen inches thick, with white brick trim, and even the cellar beneath has a nine-foot ceiling. A verandah was added in 1925. Gordon and Viola Bothwell still have the architect's plans for the house, which was designed by George Staples of Owen Sound.

The present furnishings, admirably in keeping with the period, reflect Viola Bothwell's interest in the past, an interest she maintains by working in the County of Grey and Owen Sound Museum. The walnut dining-room buffet and chairs were inherited from the Bothwell family, as well as other pieces including the sitting-room sofa and a bonnet chest.

John Bothwell, who built the house, was the son of a Scottish farmer and was born in Aberdeenshire in 1828. He served an apprenticeship to a draper and was sent by his firm to establish a store in Newfoundland in 1852. Later, he was transferred to Montreal and afterwards to Newmarket. While in Newmarket he decided to strike out for himself. He took the Northern Railway to Collingwood and from there walked the forty-odd miles to Owen Sound.

There John Bothwell set up a store on the corner of Poulett and Division streets, and in 1862 he bought a farm for four thousand dollars from Hugh Gun Campbell. This farm — Lot 19, Concession 10, of Sydenham Township — had been purchased from the Crown by Campbell in 1846 for eighty pounds, the equivalent of four hundred dollars. The tenfold mark-up in sixteen years reflects the rapid growth in the Owen Sound area at that period.

In the same year that he purchased his farm, John Bothwell made a trip to Scotland. He returned to find that a fire had gutted his store and that his farm manager had left. It was then that he moved his family to the farm and decided to work it full time.

There was a ten-roomed log house on the place and this John Bothwell must have needed, for he married twice and produced a family of ten sons and five daughters. At some time prior to 1886 a large barn had been built, one that is still standing.

When John Bothwell took over the farm, only fifteeen acres had been cleared. He went to work, and when about a hundred were ready for the plough he divided the land into twelve-acre plots with a high board fence round each plot. It took one man almost a whole year just to dig the post-holes, for which he was paid seven cents a hole.

To square off his holding, John Bothwell bought Mander's Corner in 1889, now known as Bothwell's Corner, and replaced an old hotel that had been standing there with a two-storey building, later to be used as a dairy. Before it was demolished in 1955, it also served as a community hall, a store, and the Sydenham Township Council Chamber. George Bothwell, who succeeded John Bothwell, served on the Sydenham Township Council as treasurer for twenty-four years and his son, Gordon Bothwell, the present owner of the farm, has served on the Council since the 1950s.

In 1911 the Bothwells bought four acres of a rocky outcrop a mile to the east, and from here water runs down to the farm some hundred or so feet below. Through the farm, too, runs Bothwell's Creek, one of the finest rainbow-trout streams in the province and well known to ardent fishermen throughout Ontario. The creek is now a fish sanctuary.

In earlier years, the Bothwells kept pigs, sheep, chickens, Shorthorn cows, and Clydesdale horses. There was a stable for fourteen Clydesdales, some of which were sold overseas. Gordon Bothwell took a Clydesdale to Britain as late as 1936. In the early part of this century, the family operated a dairy and sold the first pasteurized milk north of Guelph. In a photograph of the Bothwells' two horse-drawn milk-delivery rigs taken about 1912, the delivery men are smartly dressed in suits and hats, one of them a bowler.

The Bothwells are now in the feeder-cattle business, keeping between five and seven hundred head of beef cattle. Sometimes the stock is bought in western Canada, sometimes from local dealers. For a time the cattle were sent to Burford to be "finished off" at a large feeder lot of some two thousand animals. Now the Bothwells grow enough corn to do the finishing themselves. The present 550-acre farm is managed by Gordon Bothwell and his son George, a graduate of the University of Guelph.

Fourteen acres on the west side of the farm are within the boundaries of Owen Sound, and on the east there is a housing subdivision. How long can a farm overtaken by suburbia continue to be worked with efficiency? A complex question, and, as Viola Bothwell says, the answer depends on a number of factors. It might be sensible to sell and move to better farming country elsewhere. But there is a fifth generation of Bothwells coming along and Bothwell Manor Farm is their heritage. "No other farm would be the same."

The Lipsett Family
Sydenham Township
Grey County

The Lipsetts' field-stone house in Sydenham Township, Grey County, sits on the edge of the escarpment above Georgian Bay, east of Owen Sound. There is a spectacular view from the garden, where the land drops away steeply to the water of Lake Huron, blue and sparkling in the fall sunlight. In the winter it is a different story. Storms blow in from the lake, dropping a thick blanket of snow as they hit the escarpment; the roads become narrow tunnels between snowbanks so high that they tower above the school bus.

The Lipsetts have lived here since the mid-nineteenth century. Their ancestors were driven from the borders of Holland and Germany by religious persecution in the seventeenth century to seek refuge, first in England, and then near Ballyshannon in Northern Ireland. They lived nearly two centuries in Ireland and fought for the Protestant cause with such vigour that they were awarded land after the Battle of the Boyne in 1690 and a coat of arms with a motto meaning "This through merit". In 1840, one of the family, Francis Lipsett, left Ireland for Canada. He settled for a time near Toronto, moving to the Township of Sydenham in 1851 and building the field-stone house in 1863.

It is here that Ronald Lipsett, his wife, Louise, and his two young children, Robert and Julie, now live. Ronald's parents, Frank and Muriel Lipsett, reside in a new house near by, and his aunt, Elsie Lipsett, lives in a cottage down the road near what used to be the village of Silcote. It is still marked on the map, but of the Silcote that was, only the building that housed the blacksmith's shop remains; church, school, and village hall, all have gone.

So too have many of the houses and barns on the surrounding farms disappeared. The land on this upland plateau is of varying quality, with rock outcrops and areas of poor drainage, and with fertile soil scattered in pockets, conditions that encouraged the amalgamation of the original hundred-acre holdings which were too small to be worked economically. Ron Lipsett, though holding a degree in music, decided that he would rather farm than teach; with his father he expanded their small farm to fifteen hundred acres, making it one of the largest farms in this book.

The Lipsetts run a large ranch-style Charolais beef operation suited to this type of terrain, pasturing their cattle, growing oats and hay to feed them, and buying kernel corn for supplementary feed. There are four hundred head in the Lipsett herd, of which about a hundred and fifty are cows and calves; of these, some twenty-five animals are "Full French" — cows and their progeny that Frank Lipsett, Ron's father, bought in France.

It is a pity, Louise says, that even with a herd of this size a farmer cannot earn a better living for the number of hours he works — from six in the morning often until ten o'clock at night. "There's the land, of course, but this is not money in the bank. The only way you can get the money is to sell the land. The reason we went into Charolais is because you make a little extra; the animals are larger and a premium is being paid for better-quality meat. . . ."

It is pleasant to sit in the old house. From the living-room a door leads into the "birthing" room, a room in which previous generations of Lipsetts were born. Between happy arrivals, the space became a bedroom for visitors or for the hired man.

Even now, with central heating, the old house can be cold when storms blow in from the lake in winter. When Elsie Lipsett lived there as a small girl, and when there were only wood stoves to heat the house, it must have been colder still. "My father was never one to go to bed and leave the stove burning." Her brother was ten years younger and she and her sister helped with the chores. "Filling up the wood-box, filling the reservoir of water on the stove, holding the lantern in the barn for my dad when he went to do the evening chores." There was no electricity, and in the evenings they made their own amusements. "Apples were brought up from the basement for treats. My mother read stories and we learned to crochet and to knit."

Elsie Lipsett recalls the busy household with some nostalgia, but acknowledges the particular hardships of early farm life for women.

"My mother and my grandmother made the men's overalls, shirts, and smocks. The smocks were like a man's jacket, buttoned down the front and made of 'duck' — a strong cotton fabric. Sometimes black, sometimes blue, sometimes lined with plaid or plain grey flannelette." Ever practical, her grandmother's wedding gift to her mother had been a sewing machine.

"Our cistern was out under the roof of the back kitchen. If we wanted soft water, my dad had to break the ice in winter and hand it out by the pailful. Otherwise we brought water in from the well outside. There was no bathroom. At first we used to bathe in the galvanized tub that we had for washing clothes. Then my grandparents bought a folding rubber bath with wooden legs. We used that until it wore out. Then we got a galvanized one just like a bathtub." In summer, water was put outside in containers — sometimes the big pans used for boiling maple syrup — and by evening it was warm enough for a bath.

Then there was washing and drying long hair. Egg yolk, lemon juice, and vinegar could all be used to make the hair shine. Elsie Lipsett's mother had "rats", bun-shaped knobs made from combings, over which the hair was arranged.

When she was a small girl, Elsie Lipsett went to the bush with her father, and her toes were frozen. "From then on I couldn't take much cold." And cold it was on the two-and-a-half-hour drive by horse and sleigh to Owen Sound. "We generally heated a block of wood or stone in the oven and wrapped it up to keep our toes warm.

"We went to Owen Sound perhaps once a month, though there were times when we just had to stay here and make do. We never thought of having the roads kept open. In spring the water would run under the snow and the horses would break through and if there were patches of snow and bare ground, you wouldn't know whether to take a sleigh or a wagon.

"I was afraid of horses for some reason. When it came to field work, my sister would drive the horses and the implements, but I'd take the fork and help with the hay or in the mow."

Just as Elsie Lipsett performed her share of heavy farm labour, Louise Lipsett, a modern farmer's wife, is frequently found on the tractor, or seen helping with the baling. She enjoys it. "To us, farm life is something special. It's a wonderful place to raise the children, yet in twenty minutes I can be in town. . . . We have the best of both worlds."

CHAPTER THIRTEEN

Farming on the Urban Fringe

*T*he settlement of the Place whether it becomes the Capital of the Province or not will be attended with no difficulty. . . . The soil between this [place] and Lake Simcoe is perfectly calculated for farming and before the summer the Road of communication will probably be thickly settled. . . . The inhabitants will soon raise an abundance of provisions [and the] Rivers and Bays abound with salmon. . . ."[1]

So wrote John Graves Simcoe, in a report dated December 2, 1793. The settlement to which he refers developed into the Toronto we know today and as the city grew much of that "soil . . . perfectly calculated for farming" was lost. As Toronto and the megalopolis of which it is now a part continue to expand, more of the soil that Simcoe praised disappears each day. Ironically, it was Simcoe himself who "saw Upper Canada as a favoured land, bound to prove attractive to farmers"[2] and who founded the settlement that in expanding was eventually to deprive so many farmers of their land.

Simcoe was there from the start. His was the first residence in what became Toronto, and a very unusual residence it was. For not only did it shelter the Lieutenant-Governor himself with all his family, but it was made of canvas. More than just a tent, it was over twenty feet long and all of fifteen feet wide. Floored with wood, papered within, and with windows and doors, Simcoe's canvas house created a stir in Upper Canada, then only a couple of years old.

The house was located on the shore of Lake Ontario, where, according to Thomas Talbot, "a most magnificent city" was to be built, one that Simcoe had already decided would be called York. Around the governor's residence, men of the Queen's Rangers were felling trees and putting up for their own use the first log buildings on the site.

His Excellency's canvas house was admired by some; earlier at Niagara, where Simcoe had first put it up, a visiting American general was most intrigued by it, calling it "quite a curiousity" and remarking that "you would suppose you were in a common house." Others were not so impressed. Peter Russell, later Administrator of the province, referring in a letter to the Simcoes' situation at York in the fall of 1793, wrote "you have no conception of the Misery in which they live — The Canvas house being their only residence — in one room of which they lie and & see company — & in the other are the nurse & Children squalling Etc. — an open Bower covers us at Dinner — & a Tent with a small Table & three Chairs serves us for a Council Room. . . ."[3]

The Simcoes' canvas house was probably the world's most travelled residence. It was said to have been the one that was used by Captain Cook himself on his voyage of discovery in the Pacific, and as such would have been a link with John Graves Simcoe's father, Captain John Simcoe, R.N., under whom James Cook had served as sailing master in the months prior to Captain Simcoe's death at sea off Anticosti Island not long before the British took Quebec in 1759.

Shortly before his death, Captain Simcoe had supervised the preparation of the chart of the St. Lawrence that was to do much towards the success of British operations at Quebec. The men who did the leg-work — or perhaps it should be called the boat-work — were Samuel Holland, the same Major Holland who as Surveyor-General of Quebec was later to lay out the Six Nations lands at Deseronto, and James Cook.

Seen in historical perspective the lives of the two men, John Graves Simcoe, the professional soldier who always had more ideas than he seemed to know what to do with, and James Cook, great seaman and brilliant navigator, offer a contrast that reflects the strange turn of events that saw the one extending the new British empire through his discoveries in the south Pacific at the same time as the other was strenuously trying to preserve what was left of the old one. One man's life lived out for the most part to the insistent calls of army bugles and the rub-a-dub-dub of its drums, the other to the quiet creak of tackle and the groan of ship's timbers as he made his way towards yet another distant horizon.

John Graves Simcoe was a schoolboy at Eton when Lieutenant Cook sailed on his first voyage to the Pacific in August 1768, returning three years later with both Australia and New Zealand claimed for Britain. By this time John was on the threshold of his army career. Born in Northamptonshire and with a middle name that honoured his godfather, Samuel Graves, later an admiral, he was already an only son. Two brothers had died in infancy, a third in a drowning accident. From Eton, John Graves had gone to Oxford, though it seems he took no degree there. By the age of nineteen he was an ensign in the 35th Foot, and in 1775 he arrived in Boston with his regiment two days after the Battle of Bunker's Hill had been fought.

Meanwhile, James Cook, now a captain, had completed his second voyage, and following it there was little of significance left to discover in the southern hemisphere. However, there was still another outstanding geographical problem that needed elucidation — the presence or otherwise of the North-West Passage — and Captain Cook was sent to search for it from the western end.

It is an interesting comment on the complacency with which the British government apparently regarded the rapidly deteriorating situation in the American colonies that the Admiralty went calmly ahead with the preparations for Cook's third voyage. Revolution or no revolution, Captain Cook sailed for the Pacific in July 1776. "It could not but occur to us as a singular and affecting circumstance," observed Cook on his way down the Channel, "that at the very moment of our departure, the object of which was to benefit Europe by making fresh discoveries in North America, there should be the unhappy necessity of employing others of His Majesty's ships . . . to secure the obedience of those parts of that continent which have been discovered and settled by our countrymen in the last century."[4]

John Graves Simcoe had by now purchased a captaincy in the 40th Foot to take part in the operations that followed the capture of New York and forced Washington to retreat across the Delaware to Philadelphia, and it was in the battle on the Brandywine that he was badly wounded. Upon his recovery he was given command of the Queen's Rangers, something he had been hankering after for some time. Under Simcoe's command the Rangers grew to a regiment of eleven companies, including a mounted arm — Simcoe was never a man who could leave anything alone that could possibly be improved.

Before the war ended Simcoe had the satisfaction of seeing his regiment given regular status as the 1st American Regiment. He himself had been wounded again twice, and on another, and as far as he was concerned unforgettable, occasion he had been taken prisoner to face execution as a hostage before his exchange was providentially arranged.

The Rangers were with Cornwallis at Yorktown. Because of ill-health Simcoe was permitted to return to New York, and from there he sailed for England late in 1781. His beloved regiment was disbanded two years later.

Cook's ships had arrived home some years earlier — but without their great captain, who had been killed in Hawaii in the course of a quite trivial dispute with the natives. In 1788, five years after the War of Independence ended, a fleet of ships laden with convicts arrived in Botany Bay, there to found the first colony in Australia.

In the best romantic tradition of a soldier coming back from the wars, John Graves Simcoe fell in love with a young heiress within a few months of his arrival home and married her. Only sixteen years old, Elizabeth Gwillim was a ward of Simcoe's godfather, Admiral Graves — her mother had died at the time of her birth, her father before she was born; hence her rather curious middle name of Posthuma.

The couple went to Exeter to live; then to a five-thousand-acre estate near Honiton in Devon, which Elizabeth's fortune enabled them to purchase. Children started to arrive — Elizabeth was to have eleven in a space of fourteen years. John Graves by no means became a retiring country gentleman, however. Before long he was writing to William Pitt, the Prime Minister, suggesting a way of capturing Cadiz and outlining a scheme for raising a multi-purpose regiment on the lines of his old one.

With his deep involvement in the war against the American revolutionaries and with so many of ex-comrades-in-arms now settling in Canada, it comes as no surprise to find Simcoe evincing an interest in what was left of the British empire in North America and, being the sort of man he was, coming up with numerous suggestions as to how that remnant of the empire could be made secure and prosperous. And it seems it was these suggestions, communicated at his customary length to his contacts in Whitehall, that brought his name to the fore when candidates were being considered for the post of lieutenant-governor of the new province of Upper Canada, then in the process of formation.

Lord Dorchester, the governor-general, had his own candidate in Sir John Johnson, but by the time his recommendation reached London, Simcoe had already been selected. And no sooner was he selected than he started to fire off letters to Whitehall concerning his plans and requirements. One of these, written in November 1790 to Henry Dundas, the Secretary of State, states his intentions of raising a new corps which "officered by chosen young Gentlemen . . . would probably be raised in the Winter and embarked in April next. . . ." The new corps, like Simcoe's old regiment, was to have its cavalry arm, and Simcoe even had ideas on the raising of suitable horses.

It was in this letter that Simcoe first broached the idea that the men of his proposed regiment should be only part-time soldiers, with two days a week devoted to military duties, two to labour on public-works projects, and two to clearing land on their own account — which individual soldiers could then sell to settlers and in this way augment their pay.

Simcoe's plan for a quasi-military work-force was to be one of the many ideas that Lord Dorchester was to frown on. Simcoe was granted his corps, however, which was given the not altogether unexpected name of the Queen's Rangers, and which in due course followed him to Upper Canada.

Another letter written by Simcoe to the Secretary of State late in 1790 — on Christmas Eve, as a matter of fact, when one would have thought that his mind would have been occupied by less mundane things — brings us back to the subject of the canvas house. In this letter he suggested "That a Canvass House similar to that sent with the Governor of Botany Bay might be highly convenient, if not necessary, in the various expeditions 'twill be proper that I should make . . ."[5] and he ended his letter that, if agreeing, His Lordship should issue instructions for such a house to be issued to him. In the event the house that Simcoe ended up with and that caused so much interest in Upper Canada seems to have been bought by Simcoe himself at a sale of Captain Cook's effects.

The Simcoes arrived in Quebec on November 11, 1791, and a week later the creation of Upper and Lower Canada, as of December 26, 1791, was proclaimed. Impatient though he was to get on with things, Simcoe had to wait until the following June before a sufficient number of his executive arrived from England to administer the necessary oath of office. With their arrival, events moved swiftly. After a short stop at Montreal, the Simcoes went on to Kingston, where John Graves was sworn in as Upper Canada's first lieutenant-governor. A week later Upper Canada was divided into nineteen counties, stretching from Glengarry in the east to Essex in the west. These were allocated among electoral districts in which elections were to be held without delay. After only another week in Kingston, Simcoe was off again — to Niagara, where, as we have seen, a settlement of some size was already growing. This Simcoe renamed Newark, and it was there a couple of months later, in September 1792, that the first legislative assembly was held.

John Graves Simcoe had a very clear idea of the sort of colony that Upper Canada should become. In his view — and many were to agree with him — the revolution in the American colonies had been brought about by a small clique, which, while successful in disseminating their republican ideas, did so in the face of an American population largely indifferent to their ideals, if they were not actively hostile to them. Given an Upper Canada thriving under the British Crown, Simcoe was convinced that the many Americans who detested the Republicans as much as he did would flock north, eventually to build up an outpost of the empire that would be the envy of the United States, if it did not actually emerge as the dominant country in North America.

Thus, even before his legislative assembly had met at Newark, Simcoe had issued a proclamation inviting settlers to take up land in Upper Canada, with farm lots of two hundred acres to be granted to those who would take an oath of allegiance to the King, such lots to be laid out in township blocks, along with the Crown and Clergy Reserves that, as we have seen, were to cause so much trouble in the future. As Simcoe hoped, the news of his proclamation, supplemented by a letter to the British consul in Philadelphia, soon reached interested ears south of the border.

In taking these steps, Simcoe had the approval of the home government. However, the broad principles that Simcoe felt should underlie the development of the new province were regarded with some misgiving. To keep pernicious republican ideas from seeping north and taking root in Upper Canada, and indeed to guard against any untoward liking for democracy on the part of the common people, it was essential, in Simcoe's view, to foster a local aristocracy which would guide the province's affairs with as little interference as possible from the electorate. Such an aristocracy, bolstered by a strong established church and perpetuated by suitably educated youths, should lead, Simcoe concluded, to the establishment of an unassailable bastion of the British empire.

Simcoe's plan for the future of what he considered to be his province, indeed any plans for its future, presupposed that it would remain secure in the face of a United States that was not only in an expansive and ebullient mood, but in an increasingly angry one over the British refusal to vacate several forts that, according to the peace treaty, were now in the United States, that at Detroit among them, as mentioned earlier.

Ostensibly the British were hanging on to these forts as a bargaining-point in their efforts to obtain compensation from the Americans for property losses suffered by Loyalists during the war. In fact there were other reasons. The bulk of the Six Nations Indians had, as we have seen, accepted the British invitation to take up land in Upper Canada. Those beyond the western frontier south of Lake Erie, however, had hopes of keeping their homeland and in 1790 had defeated an American force that had encroached upon it. In 1791, the year that Simcoe arrived, a second American force was defeated. It was thought that a continuing British presence in the forts in question would at least give the illusion of a Britain sympathetic to the interests of these Indians who, if they lost their land to the Americans, might well turn in their anger on a weakly defended Upper Canada. Apart from all this and perhaps more to the point, the lands of the Ohio were still yielding a profitable crop of furs, and the influential merchants of Montreal were understandably anxious that such should continue to come their way.

These problems were not to be resolved until Simcoe was nearing the end of his time in Canada; thus the new province that he was so busily putting on its feet was under threat of war almost the whole time he was there. Its state of military preparedness was always uppermost in Simcoe's mind, and in coming to his decisions, military considerations were paramount.

Newark, he decided, was no place for the province's capital, located as it was within cannon-shot of the Americans on the other side of the Niagara River. In Simcoe's view the ideal spot for a capital would be on the river that the French called La Tranche and that he renamed the Thames, where a town to be called Georgina would be founded. Later, he had second thoughts about the name and decided that it should be called London instead, which with Chatham as a naval dockyard established further downstream would form a pleasing parallel with that other London and Chatham on England's River Thames.

Toronto, with its fine harbour protected by a curving spit of land and strategic location, would make an excellent naval base and a start should be made on a settlement there. Kingston, though already fortified, was in Simcoe's view dangerously close to the Americans.

Such were some of the conclusions arrived at by Simcoe before he had even arrived in Upper Canada. Once on the job, he wanted to see things for himself, and not long after the ending of the first session of the legislature in Newark he was off on one of the many jaunts that were to exasperate his subordinates anxious for His Excellency's decision on this or that, or perhaps impatiently waving papers or orders that were worthless without his signature.

The first trip was quite a short one. He walked from Niagara to Burlington Bay and back, covering the hundred miles in a week. Along the lakeshore the Loyalist settlements were now ten years old, and land was being cleared back to the foot of the escarpment and even on its crest. The first of the Mennonites had settled on the Twenty some years before, joining Loyalist settlers from New York who had arrived even earlier. According to Elizabeth Simcoe, her husband "was delighted with the beauty of the Country & industry of the inhabitants."

Simcoe got back in the middle of December. At the beginning of February he was off again on a much more ambitious trip. With six officers and twenty men he travelled by sleigh to Brant's Ford, there to be joined by Joseph Brant and some Indians who were to guide him down the Thames River to Detroit — a journey yet to be taken by a white man. No doubt anxious over the state of his health — which was never good and which was to get worse — Mrs. Simcoe noted that "The Gov. wore a fur Cap tippet & Gloves & maucassins no Great Coat."

Detroit was duly reached and on the way Simcoe was "confirmed in his opinion that the forks of the Thames is the most proper scite [sic] for the Capital of the Country, to be called New London on a fine dry plain without underwood but abounding in good Oak trees."

Simcoe was away for five weeks, having walked most of the way to Detroit and back, a total distance of some six hundred miles. With the site of the new provincial capital selected, at least to his satisfaction, Simcoe lost no time in taking his first look at York, already selected, sight unseen, as an appropriate place for a naval installation.

From earliest times the Indians had reached Lake Ontario from Georgian Bay via Lake Simcoe, from which they travelled south on the Holland River to a portage that took them to the Humber River and from there to Lake Ontario. In 1750 the French built a fort at the mouth of the Humber in order to make sure that any furs the Indians might bring did not fall into British hands. The French called their new fort Fort Rouillé or, sometimes, Fort Toronto — an Indian name the exact meaning of which is still the subject of scholarly dispute. "Place of meeting", "trees in water", or, more evocatively, "place where trees are reflected in water" are all possibilities, it seems.

Shortly afterwards the French built another fort with a garrison of ten men further east, more or less where Dufferin Street meets the Exhibition grounds today. The French destroyed this fort themselves at the time of the conquest of Quebec, but the ruins were still there in Simcoe's day.

Simcoe was well pleased with what he found at Toronto. Lord Dorchester was away in England at the time, so it was to his deputy that Simcoe addressed his letter. "I lately . . . examined this Harbour . . . and upon minute examination I found it to be without Comparison the most proper situation for an Arsenal in every extent of that word that can be met with in this Province. . . . At the bottom of the Harbour there is a Situation admirably adapted for a Naval Arsenal and Dock Yard and there flows into the River [the present Don] the Banks of which are covered with excellent Timber. Upon this River I purpose to construct a Saw Mill. . . . I have fixed upon the Scite for a place for a Town on the main shore — and another [for] barracks for the King's troops. . . ."[6]

Simcoe returns to the matters of defence at the end of the letter when he puts in a request for heavy guns and ten-inch howitzers. It transpired that howitzers were in rather short supply, and as for ten-inch ones, there were none in stock. In the event, Lord Dorchester on his return was to bring Simcoe's attempts to fortify York, as he was already calling it, to an abrupt end, though not before the latter had managed to scrounge a few guns and gunners from Kingston and elsewhere.

At the end of July, Simcoe moved to York with his family and there they were to stay in their canvas house for the rest of the summer of 1793, through the next winter, and into the spring of 1794.

Elizabeth Simcoe was enchanted with York. "We went in a Boat 2 miles to the bottom of the Bay and walked through a grove of fine Oaks where the Town is intended to be built. A low spit of Land covered with wood forms the Bay & breaks the Horizon of the Lake which greatly improves the view which is indeed very pleasing. The water in the Bay is beautifully clear and transparent. . . ."

And a few days later: "We rode on the Peninsula so I called the spit of land for it is united to the mainland by a very narrow neck of ground," a neck destined to be washed away in a storm in 1858 which produced Toronto Island. After their ride on the "peninsula", Elizabeth and her friends explored the coast east of Toronto. "The shore is extremely bold & has the appearance of Chalk Cliffs. . . . They appeared so well that we talked of building a summer Residence there & calling it Scarborough . . . " after, of course, the Scarborough on England's north-east coast noted for its tall white cliffs.

As for Simcoe himself, he was extremely busy. Shortly after his arrival, he was joined by his Rangers, some of whom had already been put to work earlier that summer building Dundas Street, a military road that headed westward from Burlington towards the Thames River, where Simcoe's capital was intended to be. Now the rest of the Rangers assembled at Toronto, which officially became York on August 26, 1793. The name was chosen by Simcoe in honour of one of the many royal dukes, the second son of George

III, who as commander-in-chief of the army had lately emerged victorious in a series of rather minor engagements with the French. The Duke of York, though said to have been the only one of the royal dukes with the feelings of a gentleman, was to be dismissed in 1809 because of a scandal involving his ex-mistress, who had sold commissions in the army. Nevertheless, York kept its name until 1834, when it again became Toronto at the time of the town's incorporation.

After less than two months at York, Simcoe was off on his travels once more, leaving his Rangers to build their barracks roughly where Fort York is now, and to lay out a small settlement a mile to the east, south-east of what is now the intersection of Queen and Jarvis streets. Almost as soon as the town plan became available, there was a rush to take up lots, for it was already apparent that York was to be at least the temporary capital.

This time, Simcoe headed north to Lake aux Claies, which he renamed Lake Simcoe after his father, and then he struck west to come out on Georgian Bay, tracing the route of another strategic road that he felt should be built as soon as possible.

Work on the southern half of this road was to begin the next year, 1794, when William Berczy started a settlement in Markham Township, a settlement that was to attract a number of Plain People to the area. A couple of years later, the indefatigable Rangers were brought in to help push the road north, which Simcoe decided to call Yonge Street after his friend Sir George Yonge, member of Parliament for Honiton where the Simcoes lived in England. Yonge, then Secretary of War, was a rather shadowy figure, but with influence, it was said, with George III.

With Simcoe back once more in York it became clear to disgusted officials that their elusive chief was intending to spend the winter there. However, no canvas tents for them, even if they did have stoves in them, and so the various senior officials scattered to the comfort of their homes in Niagara for the winter months. "Our Government is to spend the Winter at a respectable distance," was one sour comment.

Much of what Simcoe managed to accomplish was done in the face of Lord Dorchester's disapproval, while some projects, such as the fortification of York, were simply vetoed. As for Simcoe's plans for developing London as the provincial capital, they were to come to nothing. There were just not enough men or guns to go round, at least according to Dorchester. In any case, Dorchester favoured Kingston as the projected capital, already a thriving town and fortified into the bargain.

Dorchester was not alone in his opinion of some of Simcoe's schemes, which became, for many citizens less far-sighted than he, merely something to poke fun at. Thus, Simcoe's laudable if impractical attempt to introduce a measure of good urban design in his new town was to provoke one Kingston businessman into writing: "You will smile perhaps when I tell you that even at York, a Town Lot is to be granted in the Front Street only on Condition that you shall build a House of not less than 47 feet Front, two stories High & after a certain Order of Architecture. . . . it is only in the back Streets and Allies that the Tinkers and Taylors will be allowed to consult their own Taste and Circumstances in the Structure of their Habitations. . . . Seriously our good Governor is a little wild in his projects. . . ."[7]

Meanwhile, just about the time that Simcoe had been having his first good look at Toronto and its environs, news had reached the province that war had broken out — the start of that long war against Napoleonic France that with its aftermath was, as we have seen again and again, to have such a profound effect on the development of Upper Canada. The outbreak of war underlined the need for setting up a militia system in the new province — something else that Simcoe had to see to.

In all his comings and goings, Simcoe had been attending the annual sessions of the new legislature at Newark, which, with the executive council, had not only the basic apparatus of government and the legal system to set up, but a multiplicity of other matters to attend to if Upper Canada were to become a going concern, everything from the regularization of marriages performed in earlier days without benefit of clergy, to placing a bounty on wolves and bears, from millers' tolls to the abolition of slavery in the province. In connection with the latter, of which Simcoe had long been an advocate, it was decided that slaves would not be freed — many Loyalists had brought slaves with them — but no new ones could be brought into the province.

In early 1794, matters more urgent than these, or the progress of his settlement at York, claimed Simcoe's attention. The United States were sending another and more formidable army to deal with the Indians in the Ohio Valley. The British response was not only to bring the forts they still held on American soil to a greater state of preparedness but, in an interesting exercise in brinkmanship, to build *another* fort well inside what the Americans were claiming as their territory, at Maumee on the river of that name, south-west of the present Toledo in northern Ohio.

A couple of weeks after the shocking news reached York that

Marie Antoinette had died under the guillotine, Simcoe received urgent orders from Lord Dorchester to build the new fort, which became known as Fort Miami. Simcoe was against it, considering it to be too provocative, but orders were orders and on March 18, 1794, he was off to Detroit to see about it.

He was away until May and returned to York to take his wife and family back to Niagara, which was now seething with military activity. Simcoe was everywhere: now inspecting forts on the American side; now off to Detroit; or travelling to Long Point, where he had hopes of establishing a fortified settlement — yet another project that Lord Dorchester was to veto.

The events of a nerve-wracking spring and summer came to a climax in August when General Wayne, after defeating the Indians at Fallen Timbers, appeared before Fort Miami in the hopes of intimidating the garrison and forcing its evacuation. But the British, under a Major Campbell, stood firm, and after his show of strength General Wayne went away again.

From then on the situation was to ease until Jay's Treaty was signed in November. In the meantime, after attending another session of the legislature, Simcoe took himself off once more, this time to look at Kingston and the Lake Ontario shore, early in 1795 to be reunited with his wife, who had been sent to Quebec for safety during the war scare.

Shortly afterwards Simcoe's health, which had been deteriorating throughout his stay in Upper Canada, broke down completely and it was to be several weeks before he could leave his room. Following another summer at Newark and further bouts of illness, he applied for leave of absence on the grounds of ill-health. But it was more than that. The antagonism between Lord Dorchester and himself had reached the point where his letters to the former were barely civil and on occasion filled with very thinly veiled sarcasm. Apart from anything else, following the signing of Jay's Treaty in November 1794, Lord Dorchester had decided to withdraw all troops from Upper Canada except the Rangers and men of the Royal Artillery. Simcoe's many plans were going to be even harder to bring to fruition.

Simcoe was at York when his anxiously awaited leave of absence came through in July 1796. He left with his family less than a week later, sailing from Quebec in September. Elizabeth Simcoe wrote of her arrival in England: "The weather is damp raw & unpleasant . . . the fields looked so cold, so damp, so chearless, so uncomfortable from the want of our bright Canadian Sun that the effect was striking & the contrast very unfavourable to the English climate."

The Simcoes were never to return to Upper Canada. At the time of his departure, York was still a temporary capital as far as John Graves Simcoe was concerned, though not long before he left he was planning buildings there to serve the legislature — such, with his usual foresight, to be sold when "the seat of Government be ultimately established on the River Thames as in my opinion every public Consideration & the King's Service requires. . . ."[8] He had his heart set on London as his capital to the last.

Moving the seat of government from Newark to York was not at all popular among the men most directly concerned, and it was to be a couple of years before the last grumbling official was persuaded to move across the lake from the comfort of his home in Niagara. And so as time went by, York came to be accepted as the capital of Upper Canada. Toronto's beginnings were as casual as that.

Within a few months of his arrival in England, Simcoe was promoted to major-general in command of British operations in San Domingo, the island in the West Indies that now comprises the Dominican Republic and Haiti. The French had acquired the western or Haitian portion and there in 1791 the blacks revolted against their French masters. The whites appealed for help to the British governor of Jamaica, who sent troops in late 1793.

The San Domingo operation, which became part of a wider compaign to oust the French from the West Indies and which saw the loss of forty thousand British troops, mostly from yellow fever, had dragged on for two years before Simcoe took over at the request of Pitt.

He arrived early in 1797 and seems to have thrown himself into his job with all the energy he had shown in Upper Canada and to have achieved some successes — not only in the military field, but in matters of administration. Then something went wrong. With insurgents starting to gain the upper hand, and hurt by rumours touching on the efficiency of his troops, Simcoe asked for leave of absence, arriving back in England under something of a cloud. He had been in San Domingo less than a year.

Although he had left Upper Canada two years before, he was still, at least nominally, its lieutenant-governor, his duties in his absence being carried out by Peter Russell, who acted as Administrator. He did not formally resign from the post until after his return from San Domingo. It seems he had some hope of succeeding to the governorship of British North America — in place of General Prescott, who in his turn had taken Lord Dorchester's place — but nothing came of it, and for several years Simcoe resigned himself to serving with the home defence forces in southern England.

Then in 1806 his star seemed to be in the ascendant again when he was given command of the British forces in India. A sudden change of official plans, however, required him to join a force that was forming in Portugal to resist a possible French invasion, and it was on the way there that he became suddenly ill and was hurriedly taken back to England. He died not long after landing at the house of a friend in Exeter. Elizabeth Simcoe, whose diary and sketches enrich immeasurably our knowledge of her husband's régime in Upper Canada, survived him by forty-four years.

John Graves Simcoe had been in Upper Canada for only four and a half years and his immediate successors were to be lesser men. Yet he had done his work well; and for much of what we now take for granted in Ontario, we have John Graves Simcoe to thank.

The Upper Canada that John Graves Simcoe worked so hard to set on its feet is now the home of nearly eight and a half million people, over a third of whom live in Metropolitan Toronto, the city that was to grow around the place that he wanted for his naval base.

At the time of Simcoe's departure for England in 1796, York was little more than a village, with fewer than 250 inhabitants. By the turn of the century there were about 400, rising to 700 at the outbreak of the War of 1812. Then with the ending of the Napoleonic Wars, York started to grow, and at an increasing pace. In 1818 the population was over the thousand mark. It took about ten years to double that figure, and only three years after that to double again. By 1833 York was a thriving town of over 6,000, and by mid-century it was one of more than 20,000 inhabitants.

At this time Ontario was still predominantly rural. The first decennial census after Confederation in 1867 gave a total population for the province of 1.6 million, of which less than a quarter was living in the towns. Then, as in all industrialized western countries, the flight to the cities began. By 1901, of the 2.2 million people living in Ontario, over forty per cent were now urban dwellers. And then some time in the first decade of the twentieth century, the watershed was passed. More people were living in the towns than in the country.

By 1951 the rural population had shrunk to twenty-nine per cent of the total. In 1971 it was less than eighteen per cent. In those two decades following the Second World War, not only did the proportion of country dwellers fall, but so did the numbers and the proportion of those actually farming.

From 1951 to 1971 the number of people on the land in Ontario fell from 678,000 to some 363,000: in other words, the farming population was almost halved in a matter of twenty years — and this during a period when the total population in Ontario rose by 3.1 million to its 1971 total of 7.7 million. In 1971 fewer than five people out of a hundred were on the land, and the number is probably less today. With the total population of Ontario at almost 8.5 million, one begins to understand why the voice of the farmers often goes unheard.

The dramatic changes in both the size and the character of Ontario's population since the Second World War are principally associated with the growth of the megalopolis that straggles along some 150 miles of the Lake Ontario shore from Oshawa to Niagara-on-the-Lake and into which some four million people are now crammed — about one-seventh of the entire population of Canada. And the megalopolis continues to grow as it draws to it one out of every three immigrants to Canada.

The towns and villages between Metropolitan Toronto and Hamilton — Port Credit, Lorne Park, Clarkson, Oakville, Bronte, Burlington — in coalescing in the years since the Second World War destroyed one of the prime fruit-growing regions of southern Ontario. Already forgotten by many — if indeed as newcomers they ever knew of it — are the fifteen thousand acres of the fruit belt, once well known for its small fruits such as strawberries, raspberries, and currants as well as for its vegetables and its orchards of apples and pears.

As late as the 1940s there were still about one thousand fruit and vegetable farms in the lakeshore region, besides farms of a less specialized nature. They are all gone now, though there are still a few producing orchards among the houses, and here and there small holders are still to be found growing their vegetables, though there are fewer of them each year.

With the process of in-filling between urban centres along the lakefront all but complete, the megalopolis had nowhere to go but north. With Metro Toronto showing the way in the immediate post-war years, the northerly advance of the city has continued since, engulfing huge acreages of farmland and bringing more and more farmers into the urban shadow.

As pointed out earlier, even a distant threat of urbanization brings an uncertainty about the future that may set a farmer thinking about the continuing viability of his operation long before someone appears on his doorstep with an offer for his land. The various agricultural support industries have their living to earn as well, and with the approach of the city the services they offer, services the farmer cannot do without, may start to dwindle. Then comes the more

Jerker rods of black ash run across country from a central engine and spider-wheel to work this nineteenth-century pump-jack, still operating at Petrolia, Lambton County. Once there were pump-jacks similar to this one on the Kells farm in Enniskillen Township.

(above) The Botsford family left England for the American colonies in 1637 rather than pay "Ship Money" to King Charles I. As Loyalists during the War of Independence, some came north to Upper Canada. David Botsford, local historian and genealogist, reads in his study on a farm near Amherstburg.

(below) Roland Belanger, French farmer from Paincourt, near Chatham, Kent County. His ancestors came to Quebec from Normandy in the mid-seventeenth century, and to Paincourt in 1833.

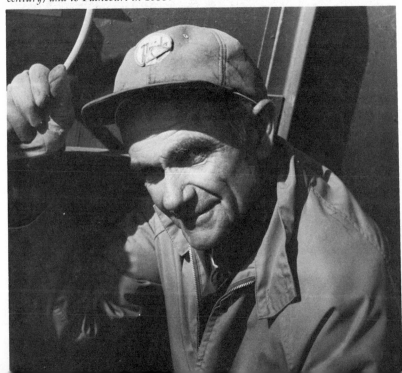

(above) Baby mink in a pen on the Stevens farm at St. Mary's. There are usually four mink kits to a litter.

(below) Faithful Stevens from Cornwall, England, took up land near St. Marys in Perth County in 1853. Today, his descendant, David Stevens, has a mink ranch and a hog operation. In addition, he is a Master Breeder of Holstein cattle.

(above) The ninety-year-old Dolson house faces the River Thames near Chatham, Kent County. During the War of 1812, the British with their Indian allies passed by this farm on their retreat up the river, to be overrun by American forces at Moraviantown, where the Indian chief, Tecumseh, was killed.

(right) Family tragedies left Margaret MacMillan Whyte of Huron County the owner of her father's farm and cattle at the age of twenty-one.

On the family's century farm near Ingleside, Stormont County, Maurice Shaver walks away from fields that were flooded when the St. Lawrence Seaway was built in 1959.

(above) *Austin Hodgins and his family live in this house on the Coursey Line near Lucan, Biddulph Township, Middlesex County. His ancestor, Lieutenant-Colonel James Hodgins, was agent for the Canada Company.*

(below) *Affection and trust are reflected in the faces of Paul Baker and his son, David. Paul Baker is the seventh generation of a Dunkard family that came north from Brothers' Valley, Pennsylvania, at the invitation of Upper Canada's first lieutenant-governor, John Graves Simcoe.*

Once a noted breeder of Guernsey cows, Lloyd Chisholm now raises Standard-bred horses on his farm near Milton, Halton County. He helped establish the Mohawk Raceway at Campbellville.

Simeon Reesor of Markham is a member of a noted Mennonite family who has inherited all his forebears' skill with their hands. Here he is shown carving intricate chains out of wood.

immediate impact of new roads built or old ones widened and improved to carry more commuters into the growing city. Cattle and traffic do not mix. In some cases the farmer may use public roads to get his equipment from one part of his farm to another — and to get his crops out. And again there comes a point where slow-moving farm vehicles and cars in growing numbers become incompatible. In the meantime, the efficiency of the farming operation has been reduced while the motorist, perhaps, has become more vociferous in his complaints.

The approach of the city brings more trespassers who trample crops and break down fences. Woodlots in the summer are a temptation to walkers and picnickers, while in the winter they attract those in search of firewood, and to those farmers who rely on obtaining a good yield of maple syrup, a damaged woodlot is a serious matter.

Expropriation may occur anywhere and for a variety of reasons but is more likely in the vicinity of growing towns and cities. And so farmers lose their land in part or in total to highways, hydro lines, and airports, or perhaps to large-scale recreational complexes.

In some farming areas the prevailing voice may come to be that of the suburbanite, and the farmer may start to find himself hedged about by restrictions that may well affect the efficiency of his operation.

And so the attrition of the farmer's will to survive continues, until the prospect of selling his land, perhaps to a developer, comes as a release from what may have been years of increasing worry, though the decision to sell out may well be a painful one.

In this process it is the smaller family farm with its greater economic vulnerability that may be the first to go under. However, all farms that change hands are not within the urban shadow. Much as it was in nineteenth-century Ireland, "consolidation" is now the cry, for larger farms can be run more efficiently. Mechanization demands economies of scale in the agricultural industry as in any other. But what may well be lost when smaller farms are merged into that larger and economically more desirable, if impersonal, whole is that commitment to the land which brings such century farmers as we have met in this book to cherish and get the most out of the soil that is theirs.

But when a century farm sign is taken down for the last time, something more than just a farm is lost. Cicero, the great Roman, wrote: "I care more for that long age that I shall not see than for the little that I hold of time." There are not many of us who can say that in all sincerity. Yet for many generations of century farmers,

Cicero's words sum up, perhaps as no other words can, the attitude of those men and women towards their land and those who will inherit it.

The Chisholm Family
Arawana Farms
Nassagaweya Township
Halton County

Lloyd Chisholm, his wife, Mary, and his daughters, Frances and Lenore, live on a farm north of Milton in the Township of Nassagaweya. Travelling by Highway 401, which runs through their backyard, it is less than an hour's drive to Toronto, just over the horizon to the east. On the other side of the highway is the lake formed by the Kelso Dam; beyond it rise the steep cliffs of the Niagara Escarpment.

Lloyd Chisholm inherited the farm from his mother's family, the Moffats, members of a widely dispersed Scottish family with branches in Canada, Australia, and Africa. Robert Moffat and his wife, Mary, a devout and courageous young couple, founded the famous mission station at Kuruman in South Africa in the 1820s. Their daughter, Mary, "a little, thick, black-haired girl, sturdy and all I want", became the wife of David Livingstone, the famous explorer. She died of fever at the age of forty-one and is buried in a remote and alien place, under a great baobab tree on the banks of the Zambesi River.

In the 1877 *Historical Atlas of Halton County* there is a picture of the "Farm Residence of James Moffat, Milton". It shows the brick house in which the Chisholms now live. The silver maples that line the picket fence were planted by Lloyd Chisholm's grandfather, and some of them are still standing. Horses graze contentedly in the field to the side of the house.

The Chisholms came from the Highlands of Scotland west of Inverness. One of the Chisholm clan, George, was born in 1752 in the Parish of Croy in Inverness-shire, not far from the place where the Battle of Culloden had been fought six years earlier. Chisholms had fought on both sides of the battle, with the chief's youngest son, Roderick, leading the Chisholm clansmen for Prince Charles and two other sons serving as officers in the Royal Scots under the Duke of Cumberland. It seems that the cunning old chief arranged it thus so that whatever happened he would not lose his lands. Young Roderick was killed, and after the battle it was his brothers who looked for and found his body, saving it from possible mutilation by Cumberland's vengeful men.

George Chisholm emigrated to the American colonies in 1773, settling on the frontier of New York. After fighting in the Revolutionary War as a Loyalist under General Burgoyne and being taken prisoner at Saratoga, he came to Canada and settled on the north shore of Burlington Bay. His son, William, bought land where the town of Oakville now stands.

Other Chisholms, perhaps a thousand of them, came to Canada in the early part of the nineteenth century. They had been driven out of Scotland by their own chieftain, and later by his heirs, who evicted the clansmen from Strathglass, north of Loch Ness, and burned their homes. Only Mary Chisholm, the spirited daughter of the twenty-third chieftain, and her mother championed their people, but they were powerless to help them.

When Lloyd Chisholm took over the farm, the original Moffat grant of two hundred acres had been reduced to a hundred and fifty. It was further reduced in 1958 by the expropriation of a hundred acres for the building of Highway 401 and the Kelso Dam. Lloyd Chisholm was paid two hundred dollars an acre for his land, but the irreplaceable fields that his grandfather had worked and the remains of the first log house disappeared under the water of the dam. "They say it's progress, but I say it's destruction."

The fifty acres remaining did not constitute a viable farm; however, Lloyd had bought another farm in 1941, so he was able to carry on. As it happened, this second farm had been in his father's family at one time. "When I was a boy, about twelve years old, my grandmother showed me a photograph of the old place and told me that she wanted me to buy it when I grew up. At that age, I didn't pay any attention to it. But, lo and behold, the time came when the owners were in trouble financially and they came to see my father. My father said, 'No, I don't want to buy it; it's up to Lloyd.' And I did buy that farm, though I didn't know how I was going to raise the down payment, money was so scarce at the time. Well, we managed and got it paid for. In 1958 when the land went for the highway, I sent some of the milking herd to that farm and kept the dry cows and heifers here."

Lloyd Chisholm has been a livestock breeder since he left school, beginning with a pure-bred Shorthorn herd and later moving into the milk business with Guernseys. "At that time you got full price for Guernsey milk and you could sell a hundred per cent of what you produced because of its better quality. . . . I bred and showed four generations of Guernseys, quite a feat if I do say so. I am one of the few farmer-breeders who have bred a cow and showed her through to the Grand Championship. I bred several All-Canadian Grand Champions."

Lloyd Chisholm went out of Guernseys in 1965 when the Ontario government ruled that milk was milk whatever breed it came from, thereby destroying the high demand for Guernsey milk. "But I showed the herd right up to the last."

During the time he was a Guernsey breeder, Lloyd Chisholm was active in several associations connected with livestock-breeding, and he judged Guernseys from coast to coast. He has served as a director of the Royal Winter Fair at Toronto and as chairman of the Canadian National Livestock Records in Ottawa.

It was to the breeding of Standard-Bred horses that Lloyd Chisholm turned when he went out of Guernseys. For twenty-seven years he had always had a brood mare and raised a few colts.

Leslie Frost, Premier of Ontario at the time, had instituted a ruling that there was to be no night racing in the province — a serious deterrent to harness-racing. "In those days the horses were owned by farmers, and farmers couldn't race during the day. Harness-racing was just a pastime, and there weren't too many city people involved because there was no money in it."

Working with representatives of the Canadian Trotting Association and sympathetic members of the provincial legislature, Lloyd Chisholm and his friends were able to reverse the ruling, thereby opening the door for night racing in the province.

Not surprisingly, a movement to establish a racetrack in the area gained strength in the years following. In 1963 the Mohawk Raceway at Campbellville was opened under the able management of the Ontario Jockey Club, thanks in large measure to the persistence of Lloyd Chisholm. As the only breeder of Standard-Bred horses in Nassagaweya Township, he headed a committee to see that a carefully planned proposal was put to the people of the township, some of whom expressed concern about the impact of the track on the community. Earl Rowe, later lieutenant-governor of the province and a harness-racing enthusiast, addressed a township meeting on the issue, where a capacity crowd voted in favour of the enterprise.

Lloyd Chisholm has had nothing to do with running the racetrack, but he thinks it has been a great success. In the past it generated thirty per cent of the taxes for the Township of Nassagaweya, and since it opened, the Jockey Club has enlarged it three times.

Ontario's Sire Stakes, a series of races for two- and three-year-old Standard-Breds, is another of Lloyd's innovations. "There were six of us who sold yearling colts at New Woodbine in Toronto, but we decided they weren't selling well enough. . . . I knew about the situation in New York State, where I had attended sales in Batavia. Colts that had been selling for five or six hundred dollars were fetching five or six thousand within a few years of the introduction of the Sire Stakes there."

Lloyd and his colleagues first organized the Ontario Standard-Bred Improvement Association, then made an arrangement with the Ontario government whereby half of one per cent of the proceeds of all harness-racing is put towards the Stakes. Only colts by sires standing in Ontario are eligible, and the total prize money is now over three and a half million dollars. The main objective is to upgrade the breed, and in this, Lloyd Chisholm says, they have already made great strides.

Lloyd Chisholm and his wife, Mary, sell their Standard-Breds as yearlings; they have a stallion of their own and shares in some others. The old Moffat house contains many trophies, awards for Shorthorns, for Guernseys, and for horses. Ribbons from agricultural fairs and exhibitions dating back to the end of the nineteenth century testify to the fact that this is an Ontario farm on which agricultural and racing history has been made.

The Reesor Family
Markham Township
York County

*A*mong thousands of Canadian visitors to Europe in the summer of 1978 was a young farmer, Paul Reesor, a grandson of Simeon Reesor of Markham Township. He was one of a party of Mennonites who made a pilgrimage to those places that hold a special significance for people of their faith: the former Rhine Palatinate; Zurich, where the Anabaptist leader, Conrad Grebel, was imprisoned; the Limmat River, where the martyr Felix Manz was forcibly drowned in 1527; and Holland, where the founder of the sect, Menno Simons, had lived.

The familiar Mennonite text, *The Martyrs' Mirror*, published in 1660 and containing accounts of fifteen hundred Anabaptist martyrs, was used for reference. This volume has particular significance for Paul Reesor. One of his ancestors, Frederick Risser, was martyred for his faith in Strasbourg in 1458.

It was the sustained and relentless persecution in Europe by Catholic and Protestant alike that drove the Reesor family to seek asylum in Pennsylvania in 1739, the year in which Pieter Rieser and his wife, with two children, sailed from Rotterdam in the ship *Robert and Alice*. They settled in Lancaster County, Pennsylvania, on a farm granted to William Penn, but this was not to be the family's permanent home. In the aftermath of the War of Independence, "owing to the arbitrary acts of the associators and unfair treatment of the non-associators because of their refusal to join the Revolutionary Party," Pieter Rieser's son, Christian Reesor, "with others who held the same principles, decided to leave their homes and come to Canada, that they might live in freedom."[9]

A story is told that Christian's son, another Peter, had already been to the Home District of Upper Canada as early as 1796 looking for land. While in York, he was approached by Frederick, Baron Dehoen, an ex-army officer, who offered him six hundred acres in exchange for his horse and saddle. The deal was made, but Peter, sticking strictly to the terms of the bargain, hung on to his bridle and walked back with it to Pennsylvania.

Out of consideration for the older Pieter, who had been uprooted twice in his lifetime, the family did not move until he died in 1804. Christian Reesor and his family then came north in "a fleet of conestogas", rounding Lake Ontario on a journey that took almost seven weeks. Each wagon was pulled by four horses over what were not much more than Indian trails, and each carried a ton and a half of goods, among them a treasured heirloom — a Bible printed in Zurich by Kristoffel Froschover, with a commentary dated 1579. Accompanying the wagons was an assortment of cattle, pigs, sheep, and chickens.

The Reesors settled in Markham Township on the Little Rouge River. They chose land high up on the bank with fine views over the valley, and here they would build stone houses and dam the river for their sawmills, grist-mills, and flour-mills.

Christian Reesor met an early death in 1806. With no feed for the cattle, he was cutting down a tree so that they might eat the leaves when it unexpectedly fell and killed him. He was succeeded as head of the family by his son, Peter, the same Peter who had walked to Pennsylvania carrying his bridle.

A stone house that Peter built in the 1830s on the bank above the Little Rouge was the first in the Township of Markham. A bank barn was built at about the same time, its timbers cut from pine that yielded logs fourteen inches in diameter and forty feet in length, all hand-hewn with a broad axe. The barn stood until the late 1950s, when it was destroyed by fire.

The Reesor family "multiplied exceedingly". It was said that at the turn of the century, a third of the patrons at the local creamery were Reesors; two-thirds of those who patronized the local smithy were Reesors; and within a day's travel were five hundred of the same name. By 1950 the Reesor family in Canada were placing the number of Christian Reesor's descendants at over seven thousand.

Today, Simeon and Annie Reesor live on a century farm that came into the Reesor family in 1845. The present house was built in 1890 when Simeon's father, Isaac, married Emma Rittenhouse, who, as a girl, had lived for time with the Moyer family on their Cherry Avenue farm.

The layout of the Reesor farm owes much to Isaac and Emma, who moved the barn from its original site near the spring where the first log house had stood, and who planted the spruce windbreaks, the trees, the orchard, and the hedges that surround the house today. In time they added a "doddy-haus", or "daddy-house", to the main house for their son, Simeon, when he came to marry Annie Wideman, a descendant of the oldest family in Markham Township.

Blodwen Davies, the writer of travel books, was a longtime friend and neighbour of the Reesors. She knew the farm as it was in the 1950s with its barns, stables, chicken-houses, driving-shed, corn cribs, smoke-house, workshop, and other buildings. Emma Reesor was then over ninety but she still worked in the garden in her long-skirted, long-sleeved dress and starched sunbonnet. "One late September day," Blodwen Davies wrote, "I dropped in to see her and walked the length of the garden by her side. To the west the spruce windbreak encloses the garden. To the north the great barns lessen the force of the north winds; between the garden and the roadway stand tall trees, rows of flowering shrubs and a wide green lawn. Dividing the kitchen garden into two parts, a north and south section, there is a long row of grape vines ending at an old quince tree. . . .

"I looked all about me at the great trees of every kind — maple, spruce, walnut, apple, pear and apricot, at the old flowering shrubs, the lilacs, smoke trees, japonicas, vines leaning off their trellis wall, and here and there in the garden a long, airy plant, sparsely leaved, but bearing at the end of every small branch a great cluster of flowers of a deep cherry red.

"I thought again of all that was established here, a rich farm life, a happy home sheltering four generations, each in the privacy of its own quarters, the windbreak, the orchard, the garden. I remembered, too, that when this gentle, vigorous, busy lady first came to this farmland all this was an open, treeless field."[10]

Emma Reesor died at the age of ninety-four in 1958. Now Simeon and Annie Reesor share the house with their son, Murray, and his wife and children — a house that contains countless reminders of eight generations of the Reesor and Wideman families.

Pride, display, and vanity were frowned upon by the Mennonites; instead, they found expression for their love of beauty in the furniture they made, the quilts they wove, the linen towels they embroidered. In the Reesors' tranquil house there is much that is of outstanding historic and aesthetic value: furniture, some of it made by Simeon Reesor's grandfather; a fraktur picture, a Pennsylvania-German art form that evolved from medieval illuminated manuscripts; beautifully embroidered cover towels; handwoven quilts; and a string of roughly shaped amber beads brought from Europe and probably centuries old, worn for medicinal purposes beneath a high-necked dress.

Many utilitarian and everyday objects are just as lovingly kept: a bucket to hold axle grease made from a hollow log; a pair of bridegroom's leather boots decorated with tiny hearts; a minute hummingbird's nest; a tiny doll's hat woven from wheat straw; a small, stuffed calico bird.

For thirty years Simeon and Annie Reesor rented a stall at the St. Lawrence Market, where they sold eggs, dressed poultry, and produce from the garden, as well as running the farm, on which there have been Holstein cattle since early in this century. There are still chickens and ducks on the farm, the ducks waddling around under the trees of the orchard with their sailors' gait, quacking, stretching up to flap their wings, then dropping off to sleep, beaks under wings, motionless as decoys.

In 1972 the pattern of the Reesors' lives would be interrupted forever. In that year the government of Ontario announced plans to buy 25,200 acres of land for what was then called the North Pickering Community Development Project. The Reesors' farm lay within the boundaries of that project, but they were among the few farmers in their area who did not sell their land.

During the years following, 21,000 acres of land were bought up by the province, including the farm where Peter Reesor had settled in 1804. But in 1974, the public controversy over the new town and the proposed Pickering airport to the east resulted in a change of policy. The target population figures were modified, and 8,000 acres were set aside for a permanent open-space system.

For the present, much of the government land is leased back to farmers, some of them the original owners, so that it remains in agricultural use. In one way this has benefited those who still farm in the area, allowing them to expand their operations by leasing land, which they can do at reasonable cost. Among them are Murray Reesor and his son, Paul, who now work the Reesor farm. On the other hand, agricultural support and supply services have tended to move out of the area. Simeon Reesor thinks it would be hard for his son to carry on if he were not able to share machinery with a neighbour.

The Reesor farm lies within the boundaries of the open-space system, an area that is zoned for agricultural and other uses but that also includes linear transportation systems as well as hydro and sewer lines to service the expanding townsites to the east. Twenty acres of the Reesor farm have been acquired for new hydro lines, which will thrust pylons a hundred and seventy feet into the air. These power lines will cross both the Reesors' garden and the big field to the east where Simeon Reesor once cut wheat with a cradle scythe.

To the west of the farm are all the signs of approaching suburbia: a used-car dump; derelict farmhouses; barns advertising boat and trailer storage; and fields on which sewer pipes are laid out in neat lines. In Vaughan, York, Markham, and Whitchurch townships, the relentless advance of urbanization not only has engulfed individual farms, but has destroyed the Mennonite communities with their admirable husbandry and their exemplary religion. It may be here that we will witness an end to a unique contribution to the social fabric of the Toronto area that goes back nearly two hundred years.

The Baker Family
Vaughan Township
York County

Amos Baker and his wife, the former Edna Reaman, preserve the language and the way of life of their Pennsylvania-German ancestors on their century farm in Vaughan Township, York County. The Bakers wear the traditional Old Order dress, derived from the folk costume of Alsace-Lorraine, and so real is the sense of the past in their home that after driving away down their maple-lined laneway, it comes as a shock to see the apartment blocks of Toronto crowding the skyline just to the south.

The Reamans and the Bakers were neighbours in Vaughan Township from 1816 onwards. Both families were members of the Church of the Brethren, a religious group also known as Dunkards, Tunkers, or Dunkers, and sometimes as River Brethren, a reference to their settlements on the banks of the Susquehanna River in Pennsylvania.

The Reamans came originally from Switzerland. They moved first to the Rhine Palatinate, and from that troubled region they emigrated to Pennsylvania about 1773, eventually crossing the Allegheny Mountains into Somerset County in western Pennsylvania, where in an area known as Brothers' Valley — the Valley of the Brethren — members of the family have farmed for more than two hundred years.

After the War of Independence, when the Brethren were being persecuted for refusing to take the oath of allegiance, a John Reaman and his family travelled north to Upper Canada to take advantage of John Graves Simcoe's offer of asylum. His deed to land in Vaughan Township is dated February 16, 1804. Edna Reaman is a descendant of this first Reaman to come to Canada.

Around 1800, a Jacob Baker, accompanied by his wife, eight children, and sixteen grandchildren, left Pennsylvania's Somerset County for Upper Canada. They travelled north in a Conestoga wagon that the family still has, one of only two known to be preserved in Ontario. Jacob Baker disappeared on the way north, feared taken by Indians. His wife waited two and a half years for him at Black Creek near Niagara Falls, but he never came. Finally she and some of her children and grandchildren moved to York County. It was one of the grandchildren who bought the present Baker farm in 1816, a year long remembered for weather of appalling severity.

"When our people came from Pennsylvania," Edna Baker says, "they found an endless bush filled with huge pine trees. The white pines were at least a hundred and fifty feet tall, about three times as high as the present trees in the bush."

One of the first tasks of the settlers was to cut trees for fences to confine the animals they had brought with them. As the land was cleared, primitive fences were made from the stumps of trees. Then came the split-rail fences. "Any rails you see around here are at least a hundred years old or more," Edna Baker says. "It was an art to know how to split rails . . . and the fences were of different types; the stake-and-rider fence, the snake fence, and the ordinary straight-rail fence. It was a sign of a good farmer to have the farm well set up with rail fences."

The first Bakers cut trees in the bush for ships' masts, which were hauled by horses to Lake Ontario for shipment to England. "This was quite an industry for the early settlers — another was making potash. They burned that beautiful hardwood and sold the ashes. It was their first cash crop."

Much of the early pine from the bush went into the buildings on the farm, including a house that was built before 1816. This early shelter is made of white-pine boards, seven inches in width, laid one on top of the other from the ground to the roof, plank on plank, with siding on the outside. Although unusual in Upper Canada as a whole, this type of building was not uncommon in Vaughan Township.

The pine was used also for furniture. Jonathan Baker, one of the grandchildren to come north in the Conestoga wagon around 1800, began to make furniture for members of his family soon after he arrived. His pieces, with their fine proportions, panelled doors, and wooden pulls, were typical of the Dunkard furniture of Pennsylvania. A skilled and versatile craftsman, he made the locks and hardware used on his furniture, and a rare example of inlay, stars surrounding the brown flint knobs on a small chest of drawers, has been attributed to him. Jonathan Baker's skill was inherited by his great-nephew, another Jonathan, Amos Baker's grandfather. He built chests for all his children and grandchildren and finished one cupboard the day he turned eighty. The couch in the Bakers' kitchen was built by him, and a dry sink that bears the date 1857. The skill of the two Jonathans would make the Baker furniture famous.

The old plank house is now an outbuilding. Amos and Edna Baker live in a brick house built about 1852 from bricks made on the farm and white-pine lumber taken from their bush. The pattern of the bricks on the front, or south side, differs from that of the remainder, the front deserving special treatment. The house is typical of a Pennsylvania-German house in that it has a "gross-doddy haus", an addition built for the grandparents, for there are often three generations living in a typical Pennsylvania-German home.

In the Baker household all of the heating and cooking is done with wood stoves. The house is warm on a winter's day and smells deliciously of apples. Outside there are a number of smaller buildings, such as a wash-house, a leach-house for making soap, and a smoke-house for curing meat, the latter built of squared logs and so old that no one knows its date. The Bakers use all of these buildings, for the family is still almost totally self-supporting. They do their own butchering, smoke their meat, make soap and butter, grind their own wheat for flour, tap the bush for maple sugar, and grow their own fruit and vegetables.

Amos Baker and his son, Paul, who lives with his wife and family in the old Reaman homestead, keep about thirty beef cattle, three hundred and fifty Yorkshire hogs, enough cows to keep the family supplied with milk, and some sheep. Horses were used until about twenty years ago; today their work is done by tractors. In summer, the sheep keep down the weeds in the orchard, where there are apple trees of varieties whose names have long since disappeared from commercial orchards — Pumpkin Sweet, Seek No Further, King, Rambo, Bellflower, Talman Sweet, Spitzenberg — and a pear tree that was old when the second Jonathan was a boy in the late 1830s.

A hundred acres of the "endless bush" that absorbed so much of the early settlers' energies still dominates the farm. From it the Bakers tap some fifty thousand gallons of sap in the spring and boil it down to a thousand gallons of syrup and about six hundred pounds of maple sugar, all of it sold "right here at the door".

During the sugaring-off, the Bakers are hosts to numerous schoolchildren. "There is hardly a day when there isn't somebody here to see us making syrup. We still have the old tripod with the kettle on it so children can see how syrup was made, and we have a few buckets so that they can see the sap dripping. But most of the tapping is done through tubing. The sap runs directly from the trees through underground pipes to one central gathering-place."

Amos Baker expresses a deep affection for his woodlots, which he says are beautiful at all seasons of the year. "Our folks needed the woods to survive and we can still see the evidence of their care. They would not unnecessarily cut down a tree that was growing into timber. My father would never cut down a green tree. They just cut out carefully what would benefit the woods and left the valuable trees growing."

With the Plain People, the threat of persecution, their attitude towards violence, and the tenets of their religion, combined to produce close-knit, hard-working communities that tended to be self-sufficient. Individual members of these communities inherited and passed on to their children a wide range of practical knowledge and skills. Self-sufficiency of this kind implies a harmonious relationship with the natural world, an attitude we now call "conservationist". For the Bakers and others like them, this was not a philosophy adopted in the face of accelerating urban development, or a reaction to the impersonal technology of the twentieth century, but a fundamental element in a way of life that has been practised by their forebears for centuries.

For eight generations, the Bakers and the Reamans found in Vaughan Township the asylum and freedom that John Graves Simcoe promised the Plain People. Here they lived their lives of peace and piety, tending their animals and cherishing their trees and their land. Today, the buildings of the city of Toronto stretch almost to their farm, high fences have had to be erected around their woodlot, and the Reaman farm, the oldest in the continuous ownership of one family in Vaughan Township, will cease to exist when plans for a new expressway are implemented.

The Miller Family
Thistle Ha' Farm
Pickering Township
Ontario County

Occasionally one comes across a farm whose appearance is strikingly different, as if, by accident or intention, the first owners had recreated their new Canadian homestead in the mould of another country. Thistle Ha' is such a farm.

John Miller, a native of Dumfriesshire, Scotland, employing stonemasons originally from Yorkshire, built the big field-stone house, "remembering the stone cottages and castles of his native land", and the result is a farm that would fit comfortably among the hills and dales of the north of England or the Lowlands of Scotland: dry-stone walling, stone fences reminiscent of Westmorland or of Scottish field dikes, a farm gate that has to be opened to allow vehicles to reach the house, land sloping away to the east in a pattern of fields and trees.

Hugh Miller is the present owner of the farm. His grandfather, John Miller, the first owner, was born in 1817 on a croft near Annan in Dumfriesshire in southern Scotland. During the years of hardship following the Napoleonic Wars, the Miller family was so poor that they could only feed one pig a year. They always chose a pig with a large head, it is said, as that was the only part they kept to eat themselves; the rest of the carcase was sold. John Miller left this life of poverty when, at the age of eighteen, he came to Upper Canada in 1835, there to join his uncle, George Miller, on Rigfoot Farm in Markham Township. He worked for his uncle for four years, then drew his accumulated wages, consisting of two cattle and four sheep, and settled in 1839 on a two-hundred-acre lot in Pickering Township. There he continued the back-breaking task of clearing the land, for which he received the deed in 1848.

John Miller had only an axe to fell the trees, some of them maple over three feet in diameter, and when the trees were gone, in came the thistles. With wry humour, he named his farm "Thistle Ha' " ("Ha'" meaning a "small hall"). He might equally as well have named it "Stone Ha'": the ground was so rocky that one could step from one stone to another. John Miller remarked that "the Devil must surely have intended the farm to be the foundation of his house, but had made the mistake of putting a little dirt between the stones instead of mortar. . . ."

It was to take the Miller family over a century to rid the land of the worst of the stones, some of which weighed as much as two tons. Hugh Miller describes how it was done: "It would take two teams of horses to get them out. Dig a hole round them; make a ramp. Roll them up the ramp. When they had the first snow, they'd move them on a stone-boat. Or they'd keep a fire going around them all day, then at night throw on two five-gallon cans of cold water. The stones shatter with a crunch. I've done it myself."

The first crops were barley and peas, sown by hand and reaped by cradle. The fields were ploughed by single-furrow ploughs, harrowed by a tree branch, and levelled by a log dragged over them drawn by a team of oxen. Threshing was by flail in a barn, usually at night, when it was too dark to work outside. Sacks of wheat were carried through the woods to Markham some ten miles away, there to be ground into flour. One spring when the family was almost starving, they turned the cattle out into the woods, watched them to see what plants they ate — then devoured the same plants themselves. Such was their need that season that they were forced to eat the potatoes they had saved for planting.

In spite of all these hardships, it took only a few years for John Miller to establish himself. In 1852 he turned his attention to the importation and improvement of livestock, something for which the Miller family would become famous.

The first pedigreed cattle were brought to Thistle Ha' from Kentucky. They were Durham or Shorthorn cattle, descended from those raised in England by the noted breeder William Booth of Kirklevington in County Durham. They were big, rough cattle but very good milkers, and they formed the foundation of the Thistle Ha' herd of pure-breds that is now the oldest in the world.

In the 1860s, John realized that the American mid-west and some areas of Canada were eminently suitable for beef production. So he set about adapting the Booth breed to produce a beefier type of animal. To this end, animals were imported directly from Scotland to become the foundation of today's beef industry. One of his great Shorthorn bulls was Vice Consul, bred by Amos Cruikshank of Aberdeenshire, "a Quaker with an immense genius for improving livestock".

Then were was Young Abbotsford, a beautiful bull, and later two outstanding females, Cherry Bloom and Rose of Strathallan.

At the same time as he was importing cattle into Canada, John Miller was bringing in sheep and horses. The first sheep were Cotswolds and one consignment came to grief in a violent storm off the coast of Ireland, as a result of which a number of them died. At the height of the tempest John Miller wrote laconically in his diary: "I never expect to see land again."

In 1872 he brought the first Shropshire sheep to Canada. These sheep were the ancestors of what would become a famous flock, and their descendants are still at Thistle Ha'. John Miller's son, another John, became renowned as a judge of sheep throughout North America.

There were horses, too. "Americans used to come here to buy horses when they opened up the prairies," Hugh Miller relates. "At first there was a demand for big, rough horses that could pull stumps, and so we had shire horses here then. But when they stopped sowing grain by hand and used seed drills, they needed a different type of horse — smaller, easier to feed, better legs and feet. When the change came, my grandfather and one of his sons saw what was happening. They bought a stallion in Aberdeenshire, a great horse named Boydson Boy. He was a good walker and he produced colts that could step out well and pull wagons. He lived until he was twenty-five years old and left a tremendous number of colts. There's a picture of him upstairs. . . ."

Thistle Ha' farm still has two horses that are hitched up to the wagon and worked when the hay is being baled and drawn.

During the last decades of the nineteenth century, the Miller family, now the firm of John Miller and Sons, emerged as one of the most aggressive and successful promoters, breeders, and sellers of pedigreed livestock in North America. "They had the confidence and they had the conceit," Hugh Miller says. John Miller's son, Robert, Hugh Miller's uncle, helped organize many of the leading livestock associations in North America. His livestock interests took him all over the world, and wherever he went, he displayed the Millers' uncanny knack of being able to apply and profit from their knowledge and experience of breeding animals. He knew, for instance, that breeders of merino sheep in the United States, including the brothers Eugene and John Little, were having trouble with the ticks and fleas that gathered in the folds of skin around the necks of this breed. Near Paris, France, he saw some Spanish merino sheep at Rambouillet, where the noted scientist and explorer Baron von Humboldt bred sheep without the neck folds. He bought five of these sheep — four ewes and a ram — and took them back to the Littles.

Hugh Miller remembers as a boy going round the Royal Winter Fair with his uncle Robert. "He was getting up in years at the time, but he'd been everywhere, done everything, and seen everything. Pigs, cows, sheep, horses — he knew them all. He'd walk around the Fair and wherever he went, he'd have an audience of twenty to thirty people just hoping to hear what he had to say."

When John Miller married Margaret Whiteside in 1847, they lived in a rough log house. In time they were to have eight children and some larger accommodation would be needed. In 1855, work was begun on a new stone house. The stones from the fields were used as building material and lime for mortar was burned on the farm. The masons were Yorkshiremen, the Pearson brothers of Ashburn, who were paid $1.25 a day, no small amount for those days.

By the 1870s John Miller had become a noted public figure: councillor, then reeve and afterwards warden of Ontario County. In 1875 an east wing was added to the house containing a ballroom, an ash-pit, and a brick oven large enough to bake twenty-two loaves. Present-day visitors have been known to comment on the skill shown by the architect who must have designed the east wing, but Hugh Miller says that when the foundations were about to be laid his grandfather was going away on a trip and it was his uncle Robert who was instructed to "pace them out".

It is a beautiful home, substantially unchanged inside and out. Robert Miller, Hugh Miller's brother, wrote in 1973: "Today this noted rural residence still stands, one of the finest examples of the stonemason's art, with its arched lintels locked with a central keystone and walls two feet thick. The corners are as plumb as the day they were laid. It is one of the few pioneer homes that has not been remodelled; an interesting landmark in an ever-changing rural scene."

Despite its architectural dignity, the Miller house and the family farm itself have been threatened in recent years with total destruction. On January 30, 1973, Thistle Ha' was expropriated by the federal government to make way for the proposed Pickering airport. There followed four years of uncertainty, distress, and frustration amidst a well-publicized controversy. At considerable cost to themselves, the Millers finally won from the Supreme Court of Canada a decision that rescinds the expropriation order.

As a gracenote to this story, it is a pleasure to be able to add that because of the distinction of the Miller family's contribution to Canadian agriculture, Thistle Ha' Farm has been identified as a Canadian National Historic Site. "This farm was acquired in 1848 by John Miller," the text for the plaque reads, "a Scottish immigrant who became a pioneer importer and breeder of pedigreed livestock in Canada. . . . Miller's example, as well as the animals bred at Thistle Ha', played an important role in improving stockbreeding throughout North and South America in the 19th century. Succeeding generations of Millers have maintained the farm's reputation for raising fine blooded stock."

These words echo the comments of Robert Gibbons, President of the Agricultural and Arts Association, made over a century ago: "In any history which may hereafter be written of the introduction of the most valuable breeds of livestock into this country, the names of the Millers of Markham and Pickering . . . must always be honourably mentioned."[3]

Epilogue

Something like a third of the century farms in this book are affected by urban encroachment, although their selection had nothing to do with their proximity or otherwise to towns and villages.

Why did so many farms fall within the urban shadow? Part of the answer lies in the fact that some of the oldest farms are located close to what were the first embryo towns and villages, and these are the farms that continue to be absorbed as these centres grow. Another part of the answer lies with the length and breadth of the urban shadow in late-twentieth-century Ontario.

Sentiment apart, the disruptive effects of urbanization on a century farm, indeed on any farm, would be of little concern had Canada been blessed with a plenitude of good farmland. It was not. Less than half of one per cent is, to use Simcoe's words, "land perfectly calculated for farming", and of that very small percentage, half lies in southern Ontario, where the urbanizing pressures are greatest.

It seems that Ontario may be destined to import, as the years pass, more and more food and that at an increasing cost. This because of a rising population and the continuing disappearance of the most productive land — to mention only two of the variables in a highly complex agricultural, economic, and political equation. It is, therefore, in everyone's interests to help keep the urban shadow within reasonable limits. For generations, century farmers have fostered a heritage that is of value to us all. Now, because of the numerical preponderance of town and city people over the rural population, the onus of maintaining the integrity of agricultural Ontario lies largely with the urban dweller.

Clearly, the traditional character of land-ownership in the province is undergoing a profound and rapid change. This book did not set out to demonstrate anything in the statistical sense, yet it seems that of the many farms that first proudly displayed the century farm sign in 1967 in celebration of Canada's centennial year, a high proportion are no longer in existence, or have changed hands. An off-the-cuff estimate by someone who was in a position to know put the loss of these farms in one county as high as seventy per cent, in another county as high as eighty per cent. These may be exceptions, but however many century farms have already disappeared in the last very few years and for whatever reason, one cannot but regret their passing.

Notes

CHAPTER 1

1. Robert M. Calhoon, *The Loyalists in Revolutionary America* (New York: Harcourt Brace Jovanovich, 1973).
2. *The Old United Empire Loyalists List* (Baltimore: Genealogical Publishing Co. Inc., 1976).
3. Wallace Brown, *The King's Friends* (Providence: Brown University Press, 1965).
4. *Ibid.*
5. Calhoon, *The Loyalists in Revolutionary America.*
6. *Ibid.*
7. Brown, *The King's Friends.*
8. Winston S. Churchill, *The Age of Revolution* (Toronto: McClelland and Stewart, 1957).
9. E. A. Cruikshank, ed., *The Settlement of the United Empire Loyalists on the Upper St. Lawrence and Bay of Quinte* (Toronto: Ontario Historical Society, 1934).
10. *Ibid.*
11. *Ibid.*
12. Calhoon, *The Loyalists in Revolutionary America.*
The authors are indebted to Mr. Alexander "Bud" Farlinger, Toronto, for information on the Farlinger family.

CHAPTER 2

1. Cecil Woodham-Smith, *The Reason Why* (London: Constable, 1956).
2. Mollie Gillen, "The Residences of the Duke of Kent", *History Today*, XXI: 12 (December 1971).
3. Mary Quayle Innis, *Mrs. Simcoe's Diary* (Toronto: Macmillan of Canada, 1978).
4. Richard and Janet Lunn, *The County* (Prince Edward County Council, 1967).
5. George Heriot, *Travels Through the Canadas* (Edmonton: Hurtig Publishers, 1970).
6. H. Belden & Company, *Illustrated Historical Atlas of the Counties of Hastings and Prince Edward, 1878* (Belleville: Mika Publishing Co., 1972).
7. *Pioneer Life on the Bay of Quinte* (Toronto: Rolph and Clark, 1904; Belleville: Mika Publishing Co., 1972).
8. *Ibid.*

CHAPTER 3

1. Edwin C. Guillet, ed., *Valley of the Trent* (Toronto: University of Toronto Press, 1957).
2. Helen McGregor, "Richard Birdsall", in *Peterborough: Land of the Shining Waters* (City and County of Peterborough, 1967).

CHAPTER 5

1. Terry Coleman, *Passage to America* (London: Hutchinson Publishing Group Ltd., 1972).
2. *Chicago Tribune*, Oct. 6, 1884.
The authors are indebted to Mr. Paul Moreland, Toronto, for information on the Moreland family and to the staff of Fathom Five Provincial Park and Mr. Patrick Folkes of Tobermory for information on the barque *Arabia*.

CHAPTER 6

1. John Prebble, *The Lion in the North* (Harmondsworth: Penguin Books, 1973).
2. *The MacLeods of Glengarry: The Genealogy of a Clan* (The Clan MacLeod Society of Glengarry, 1971).
3. *Ibid.*
4. Attributed to William Robertson, 1721-98, Scottish historian.
5. John Prebble, *Culloden* (Harmondsworth: Penguin Books, 1961).
6. A. F. Hunter, *A History of Simcoe County* (Barrie County Council, 1909).
7. J. K. Smith, *David Thompson: Fur Trader, Explorer, Geographer* (Toronto: Oxford University Press, 1971).
8. A. G. Morice, "A Canadian Pioneer: Spanish John", *Canadian Historical Review*, X, 1929.
9. John Graham Harkness, *Stormont, Dundas and Glengarry . . . 1784-1945* (Oshawa: Mundy, Goodfellow, 1946).
10. W. Stanford Reid, ed., *The Scottish Tradition in Canada* (Toronto: McClelland and Stewart, 1976).

CHAPTER 7

1. Charles M. Johnston, ed., *The Valley of the Six Nations* (Toronto: University of Toronto Press, 1964).
2. *Ibid.*

CHAPTER 8

1. Innis, *Mrs. Simcoe's Diary*.
2. E. A. Owen, *Pioneer Sketches of the Long Point Settlement* (Belleville: Mika Publishing Co., 1972), p. 58.
3. H. R. Page & Co., *Illustrated Historical Atlas of Norfolk, Ont.* (Belleville: Mika Publishing Co., 1972).

CHAPTER 9

1. Innis, *Mrs. Simcoe's Diary*.
2. *Ibid.*
3. Gerald M. Craig, *Upper Canada: The Formative Years 1794-1841* (Toronto: McClelland and Stewart, 1963).

4. Fred Coyne Hamil, *Valley of the Lower Thames* (Toronto: University of Toronto Press, 1951).
5. Fred Coyne Hamil, *Lake Erie Baron* (Toronto: Macmillan of Canada, 1955).
6. *Ibid.*
7. Anna Brownell Jameson, *Winter Studies and Summer Rambles in Canada* (Toronto: McClelland and Stewart, 1965).
8. H. R. Page & Co., *Illustrated Historical Atlas of the County of Elgin* (Port Elgin: Cumming, 1972).
9. V. Lauriston, *Romantic Kent* (County of Kent and City of Chatham, 1952).
10. Page, *Illustrated Historical Atlas of the County of Elgin.*
11. *Ibid.*

The authors are indebted to Mr. Duncan McKillop, St. Thomas, and to Mrs. Robert McPhedran, Toronto, for information on the McKillop family.

CHAPTER 10

1. Jameson, *Winter Studies and Summer Rambles.*
2. Robert Leslie Jones, *History of Agriculture in Ontario* (Toronto: University of Toronto Press, 1946).
3. Innis, *Mrs. Simcoe's Diary.*
4. Hamil, *Valley of the Lower Thames.*
5. *The History of Pain Court*, Kent Historical Society, Papers and Addresses, V, 1921.

CHAPTER 11

1. *Land Companies of Canada* (Public Archives Report, 1898-1899).
2. *Ibid.*
3. *Ibid.*
4. The Seaforth *News*, June 9, 1932.
5. *Ibid.*

CHAPTER 12

1. Hamil, *Lake Erie Baron.*
2. William H. Smith, *Canadian Gazetteer* (Coles Canadiana Collection, 1970).
3. W. H. Graham, *The Tiger of Canada West* (Toronto: Clarke, Irwin, 1965).
4. W. D. McIntosh, *100 Years of the Zorra Church* (Toronto: United Church Publishing House, 1930).

CHAPTER 13

1. Edith G. Firth, ed., *The Town of York 1793-1815* (Toronto: University of Toronto Press, 1962).
2. Gerald M. Craig, *Upper Canada – The Formative Years* (Toronto, McClelland and Stewart, 1963).
3. Firth, *The Town of York 1793-1815.*
4. Bern Anderson, *The Life and Voyages of Captain George Vancouver* (Toronto: University of Toronto Press, 1960).

5. John Graves Simcoe, *Correspondence . . . with allied documents* (Toronto: Ontario Historical Society, 1923-31).
6. Firth, *The Town of York 1793-1815.*
7. *Ibid.*
8. *Ibid.*
9. The Markham *Economist*, July 25, 1901.
10. Blodwen Davies, *A String of Amber* (Vancouver: Mitchell Press, 1973).
The authors are indebted to Robert A. Miller's book *The Ontario Village of Brougham* (1973) for information on the Miller family.

Bibliography

*T*he authors owe much to *A History of Agriculture in Ontario*, by Robert Leslie Jones; to *Upper Canada: The Formative Years, 1784-1841*, by Gerald M. Craig; to *The Pioneer Farmer and Backwoodsman*, by Edwin C. Guillet; and to *Early Settlement in Ontario*, by G. E. Mills.

Much of the information on the Loyalists came from *The Loyalists in Revolutionary America*, by Robert Calhoon, and from *The King's Friends*, by Wallace Brown, with both of these books providing historical material directly quoted.

John Prebble's three books, *The Lion in the North*, *Culloden*, and *The Highland Clearances*, and Cecil Woodham-Smith's *The Great Hunger* were invaluable sources of material on the Scots and the Irish. The ordeal of the trans-Atlantic emigrants is graphically described in *Passage to America*, by Terry Coleman.

Mrs. Simcoe's Diary, edited by Mary Quayle Innis, was used extensively, as were *Lake Erie Baron*, by Fred Coyne Hamil, *Winter Studies and Summer Rambles*, by Anna Brownell Jameson, and *Romantic Kent*, by Victor Lauriston.

Among works consulted were:

Anderson, Bern. *The Life and Voyages of Captain George Vancouver*. Toronto: University of Toronto Press, 1960.

Ashley, Maurice. *England in the Seventeenth Century*. Harmondsworth, England: Pelican Books, 1952.

Baker, Amos, and Baker, Edna. *"A Century Farm in Concord."* Typescript. Thornhill: Community Centre Library, 1975.

Barnett, Correlli. *Britain and Her Army, 1509-1970, a Military, Political and Social History*. Harmondsworth, England: Penguin Books, 1974.

Barry, James. *Georgian Bay, the Sixth Great Lake*. Toronto: Clarke, Irwin, 1971.

Beadle, D. W. *Canadian Fruit, Flower, and Kitchen Garden*. Toronto: Campbell, 1872.

Belden, (H.), & Co. *Illustrated Atlas of Lanark County, 1880; Illustrated Atlas of Renfrew County, 1881*. Port Elgin: Cumming, 1972.

———. *Illustrated Historical Atlas of the Counties of Hastings and Prince Edward, 1878*. Belleville: Mika, 1972.

———. *Illustrated Historical Atlas of the County of Huron, 1879*. Owen Sound: Richardson, Bond, Wright, 1972.

Britt, Kent. "The Loyalists." *National Geographic*, 147:4 (April 1975).

Brown, Wallace. "Escape from the Republic: the Dispersal of the American Loyalists." *History Today*, 22:2 (February 1972).

———. *The King's Friends, the Composition and Motives of the American Loyalist Claimants*. Providence, R.I.: Brown University Press, 1965.

———. "'Victorious in Defeat': the American Loyalists in Canada." *History Today*, 27:2 (February 1977).

Bryant, Arthur. *The Age of Elegance*. London: Reprint Society, 1954.

———. *The Years of Endurance*. London: Harper, 1942.

———. *The Years of Victory*. London: Collins, 1975.

Calhoon, R. M. *The Loyalists in Revolutionary America*. New York: Harcourt Brace Jovanovich, 1973.

Canada Company. *A Statement of the Satisfactory Results which have Attended Emigration to Upper Canada*. London: Smith Elder, 1842.

Canada and Its Provinces: a History of the Canadian People and Their Institutions. Toronto: Publishers Association of Canada, 1913-1917. vols. 3, 4, 5, 17, 18.

Canniff, William. *History of the Settlement of Upper Canada*. Toronto: Dudley & Burns, 1869; Belleville: Mika, 1971.

Chapman, L. J., and Putman, D. F. *The Physiography of Southern Ontario*. Toronto: University of Toronto Press, 1966.

Churchill, Winston S. *The Age of Revolution*. Toronto: McClelland and Stewart, 1957.

Coleman, Terry. *Passage to America*. London: Hutchinson, 1972.

Craig, Gerald M. *Early Travellers in the Canadas, 1791-1867*. Toronto: Macmillan, 1955.

———. *Upper Canada: The Formative Years, 1784-1841*. Toronto: McClelland and Stewart, 1963.

Cruikshank, E. A. "A memoir of Lieutenant-Colonel John MacDonell of Glengarry House." *Ontario Historical Society, Papers and Records*, 22:20 (1925).

———. "Petitions for Grants of Land in Upper Canada, 1796-99." *Ontario Historical Society, Papers and Records*, 26:97 (1930).

———. *Settlement of the United Empire Loyalists on the Upper St. Lawrence and Bay of Quinte in 1784*. Toronto: Ontario Historical Society, 1934.

Davies, Blodwen. *A String of Amber*. Vancouver: Mitchell Press, 1973.

Dunham, Mabel. *Grand River*. Toronto: McClelland and Stewart, 1945.

———. *Trail of the Conestoga*. Toronto: Macmillan, 1924.

Elford, Jean Turnbull. *History of Lambton County*. Sarnia: Lambton County Historical Society, 1969.

Epp, Frank. *Mennonites in Canada 1786-1920: the History of a Separate People*. Toronto: Macmillan, 1974.

Evans, George Ewart. *Ask the Fellows Who Cut the Hay*. London: Faber, 1956.

Family History of the Reesors in Canada, 1934. (Privately printed.)

Fighting Men of a Highland Catholic Jacobite Clan who fought in Canada. Toronto: McLean, 1912.

Firth, Edith G., ed. *The Town of York, 1793-1815.* Toronto: University of Toronto Press, 1962.

————. *The Town of York, 1815-1834.* Toronto: University of Toronto Press, 1966.

Fowke, Vernon C. *Canadian Agricultural Policy.* Toronto: University of Toronto Press, 1947.

Galbraith, John Kenneth. *The Scotch.* Toronto: Macmillan, 1964.

Gardiner, Herbert F. *Nothing But Names.* Toronto: Morang, 1899.

Gates, Lillian F. *Land Policies of Upper Canada.* Toronto: University of Toronto Press, 1968.

Gillen, Mollie. "The Residences of the Duke of Kent." *History Today,* 21:12 (December 1971).

Gingerich, Orland. *The Amish of Canada.* Waterloo: Conrad Press, 1972.

"Gingerich Family History." Typescript. Baden, 1975.

Graham, W. H. *The Tiger of Canada West.* Toronto: Clarke, Irwin, 1965.

Grant, R. G. M. *The Story of Martintown.* Gardenvale, Quebec: Harpell's Press Co-operative, 1974.

Guillet, Edwin C. *Pioneer Arts and Crafts.* Toronto: University of Toronto Press, 1968.

————. *The Pioneer Farmer and Backwoodsman.* 2 vols. Toronto: Ontario Publishing Co., 1963.

————. *Pioneer Settlements.* Toronto: Ontario Publishing Co., 1947.

————. *Pioneer Travel in Upper Canada.* Toronto: University of Toronto Press, 1933.

————, ed. *Valley of the Trent.* Toronto: Champlain Society, 1957.

Haight, Canniff. *Country Life in Canada.* Toronto: Hunter Rose, 1885. Belleville: Mika, 1971.

Hamil, Fred Coyne. *Lake Erie Baron: The Story of Colonel Thomas Talbot.* Toronto: Macmillan, 1955.

————. *The Valley of the Lower Thames, 1640-1850.* Toronto: University of Toronto Press, 1951.

Harkness, John Graham. *Stormont, Dundas and Glengarry, a History, 1784-1945.* Oshawa: Mundy-Goodfellow Printing Co., 1946.

Heisler, John P. "Canals of Canada." *Canadian Historic Sites: Occasional Papers in Archaeology,* No. 8, Ottawa, 1973.

Heriot, George. *Travels through the Canadas* (1808). Edmonton: Hurtig, 1971.

"History of Pain Court." *Kent Historical Society, Papers and Addresses,* 5, 1921.

Holborn, Hajo. *A History of Modern Germany, 1648-1840.* New York: Knopf, 1967.

Howison, John. *Sketches of Upper Canada.* Edinburgh: Oliver and Boyd, 1821. (Coles Canadiana Collection)

Humphreys, Barbara A., and Sykes, Meredith. "The Buildings of Canada." Reprinted from *Explore Canada.* Montreal: Reader's Digest Association (Canada), 1974.

Hunter, A. F. *A History of Simcoe County.* 2 vols. Barrie County Council, 1909.

Innis, Mary Quayle. *Mrs. Simcoe's Diary*. Toronto: Macmillan, 1965.

Jameson, Anna Brownell. *Winter Studies and Summer Rambles in Canada. Selections* (1838). Toronto: McClelland and Stewart, 1965.

Johnston, Charles M., ed. *The Valley of the Six Nations*. Toronto: University of Toronto Press, 1946.

Jones, Robert Leslie. *History of Agriculture in Ontario, 1613-1880*. Toronto: University of Toronto Press, 1946.

Lambert, Richard S., and Pross, Paul. *Renewing Nature's Wealth*. Ontario Department of Lands and Forests, 1967.

"Land Companies of Canada." *Public Archives Report*, 1898-99.

Landon, Fred. *Western Ontario and the American Frontier*. Toronto: McClelland and Stewart, 1967.

Lauriston, Victor. *Romantic Kent*. County of Kent and City of Chatham, 1952.

Lesstrang, Jacques. *Seaway*. Seattle: Superior Publishing Company, 1976.

Lewis, Jennie Raycraft. *Sure, an' this is Biddulph*. Biddulph Township Council, 1964.

Lizars, R., and Lizars, K. M. *In the Days of the Canada Company*. Toronto: Briggs, 1896.

Longford, Elizabeth. *Wellington: Years of the Sword*. London: Book Club Associates, 1972.

Lunn, Richard, and Lunn, Janet. *The County*. Prince Edward County Council, 1967.

McIntosh, W. D. *100 Years of the Zorra Church*. Toronto: United Church Publishing House, 1930.

MacLeods of Glengarry: The Genealogy of a Clan. The Clan MacLeod Society of Glengarry, 1971.

Mannion, John J. *Irish Settlements in Eastern Canada, a Study of Cultural Transfer and Adaptation*. Toronto: University of Toronto Press, 1974.

Mathews, Hazel C. *Oakville and the Sixteen*. Toronto: University of Toronto Press, 1971.

Mika, Nick, and Mika, Helma. *United Empire Loyalists: Pioneers of Upper Canada*. Belleville: Mika, 1976.

Miller, Robert A. *The Ontario Village of Brougham. Past! Present! Future?* Brougham: The Author, 1973.

Mills, G. E. 1971 and 1972. *Early Settlement in Ontario*. Manuscript Report Series, No. 182. Parks Canada, Ottawa.

Moodie, Susanna. *Roughing It in the Bush* (1852).Toronto: McClelland and Stewart, 1962.

Morice, A. G. "A Canadian pioneer: Spanish John." *Canadian Historical Review*, 10, 1929.

Nykor, Lynda Musson, and Musson, Patricia D. *The Ontario Tradition in York County Mennonite Furniture*. Toronto: Lorimer, 1977.

The Old United Empire Loyalists List. Baltimore: Genealogical Publishing Co., 1976.

Owen, E. A. *Pioneer Sketches of the Long Point Settlement*. Toronto: Briggs, 1898; Belleville: Mika, 1972.

Page, H. R., & Co. *Illustrated Historical Atlas of Norfolk, Ont.* Toronto: Page, 1877; Belleville: Mika, 1972.

———. *Illustrated Historical Atlas of the County of Elgin.* Toronto: Page, 1877; Port Elgin: Cumming, 1972.

Palmer, Eve. *The Plains of Camdeboo.* London: Collins, 1966.

Peterborough: Land of Shining Waters. City and County of Peterborough, 1967.

Phelps, Edward. *Petrolia, 1874-1974.* Petrolia Print and Litho Limited, 1974.

Pioneer Life on the Bay of Quinte. Toronto: Rolph and Clark, 1904; Belleville: Mika, 1972.

Plumb, J. H. *England in the Eighteenth Century.* Harmondsworth, England: Pelican Books, 1950.

Pope, John Henry. *Illustrated Historical Atlas of the County of Halton, 1877.* Port Elgin: Cumming, 1971.

Prebble, John. *Culloden.* Harmondsworth, England: Penguin Books, 1973.

———. *Highland Clearances.* Harmondsworth, England: Penguin Books, 1977.

———. *The Lion in the North.* Harmondsworth, England: Penguin Books, 1973.

Prince Edward Historical Society. *Historic Prince Edward,* 1976.

Raddall, Thomas H. *The Path of Destiny.* Toronto: Doubleday, 1957.

Read, D. B. *The Life and Times of Gen. John Graves Simcoe.* Toronto: Virtue, 1890.

Reaman, George Elmore. *A History of Agriculture in Ontario.* 2 vols. Toronto: Saunders, 1970.

———. *History of the Holstein-Friesian Breed in Canada.* Toronto: Collins, 1946.

———. *A History of Vaughan Township.* Vaughan Township Historical Society, 1971.

———. *Trail of the Black Walnut.* Toronto: McClelland and Stewart, 1976.

———. *Trail of the Huguenots.* Toronto: Allen, 1963.

Reesor Family in Canada, 1804-1950. Reesor Family Reunion Genealogical Committee, 1950.

Reid, W. Stanford, ed. *The Scottish Tradition in Canada.* Toronto: McClelland and Stewart, 1976.

Rennie, James A. *Louth Township.* Louth Township Citizens' Centennial Committee, 1967.

Riddell, William Renwick. *The Life of John Graves Simcoe, First Lieutenant-Governor of the Province of Upper Canada, 1792-96.* Toronto: McClelland and Stewart, 1926.

Roth, Lorraine. *150 Years. Sesquicentennial of the Amish Mennonites of Ontario.* Mennonite Historical Society of Ontario and the Western Ontario Mennonite Conference, 1972.

Scott, James. *The Settlement of Huron County.* Toronto: Ryerson Press, 1966.

Scott, William Louis. "A U.E. Loyalist Family." *Ontario Historical Society Papers and Records,* 32 (1937).

Simcoe, John Graves. *The correspondence of Lieut. Governor John Graves Simcoe, with Allied Documents Relating to His Administration of the Government of Upper Canada.* 5 vols. Toronto: Ontario Historical Society, 1923-31.

Smith, James K. *David Thompson, Fur Trader, Explorer, Geographer.* Toronto: Oxford University Press, 1971.

Smith, Paul H. *Loyalists and Redcoats: a Study in British Revolutionary Policy.* Published for the Institute of Early American History and Culture at Williamsburg, Va., by the University of North Carolina Press, 1964.

Smith, W. L. *The Pioneers of Old Ontario.* Toronto: Morang, 1923.

Smith, Wm. H. *Smith's Canadian Gazetteer comprising Statistical and General Information Respecting all Parts of the Upper Province, or Canada West.* Toronto: Rowsell, 1846. (Coles Canadiana Collection)

Stanley, George F. C. *Canada Invaded.* Toronto: Hakkert, 1973.

Tait, Lyal. *Tobacco in Canada.* Tillsonburg, Ontario, Flue-Cured Tobacco Growers' Marketing Board, 1968.

Thomson, David. *England in the Nineteenth Century.* Harmondsworth, England: Pelican Books, 1950.

Timothy, H. B. *The Galts.* Toronto: McClelland and Stewart, 1977.

United Empire Loyalist Centennial Committee. *The Centennial of the Settlement of Upper Canada by the United Empire Loyalists, 1784-1884.* Boston: Gregg Press, 1972. (Reprint of the 1885 edition.)

Upton, L. F. S. *The United Empire Loyalists: Men and Myths.* Toronto: Copp Clark, 1967.

Weaver, Emily P. *The Story of the Counties of Ontario.* Toronto: Bell and Cockburn, 1913.

Whitridge, Arnold. "The Miracle of Independence." *History Today*, 24:6 (June 1974).

Whitton, Charlotte. *A Hundred Years A-Fellin'; Some Passages from the Timber Saga of the Ottawa in the Century in which the Gillies have been Cutting in the Valley, 1842-1942.* Braeside, Ontario: Gillies Brothers, 1943.

Wilcox, Desmond. *Explorers.* British Broadcasting Corporation, 1975.

Wood, J. David, ed. *Perspectives on Landscape and Settlement in Nineteenth Century Ontario.* Toronto: McClelland and Stewart, 1975.

Woodham-Smith, Cecil. *The Great Hunger.* London: Harper and Row, 1962.

————. *The Reason Why.* London: Constable, 1953.

Index